Kentucky
Politics

Kentucky Politics

Malcolm E. Jewell &

Everett W. Cunningham

1968 | University of Kentucky Press

Acknowledgments

It is impossible to carry out a realistic study of politics in a state without the help of politicians. The authors communicated with approximately two hundred party leaders, about evenly divided between Democrats and Republicans, either by questionnaires or by personal interviews. They included more than half of the county chairmen in each party and many additional leaders active in party affairs at the state level and in several of the larger cities. In addition, questionnaires were returned by almost two hundred candidates who ran in Democratic legislative primaries in either 1961 or 1965. These many individuals are not listed by name because they were promised anonymity in answering questions posed by the authors. But we want to make it clear that our greatest debt, as authors, is to these many Kentucky political leaders who were so generous of their time and so frank in their answers to us.

The questionnaires to Democratic legislative candidates were prepared, and the preliminary analysis conducted, by two graduate students, Edward Angus and John Duvall. Professor Robert Snyder of Georgetown College and two graduate assistants, Arthur Stevens and John Baden, provided indispensable help in carrying out voter surveys. The authors are also grateful to a large number of under-graduate students at the University of Kentucky who have contrib-uted to the fund of knowledge about Kentucky politics by their participation in the polling of voters and their term papers on local politics in their counties.

Professor John E. Reeves read most of the manuscript, providing helpful comments; moreover, he has shared his extensive knowledge of Kentucky government and politics for many years and has helped to stimulate our interest in the subject. Hugh Morris and Allan M. Trout of the Louisville *Courier-Journal* also took the time to read a large proportion of the manuscript and to comment on it. Professor William J. Crotty of Northwestern University made available data on North Carolina that was valuable for comparative purposes.

The authors, like all who are interested in Kentucky politics, have found the *Courier-Journal* to be an invaluable source of Kentucky political history. Instead of citing, through footnotes, each and every instance in which we have used the *Courier-Journal*, we want to make it clear that this newspaper is the source of most of our information concerning those aspects of modern political history in the state that are a matter of public record, such as election campaigns and legislative action.

Table 4.1 and part of Table 4.3 appeared earlier in *Legislative Representation in the Contemporary South* and are used with permission of the Duke University Press.

The Kentucky Research Foundation and the University of Kentucky provided funds for travel to conduct interviews and for typing expenses, and the University of Kentucky also made available a summer research fellowship.

Mrs. Lois Summers deserves more than routine acknowledgment for her typing assistance.

Final responsibility for this volume, of course, must rest with the authors. Those who have helped us by submitting to interviews, reading the manuscript, and providing financial resources bear no responsibility for our errors or our interpretive judgments. Professor Jewell wrote the initial draft of chapters 1, 2, 4, 6, and 7; Professor Cunningham drafted chapters 3 and 5. But it should be understood that the final product is a joint one and represents our combined assessment of the political system in Kentucky today.

Contents

The moonlight falls the softest in Kentucky;
The summer days come oftest in Kentucky;

   .   .   .   .   .   .

The song birds are the sweetest in Kentucky;
The Thoroughbreds are fleetest in Kentucky:
Mountains tower proudest,
Thunder peals the loudest,
The landscape is the grandest—
And politics—the damnedest, in Kentucky.

1 | Introduction

Kentuckians, who are always fond of quoting Judge Mulligan's poem, take particular delight in the superlative about politics that climaxes the final stanza. Although some Kentuckians might admit the possibility that other states have prouder mountain peaks or even fleeter Thoroughbreds, most would argue that the politics of Kentucky is unique—its politicians more flamboyant, its courthouse gangs more powerful, and its scandals more scandalous than anywhere else in the country. They recall that one of the few Republican governors fled the state in 1900 after the Democratic candidate challenging his election had been murdered. They tell stories of the dominant political role played by the Louisville and Nashville Railroad and the Jockey Club earlier in the century, and every Kentuckian has heard of politicians who refused to report election returns until they had discovered how many votes were needed by their candidate.

Kentuckians recall with pride a long line of colorful politicians. Henry Clay, though denied the presidency by the voters, played a dominant role in Congress from 1811, when he was elected speaker of the House as a freshman, until he drafted the Compromise of 1850 in a futile effort to preserve the Union. John Crittenden, a longtime political ally of Clay, carried on the efforts to compromise the differences between North and South until the fighting broke out. John Cabell Breckinridge served as vice president immediately before the Civil War, ran for the presidency against Lincoln, tried to persuade Kentucky to join the Confederacy, and then served as a general in the Confederate army. Cassius Clay preached the cause of abolition in Kentucky during the 1840s and 1850s, appearing on platforms armed with a pistol and a bowie knife to insure his freedom of speech.

In recent decades Alben Barkley, who served in Washington as Senate majority leader and vice president, was known in the cities and towns of Kentucky for the power of his oratory and his inexhaustible fund of stories. A. B. "Happy" Chandler, probably the most colorful Kentucky politician of the twentieth century, is also gifted with the skills of an orator and the instinctive sense of a performer that for years have made him a favorite among the crowds that come to political rallies. In recent years, however, rallies have been relatively few and sparsely attended, and oratory has declined in importance. Kentucky politics has lost some of its color and flavor, and some of its distinctive character. The successful Kentucky politician of the present is more often the one who knows how to use the techniques of television and modern public relations.

The unique style of Kentucky political history is more poetry than truth, however. Other states have had equally colorful political leaders, equally powerful lobbyists, and equally entrenched local machines. Voters have been bought, elections stolen, and the public treasury stripped at one time or another in nearly every state and county in the country. The theme of this book is not the uniqueness, but the representative character of Kentucky politics. Despite the features that have made its politics distinctive, the state's history has been shaped by the major trends and crosscurrents in American political history. Kentucky was settled not only by many natives of Virginia and North Carolina, but by those of Pennsylvania and Maryland; the settlers represented a variety of economic and social backgrounds and interests. As early as 1813 Kentucky "epitomized in miniature the political struggles that were soon to rock the nation." "Kentucky politics were complex not only because of the early presence of contending social and cultural interests there but because of its position as a border state. The distinctions already emerging between the agrarian South and the burgeoning industrial North were cultural streams that flowed together in Kentucky."[1]

[1] Albert D. Kirwan, *John J. Crittenden* (Lexington: University of Kentucky Press, 1962), 26, 28-29.

HISTORY OF THE TWO-PARTY SYSTEM

Kentucky is a border state, stretching from Ohio and Indiana to Tennessee, Missouri, and almost to Arkansas. No state more poignantly exemplified the bitter divisions of the Civil War than Kentucky, where brothers debated the issues of slavery and secession and finally took up arms on opposing sides. Although it was a state where slaveholding was extensive, Kentucky never seceded. The state's leaders strove to find a compromise that would preserve the Union and, when they failed, tried to maintain a posture of political neutrality between the Lincoln administration and the Confederacy. Kentucky became both a battlefield and a jungle for guerrilla warfare, but as the war progressed, the Union army consolidated its hold on the state. During the last years of the war Kentucky was under military occupation. The writ of habeas corpus was suspended in July of 1864, and Kentuckians were often imprisoned arbitrarily by military authorities. Although the Emancipation Proclamation did not apply to Kentucky, officials of the Union army used it as an excuse to free slaves in various parts of the state. These events had the effect of alienating many of those Kentuckians who had been sympathetic to the Union cause, and in the 1864 election Abraham Lincoln won only 30 percent of the vote. After the war ended, Kentucky was subjected to some of the repressive policies and the racial turmoil that characterized the Reconstruction era. Anti-Republican feelings hardened, and only one-fourth of the voters supported Grant in the 1868 election.[2]

The Civil War and Reconstruction had an enduring effect on partisan politics in Kentucky. The return of ex-soldiers from both armies, with their wartime loyalties transferred into partisan loyalties, increased the bitterness of partisan conflict. The strongest resistance to slavery and the greatest sympathy for the Union had been found in the southeastern mountains, where the terrain made a slave-based agriculture impossible, and it was here that the Republican citadel developed which has persisted to this day. Western Kentucky and the Bluegrass area in the center of the state, where slavery had flourished, became predominantly Democratic,

[2] The impact of the Civil War and Reconstruction on Kentucky is described in Thomas D. Clark, *A History of Kentucky* (Lexington, Ky.: John Bradford Press, 1960), chaps. 18 and 19.

although there were pockets of Republican strength in many of the counties where slavery had not been common or where the effects of military occupation and Reconstruction had not been deeply felt. Another source of Republican votes in western Kentucky and in the Bluegrass was the Negro, who voted for the first time in 1872. In that election the Democratic percentage dropped by 20 to 30 points in a number of counties where the Negroes constituted a substantial proportion of the voters. The Republican party usually carried only a few counties outside of its mountain stronghold, but it consistently won a substantial minority in many other counties with the help of the Negro vote. Although Kentucky was predominantly Democratic for three decades after the Civil War, the Republican party did not degenerate into a small patronage-minded clique as it did in most of the southern states. In Kentucky it possessed a strong base of support that seldom fell below 40 percent of the electorate. From 1872 through 1892 the Democratic party consistently won presidential elections, but with a median percentage of only 54. The Republican party ran its first gubernatorial candidate in 1871, gaining a respectable 41 percent of the vote, and in the next five gubernatorial elections its support never fell below 39 percent.[3]

The election of 1896 transformed the politics of Kentucky and made it a two-party state. When the national Democratic party adopted William Jennings Bryan as its candidate and free silver as its platform, the Democratic party in Kentucky was split apart. William McKinley carried the state by just 281 votes, as conservative Democrats, particularly in the larger cities and more prosperous agricultural counties, voted Republican. In the eight presidential elections from 1896 through 1924, Kentucky went Republican only twice, but the Democratic margin was never over 52 percent and was usually slightly less than a majority. Strong two-party competition extended to state elections as well. The Republican party won five of the nine gubernatorial elections from 1895 through 1927, including the disputed election in 1899 following which the Republican governor was forced to flee the state without serving out his term.

Although the 1896 election reinforced Democratic domination of southern states and established a pattern of Republican control in

[3] Jasper B. Shannon and Ruth McQuown, *Presidential Politics in Kentucky, 1824-1948* (Lexington: University of Kentucky Bureau of Government Research, 1950). This volume contains county-by-county election returns and an analysis of each presidential election in Kentucky.

many northern states that lasted for three decades, yet it established strong two-party competition in Kentucky. The paradox is explained by Kentucky's position as a border state. The fear of "radical" policies advocated by the Bryan Democrats drove many Democratic voters—in Kentucky as in northern states—into the Republican camp, where they often remained. But the Democratic tradition was stronger in Kentucky than in the northern states, and as a consequence, party strength became more equally divided.

In one respect the political patterns of Kentucky were typical of those throughout the nation. The partisan allegiance of most counties remained stable during this period, as most of the voters apparently adhered to the traditional voting habits of family and community. During the eight presidential elections from 1896 through 1924 there were 53 counties that always voted Democratic and 41 that always voted Republican. The Republican counties were in the southeast and the eastern mountains and in an irregular band stretching through parts of western Kentucky. Only 26 counties were not consistent during these eight presidential elections, and 14 of these voted for one party (8 Democratic and 6 Republican) in seven of the eight races. Most of the inconsistent counties were stretched along the borders between the centers of Republican and Democratic strength. Among them were the four major urban counties—Jefferson, Fayette, Kenton, and Campbell. The Democratic proportion of the two-party vote in these urban counties varied from 41 to 54 percent in the eight elections, and they provided the margin necessary for Republican presidential victories in Kentucky in 1896 and 1924. In the remaining 116 counties the Democratic percentage of the total two-party vote never fell below 50 percent or rose above 52.5 percent, a remarkably consistent record for eight elections.[4]

The close competition that characterized the Kentucky two-party system was washed away by the tidal wave of the New Deal. In the five presidential elections from 1932 through 1948 the Democratic candidates won with percentages that ranged from 54.5 to 59 percent. The Democratic party dominated presidential politics by a margin that was comparable to that in the 1870s and 1880s. The New Deal elections came as a rude shock to the Republicans because

[4] In these calculations the votes cast for Taft and Roosevelt have been combined to measure the Republican vote in 1912.

in 1928 Herbert Hoover had won 59 percent of the vote, the first Republican presidential candidate to win a majority in the state. In rejecting the urban, wet, Catholic nominee of the Democratic party, Kentucky remained in step with several of the border and southern states. The partisan percentages in 1928 were approximately the same inside and outside the four most urban counties. By 1932 Kentucky farmers were suffering from a severe drought and a prolonged recession that was reaching disastrous proportions, while the industrial depression had spread throughout the cities and mining areas. Kentucky gave Franklin Roosevelt 59 percent of its votes, the same percentage given four years earlier to Hoover, the most drastic shift in the state's voting behavior since 1872.

It is important to define more carefully the effect of the New Deal on Kentucky politics. Despite the decline in partisan competition, the Republican party continued to hold the loyalties of a large minority of the voters. The Republican party won at least 40 percent of the two-party vote in every presidential and gubernatorial election from 1932 through 1951, and it elected a governor for one term in 1943. The political map during the New Deal years was not much different from that of the earlier period; the number of Republican counties shrank and the party retreated to its customary bases of strength. The traditionally Democratic rural counties in the central and western part of the state grew more strongly Democratic as the Roosevelt administration developed programs to bolster the farming economy. But the traditionally Republican hill counties were largely isolated from the effects of the New Deal and continued to deliver Republican majorities at the polls. These voters often were suspicious of New Deal programs that appeared to be designed primarily for the labor unions and the large farmers. The great exception was a cluster of counties at the southeast corner of the state where coal mining dominated the economy and the influence of the United Mine Workers changed the partisan loyalty of many voters. Most of these Republican counties began to produce substantial Democratic majorities. In the four major urban centers the Democrats won majorities ranging from 53 to 62 percent in the five elections from 1932 through 1948. In the northern industrial states the impact of the New Deal was greatest and most enduring in the large cities. But in Kentucky the urban impact was less dramatic for several reasons: the cities were smaller, the labor unions were weaker, and the Negro voters were slower to change political allegiance than in most northern cities. Kentucky was not one of the states whose political system was revolutionized by the New Deal, both because the state was less urban and less industrialized and because it was the majority party (rather than the minority party, as in most northern states) that benefited from the national Democratic surge. The New Deal weakened the two-party system in Kentucky but did not destroy it. Traditional and local political loyalties often remained strong, and these provided the Republican party with a base, much stronger than in most southern states, on which to build in the 1950s.

The level of popular participation in Kentucky elections, which for many years was above the national average, has fallen below the

TABLE 1.1

Voters as Percentage of Persons Eligible to Vote, 1880-1964

Year	Kentucky	South	Non-South	U.S.
1880	71.0	64.9	86.4	81.2
1884	68.0	64.3	84.3	79.5
1888	79.1	63.9	87.0	81.6
1892	72.6	59.3	82.5	77.2
1896	88.0	56.9	87.6	80.6
1900	86.0	43.4	84.1	74.7
1904	76.7	28.9	77.8	66.4
1908	83.0	30.6	77.4	66.5
1912	73.7	27.8	70.2	60.7
1916	81.7	31.7	69.1	61.8
1920	71.2	25.9	56.1	49.2
1924	60.5	23.3	56.3	48.9
1928	66.6	28.0	65.1	56.9
1932	67.1	29.2	64.8	56.9
1936	59.7	30.0	69.9	61.0
1940	59.0	31.3	71.5	62.5
1944	53.1	28.1	64.0	55.9
1948	49.5	24.6	61.4	53.0
1952	58.8	38.6	70.6	63.3
1956	58.6	36.6	67.8	60.6
1960	60.5	41.2	71.1	64.1
1964	54.2	45.3	67.2	62.0

SOURCE: Unpublished data provided by Walter Dean Burnham; Jasper B. Shannon and Ruth McQuown, *Presidential Politics in Kentucky, 1824-1948* (Lexington: University of Kentucky Bureau of Government Research, 1950). Kentucky is included in the nonsouthern states.

national average since the New Deal period. The contrasts, which are demonstrated in Table 1.1, result from the different levels of two-party competition in Kentucky and in the nation. National levels of voting participation fell after the 1896 election, apparently in large part because that election led to the establishment or reinforcement of one-party systems in most of the states. Where the level of competition was low, voters had few incentives to go to the polls.[5] But in Kentucky the 1896 election inaugurated a period of close two-party competition and of unusually high turnout at the polls. The nationwide extension of the franchise to women in the 1920 election led to a drop in the proportion of eligible voters who went to the polls, but the proportion continued to be higher in Kentucky than in the nation. Since the start of the New Deal there has been a gradual and unsteady rise in national voter turnout (interrupted by World War II). This has apparently resulted from intensified two-party competition in the states, but it has been far weaker than the drop in participation that accompanied the decline in competition. In Kentucky, on the other hand, the decline of two-party competition was matched by a drop in voting turnout during the New Deal, and Kentucky has gradually fallen below the national average. Although most recent presidential elections have been closely contested in Kentucky, the turnout remains below the level in the 1920s and far below that achieved consistently during the first two decades of the century.

The most important characteristic of presidential politics in Kentucky has been the persistence of partisan loyalties within the counties despite changing statewide trends. We noted earlier that from the 1896 through the 1924 elections 53 counties always voted Democratic and 8 more deviated from a Democratic vote only once; there were 41 consistent Republican counties and 6 others with only one deviation. Throughout the eighteen elections from 1896 to 1964, of the 61 Democratic counties, 47 voted Democratic with no more than two exceptions. Most of the exceptions occurred in the 1928 and 1960 elections, when the Democratic candidate was a Catholic. All but 2 of these 47 counties trace their perfect or nearly perfect Democratic records at least as far back as 1872. Of the 47 Republican counties (from 1896 to 1924), 29 voted Republican

[5] Walter D. Burnham, "The Changing Shape of the American Political Universe," *American Political Science Review*, LIX (1965), 7-28.

with no more than two exceptions through the 1964 elections. Most of these defections occurred in 1932 or in 1964. Among the counties that dropped out of the Republican category after 1924 were the major coal-mining counties and several of the more urban counties. Only 17 of the 29 Republican counties have a record of consistency dating back to 1872; most of the others did not join the Republican ranks until the realignment of the 1896 election. Although social and economic changes are occurring more rapidly today than ever before, more than half of Kentucky's counties (62) have highly consistent voting records dating from 1872 and almost two-thirds (76) have comparable records stretching back as far as 1896. The force of tradition in voting behavior and the prolonged dominance of most rural counties by a single party are aspects of Kentucky politics that should not be forgotten, although our attention in this volume is primarily focused on the changes that are occurring in the political system.

CONFLICTS AND CONTROVERSIAL ISSUES

The review of Kentucky's bipartisan battles provides the background necessary for an understanding of the political system today, but it tells little about the issues that have dominated Kentucky politics. Because local voting habits have been so stable and Kentuckians have so often cast their votes in accord with traditional party loyalties, some of the most important political battles have been fought outside the bipartisan arena or within one of the major parties. The Civil War had a lasting impact on the partisan alignment of voters in the state, but the problems of Reconstruction—resulting from the emancipation and enfranchisement of the Negroes—were settled in Kentucky more quickly and peacefully than in much of the Deep South. In the later years of the nineteenth century the issue that dominated Kentucky politics was the same one inflaming national politics: the conflict between farmers and business interests. In the years following the Civil War there was a concerted campaign to bring industry to the state, a campaign led by the dynamic and influential editor of the Louisville *Courier-Journal*, Henry Watterson. The legislature cooperated by providing a variety of benefits and tax exemptions to business and particularly to the railroads, the expansion of which was expected to stimulate business development throughout the state. The Louisville and Nashville Railroad became one of the most powerful forces in state politics.

After the Civil War the farmers of Kentucky increasingly concentrated their resources on tobacco and so became vulnerable to changes in the market price of that single commodity. The panic of 1873 hit harder and lasted longer in Kentucky than in the nation as a whole, and one of its consequences was the development of an agrarian political movement that challenged the political power structure of the state. The Granger movement and the Greenback party in the 1870s were succeeded by the Farmers' Alliance in 1889 and the Populist party in 1891. Their programs, though not identical, had several common themes: monetary policies favorable to debtors, stricter government regulation of business and particularly of railroads, and greater popular participation in government through such devices as the popular election of United States senators. These groups sometimes sponsored candidates for political office and at other times endorsed candidates of the major parties. The agrarian politicians sometimes proved more adept at winning elections than at translating their political power into legislative victories. By 1890, however, the Farmers' Alliance had won substantial concessions from the Democratic party and had achieved some notable legislative victories against the business lobbyists. The battle was continued in the constitutional convention of 1890-1891, and the detailed provisions of the document that emerged reflected the balance of power among a variety of interests as well as the popular distrust of the legislature.[6]

The last decade of the nineteenth century was a period of political turmoil in Kentucky unmatched since the 1860s. The agrarian groups divided their support in the 1891 gubernatorial election between the Populist and Democratic candidates, and were disillusioned by the limited accomplishments of the elected Democratic governor and legislature. The issue of free silver and the nomination of William Jennings Bryan as the presidential candidate in 1896 caused a disastrous split in the Democratic party in Kentucky as well as nationally. This split was already evident in the 1895 gubernatorial election. Democratic dissension and the presence of a Populist candidate on the ballot gave the governorship to a Republican for the first time, and in 1896 enough "gold Democrats"

[6] Clark, *History of Kentucky*, 412-23.

voted Republican to give the state to McKinley. The farmers had captured the Democratic party, but the Democratic party had lost its secure majority position. Although the agrarian third-party movement gradually died out, for several years the Democratic party was so deeply divided that a virtual three-party system prevailed. One consequence was that a deadlocked legislature was unable to elect a United States senator for many months.

A new champion of the agrarian cause appeared on the scene in the person of William Goebel of Kenton County. He ran for governor in 1899 on a platform of free silver and strict control of the railroads in the apparent hope of linking the western farmers with the urban voters of northern Kentucky. His policies evoked the strong opposition of the Louisville and Nashville Railroad. But the passions that Goebel aroused grew out of his personality as much as his platform. He was an aggressive and—many thought—unscrupulous politician who had made many political enemies and had killed one of them in a duel. He won the Democratic nomination on the twenty-sixth ballot of a tumultuous convention and waged a bitter election campaign. When the state election board declared Republican candidate William Taylor to be elected, Goebel charged fraud and demanded an investigation by the Democratic legislature. As the legislature met to discuss this challenge to the election returns, hundreds of mountain Republicans thronged to the capital, many of them armed and many allegedly transported to Frankfort free by the Louisville and Nashville Railroad. Goebel was shot by an unknown assassin, was sworn in after a legislative committee had declared him elected, and shortly thereafter died. The Democratic candidate for lieutenant governor, J. C. W. Beckham, was sworn in as governor, and after a period of armed truce when the state had two governors, Taylor accepted a judicial verdict in favor of Beckham and left the state.[7]

The "Goebel Affair" left a legacy of bitterness in Kentucky politics, but it also left the business interests and their conservative allies in power. Governor Beckham, who was reelected for a full term in 1903, did not carry out the programs to which Goebel had been committed, and he won the electoral support of the Louisville and Nashville Railroad in the 1903 campaign. The Progressive movement

[7] *Ibid.*, 427-35; John H. Fenton, *Politics in the Border States* (New Orleans: Hauser Press, 1957), 41-44.

of the early twentieth century had little impact in Kentucky. The railroad, coal-mining, liquor, and racetrack interests were allied with some of the more prosperous Bluegrass farmers and the political leaders of both parties in some of the larger cities. This alliance, which in the 1920s was sometimes labeled the "bipartisan combine," threw its support to Republican candidates on several occasions when its favorite failed to win the Democratic nomination. Its ability to win elections rested on campaign contributions and on its ties to urban leaders of both parties who controlled substantial blocks of votes. Alben Barkley challenged these interests in 1923 with a campaign against parimutuel betting and in support of a severance tax on coal and other minerals. He lost the Democratic primary, but in 1927 former Governor Beckham won the primary, this time running as a reform candidate with an almost identical platform. The business interests, and particularly the racing interests, threw their support and large contributions in funds to the Republican candidate, Flem Sampson, who won the election.[8]

The New Deal changed not only the bipartisan balance of power but also the nature of interest-group conflict in Kentucky. The decline of the Republican party made obsolete the strategy of supporting a Republican gubernatorial candidate when the winner of the Democratic primary was considered unacceptable by business interests. Moreover, as the state's economy became more diversified, it became more difficult for one or a few industries to dominate the political system. In particular, the railroad interests lost their position of prominence. The prolonged agricultural depression and the New Deal programs that sought to cope with it persuaded the farmers that the solution to most of their problems lay in Washington rather than in Frankfort. The farmers remained a potent political force, but their demands no longer constituted a challenge to the power structure of the state. During the 1930s that challenge came primarily from the labor unions. The United Mine Workers were a source of continuing strife in the minefields, particularly in eastern Kentucky, as they pressed their organizing campaigns and their strikes for higher wages. The violence that frequently resulted led to pressure from both sides for intervention by the state. The national alliance between organized labor and the Roosevelt administration was duplicated in Kentucky in 1938 when Senator Alben

[8] Fenton, *Politics in the Border States*, 44-55.

Barkley, the national administration's choice, had labor support in a bitter and successful senatorial primary against Governor Chandler. Labor was divided in the 1939 gubernatorial primary, however. The AFL supported the winner, Keen Johnson, who had been lieutenant governor under Chandler. The CIO supported John Y. Brown, an ardent New Dealer who lost several statewide campaigns despite support from organized labor.

Another organized group that has assumed greater importance in Kentucky politics has been the teachers. State support for local education, and for teachers' salaries, has grown as the need for raising educational standards has become recognized and obstacles to such support have been removed from the state constitution. As educational support has become an increasing percentage of the state budget, teachers have become increasingly committed to political action. For example, in the 1947 gubernatorial primary the Kentucky Education Association supported Harry Lee Waterfield, who ran a strong second, and in 1963 Chandler's defeat in his bid for a third term as governor was attributed in part to the strong opposition of the teachers.

DEMOCRATIC FACTIONALISM

One consequence of the Republican decline in state politics in the 1930s was the growing importance of factions in the Democratic party. Democratic governors frequently have attempted to pick their successor, but their selection has usually been contested in a close primary. Democratic politicians have tended to align themselves with one of two factions—the administration or an opposition group. These have been alliances of politicians more than coalitions of interest groups, although each has had to depend on interests for financial support. The beginning of modern Democratic factionalism coincides with the appearance on the state political scene of A. B. "Happy" Chandler. As lieutenant governor, elected in 1931, he challenged the administration faction led by Governor Ruby Laffoon and his ally Thomas Rhea. He blocked the administration's plan to bypass the primary in 1935 and nominate Rhea as governor by convention. During the governor's temporary absence from the state Chandler called a special session of the legislature, which adopted a compulsory primary law, though it added a runoff feature that was expected to improve Rhea's chances. Chandler ran second to Rhea in the first primary, but defeated him in the runoff, and then as governor secured passage of a revised primary law—still in effect—without a runoff. The absence of a runoff has helped to perpetuate a bifactional pattern of competition within the Democratic primary.[9]

Though Chandler lost the senatorial primary to Barkley in 1938, he resigned as governor in 1939 and accepted an appointment by Lieutenant Governor Keen Johnson to fill a senatorial vacancy caused by the death of Senator M. M. Logan. As long as Chandler remained in the Senate, he continued to be a potent force in Kentucky politics; when he resigned to become baseball commissioner, his influence in the state waned. Keen Johnson was elected to a full gubernatorial term in 1939, but in 1943 his choice for governor, Lyter Donaldson, won the primary and lost the election.

In 1947 Harry Lee Waterfield and Earle C. Clements battled for the Democratic gubernatorial nomination. Waterfield, who lost, succeeded in building a political following that made him a potent force in subsequent elections. Clements, who won the primary and the general election, likewise was able to build a powerful statewide organization and succeeded in winning a term as governor for his lieutenant governor, Lawrence Wetherby, after he entered the United States Senate. In 1951 Chandler left baseball and returned to Kentucky, where he rebuilt his political fences and formed an alliance with Waterfield. The Chandler-Waterfield alliance and the Clements organization met head-on in the 1955 gubernatorial primary. Chandler defeated Bert Combs, the candidate selected by Clements, and Waterfield won the lieutenant governorship. A year later Clements lost his Senate seat to Republican Thruston Morton as a direct result of the heat generated by the 1955 primary. In 1959 Combs defeated Waterfield for the governorship, and the outcome was regarded as a victory for Clements over Chandler. Within a year, however, Combs declared his independence, Clements lost his post as highway commissioner, and the seeds were sown for a new alliance. In 1963 Chandler again ran for governor, with Waterfield again the candidate for lieutenant governor, and with the organizational skills of Clements devoted to their cause. But the political resources of a governor are substantial in Kentucky politics, and Combs was a governor who combined political talent

[9] *Ibid.*, 27-37.

with a varied and progressive program. Combs' choice for governor, Edward T. "Ned" Breathitt, defeated Chandler, but Waterfield won the lieutenant governorship, and after a brief pause the factional contest was renewed within the administration. In 1967, the Breathitt administration endorsed Henry Ward, who defeated both Chandler and Waterfield in the gubernatorial primary but lost the general election.

LEGAL REGULATION OF ELECTIONS AND PARTIES

Kentucky has been blessed—or plagued—with almost continuous political campaigning because primary and general elections are often close and elections are held annually. The governor, other state officials, and legislators are elected a year before the presidential election, and county officials and legislators are chosen a year after presidential elections. It is not unusual for impatient candidates to launch a campaign for the May primary only hours after the polls have closed at the November election.

The state constitution sets as qualifications for voting: United States citizenship, 18 years of age, and residence one year in the state, six months in the county, and sixty days in the precinct. In 1955 Kentucky became the second state to drop the voting age requirement lower than 21. Kentucky has not yet joined the increasing number of states that permit new residents to vote in presidential elections. The residence requirements constitute an increasingly serious limitation on voting as citizens become more mobile, and long-term Kentucky residents are frequently dismayed to discover that they have temporarily lost the right to vote by moving across the street into another precinct.

Qualified voters who are temporarily absent from the county may vote by absentee ballot. The absentee ballot has frequently been a subject of controversy in Kentucky because it has been vulnerable to fraudulent administration. In some counties the county clerk has encouraged persons to fill out an absentee ballot and has "assisted" them in doing so, whether or not they were going to be out of town. Several years ago the legislature, frustrated in its efforts to devise a fraud-proof law, abolished the right of absentee voting except for servicemen and college students, but in 1964 the legislature adopted a new absentee ballot law that was designed to limit the county clerk's authority by providing that all applications for absentee ballots be reviewed at an open hearing during which candidates could challenge applicants.

Registration is permanent in Kentucky. Once a voter has registered, he does not have to reregister unless he changes his name (by marriage, for example) or moves to another county, although he may be dropped from the rolls for failure to vote for two years.[10] The permanent registration system is a great convenience to the voter, but it may also be an invitation to fraud. State law requires county registration and purgation boards to review registration lists periodically and purge them of persons no longer eligible to vote in the county, and it authorizes a variety of techniques designed to facilitate purgation, ranging from house-to-house canvasses to grand jury investigations. But there is ample evidence that in some counties, particularly rural counties rapidly losing population, the purgation boards are ineffective and the voting rolls are crowded with names of persons no longer eligible.

Evidence of overcrowded and outdated registration lists can be gained by comparing the number of registered voters with the total population in the counties. In 1965 there were 27 counties in which the number of registered voters was larger than two-thirds of the 1960 county population. All of these were rural counties, in most of which population was declining, and most were counties under one-party domination. In a few of these counties the registration proportion surpassed 80 percent. By contrast, in the largest urban counties, where purgation procedures are usually followed more closely, the percentage was about 40 or slightly higher. Approximately 61 percent of the population in Kentucky is of voting age (18 or older), and consequently any registration figure higher than that is open to serious suspicion. It is true that the proportion of persons of voting age varies substantially from county to county, but in only one of the 27 counties with a two-thirds registration proportion does the estimated number of persons of voting age surpass the number of registered voters. In almost half of these counties (mostly in eastern Kentucky) the proportion of inhabitants of voting age is less than the statewide percentage of 61 percent. Clearly in these 27 counties, and to a lesser extent in many others, thousands of names are on the registration lists that do not belong there.[11]

[10] For a brief history of the registration system in Kentucky, see Jasper Shannon, "The Political Process in Kentucky," *Kentucky Law Journal*, XLV (1957), 414-20.

[11] Data on registration provided by the Republican State Central Committee.

Routine registration and purgation work is carried out by the county clerk, but responsibility for supervision is in the hands of a three-man bipartisan registration and purgation board appointed by a state board of election commissioners, consisting of the secretary of state and one Democrat and one Republican. This state board also appoints county boards of election commissioners, consisting of the sheriff and one Democrat and one Republican. The county board selects four election officers in each precinct, two from each party. The state board lacks the necessary staff and financing to supervise or provide service for the county boards. It also lacks the authority to insure that county boards are performing their duties competently.

Election fraud is not, of course, a problem unique to Kentucky, but it is one that has plagued the state to an unusual degree and has inspired repeated legislative efforts at reform. Several years ago Kentucky became one of the first states to require the use of voting machines in every precinct. This has eliminated several opportunities for fraud in the casting and counting of ballots. By making possible a fast compilation of the vote, it has deprived politicians of their excuse for delaying election returns until they knew how many votes were needed by a statewide candidate. Voting machines also permit a fast, economical recanvass of close elections, even in statewide contests.

One problem that cannot be solved by voting machines or by new legislative enactments is the lax administration of elections. When voters at the polls fail to sign the registration books, when electioneering takes place inside the polling place, or when a single election officer is permitted to "help" a voter cast his ballot, it is because election officers are not doing their job. The cause may be ignorance or apathy on the part of the officers, or it may be that officers representing one party or faction are willing to permit election activity that will help the other party or faction. This is a problem endemic to counties dominated by one party. Election officers representing the minority party may be persuaded, in return for some form of patronage or reimbursement, to overlook election violations encouraged by the majority party or by one faction of the majority party. It is a problem likely to decline in importance as two-party competition grows throughout the state.

The state's first statewide primary law, in 1892, provided for state regulation of the primary but did not require political parties to use the primary in making nominations.[12] Although the Republican party continued to use the convention frequently, the Democrats used the primary consistently to nominate statewide candidates (including United States Senators when they became elected) from 1903 until 1931. The use of a convention in the latter year and the debate concerning its proposed use in 1935 led to the passage of a compulsory primary law in 1935 after Lieutenant Governor Chandler took the initiative in calling a special session of the legislature. As passed in 1935 and revised the following year, the law requires both major parties to use the primary election for nominating candidates in almost all partisan elections, statewide and local. The party may use a convention or a primary to select nominees for presidential elector—and in fact both parties use a convention—and to nominate candidates to replace primary winners who die or resign or to run for office in a special election to fill a vacancy.

It is ridiculously easy to become a candidate in a primary for any office. The candidate must simply swear that he is a registered voter in his party, that he believes in its principles, and that he intends to support the party's nominees and supported them in the previous election. He must also find two members of his party willing to swear to the truth of his declaration. No signatures on petitions are necessary, and no filing fee above one dollar is required. Independent candidates for office may be nominated by petition, although the number of signatures required is relatively low: 1,000 for statewide office and 100 for state legislative or county office. Independent candidates for election must file their petitions before the primary election is held, a requirement that enhances the importance of the primary by making it impossible for the loser in a primary election to run as an independent in the general election. Candidates for judge of the Court of Appeals or a circuit court may seek nomination in the primaries of either or both political parties.

Kentucky uses the closed primary. A voter may not vote in the primary unless he has previously registered as a member of that party. The law also discourages a voter from frequently switching parties. If he changes party registration, he cannot vote in the primary of the new party until one general election has been held. The purpose of the closed primary is to assure that a party's nominations are made by the members of that party without inter-

---

[12] Shannon, "Political Process in Kentucky," 421-29.

ference or raiding by members of the other party. The consequence of the closed primary in Kentucky is that many voters register with one party even though their sympathies and often their votes in the general election are given to the other party. The Democratic primary has been so often decisive in the selection of the governor and other state officials that many Republicans register Democratic in order to have a stronger voice in choosing these officials, and a similar incentive applies to local primaries in many counties. In the smaller number of counties dominated by Republicans some Democratic voters who are more interested in local than in state contests register Republican. This misleading registration creates a problem for both parties—but particularly the minority—in identifying potential supporters during a campaign. The dominant place occupied by the Democratic primary in state elections has a more important consequence: the attention and interest of potential Republican voters are focused on the Democratic primary, and the Republican candidates find it difficult to win the support of these voters who have often identified themselves with the winning Democratic candidate.

Kentucky law defines a major political party as "an affiliation or organization of electors representing a political policy and having a constituted authority for its government and regulation, and which cast at least twenty percent of the total vote cast at the last preceding election at which presidential electors were voted for."[13] Minor parties are defined similarly if they cast at least 2 percent of the vote in the last regular election. The law also regulates a party's nominations through the requirement of a primary and authorizes the party organization itself to nominate in the case of vacancies. The law also authorizes the state central committees of the parties to submit a list of names from which the state board of election commissioners is chosen. The county committees may submit names for the selection of county boards of election commissioners and boards of registration and purgation, and they may also submit names for the choice of precinct election officers. Although the law recognizes state and county party organizations by assigning them these powers, there is no provision in the state law regulating or specifying the organizational structure of the state parties. State committees and conven-

[13] *Kentucky Revised Statutes,* 119.010.

tions, county committees, and precinct leaders may be selected in any way that the political parties choose. In a number of states the law provides rigid and sometimes impractical specifications for the organization and powers of state parties, and as a result in some states informal, extralegal party organizations have been created to do what the formal party organization is incapable of doing. In Kentucky the political parties remain free from such restrictions.[14]

THE CHANGING POPULATION

Kentucky is a land of contrasts—contrasts so drastic as to make a mockery of generalizations about its politics. For decades the people of eastern Kentucky have been isolated from the rest of the state. The mountains not only were a barrier to transportation and communication but helped to preserve a cultural heritage and a way of life that had little in common with that of the rest of the state. Today the transportation barrier is being broken, and Appalachia has attracted the attention of the national government and the national press. But the problems of Appalachia remain. Its land is too hilly and eroded for agriculture, its human and natural resources can support only limited industry, and the coal mines that brought a period of boom to parts of Appalachia a generation ago have left a legacy of unemployment and natural resources despoiled in recent years by strip mining. As the urban sectors of the state grow more prosperous, the low levels of income and education and the high levels of unemployment in eastern Kentucky stand out in sharper contrast than ever. The greatest change in eastern Kentucky is the increased pace of outmigration as the younger, better educated citizens move to the cities of Kentucky or leave the state entirely.

The Bluegrass region with its prosperous horse farms and its gently rolling agricultural land is strikingly different. Although relatively few persons own large horse farms and although there are areas of rural poverty in the Bluegrass, most of the Bluegrass counties have farm incomes that are substantially above the average. Farmers in both central and western Kentucky are primarily tobacco growers. They have been avid supporters of governmental policies designed

[14] Kentucky Legislative Research Committee, *State Regulation of Political Parties* (Frankfort, 1962).

to support prices by rigidly controlling acreage, but the restrictions that have become necessary in recent years have seriously curbed the potential earning power of Kentucky farmers.

Western Kentucky like the state itself presents a picture of diversity. Stretching along the Tennessee border are some of the more prosperous agricultural counties in the state, but the average farm income in the area is low, substantially lower than in the Bluegrass. In the center of the region is a block of counties, Hopkins and Muhlenberg in particular, with extensive coal production, most of it done through strip mining, as well as a group of other counties where oil production is high. Along the Ohio river are Owensboro, Henderson, and Paducah, cities ranging in size from 42,000 to 17,000 population.

The major metropolitan center in Kentucky is Jefferson County (Louisville), a prosperous, rapidly growing area where one out of five Kentuckians live. Fayette County (Lexington), in the heart of the Bluegrass, is growing even more rapidly. The third major population center is the suburban area south of Cincinnati; Campbell and Kenton counties have the highest income level in the state and are growing at a more modest rate. Except for Boyd County, adjacent to Huntington, West Virginia, most of the other urban centers are scattered through western Kentucky, notably in Christian, Daviess, Henderson, McCracken, and Warren counties. According to the 1960 census there were five standard metropolitan statistical areas in Kentucky, but those incorporating Boyd, Henderson, Campbell, and Kenton counties were dominated by larger cities outside the state. Only two Kentucky counties—Jefferson and Fayette— were large enough by themselves to qualify for metropolitan status. With these exceptions, Kentucky is characterized by small cities; but outside of eastern Kentucky these urban counties are growing at a steady rate and are consistently among the counties with the highest levels of income in the state.

In 1960 the state's population reached 3,038,156, a gain of only 93,350 (or 3.2 percent) since 1950. During that decade the population of the United States rose by 28 million, or 18.5 percent. Only four states had a smaller percentage gain than Kentucky did. By 1966, however, Kentucky's population had risen about 4 percent above the 1960 level. By contrast the state's population had risen at a rate of more than 8 percent between 1920 and 1940, but by only 3.5 percent between 1940 and 1950. The slow rate of growth during the 1950s was attributable to outmigration. During that decade the natural increase in population was 16.2 percent, almost half a million, but the net loss in the exchange of migrants with other states was 13.2 percent of the 1950 population, or almost 400,000.

The relative stability of total population figures is deceptive though, because the population changes within the state have been great, and it is these changes that deserve attention because of the effect they are having on Kentucky politics. During the 1950-1960 decade only 33 counties gained population and 87 counties lost, although a few of the latter made up the loss in the first half of the 1960s. The losses resulted from a rate of outmigration, to other parts of Kentucky or to other states, that outstripped the natural increase in population. In fact, 108 of the state's 120 counties had a net loss through migration. A solid block of 21 counties in southeastern Kentucky had a net rate of outmigration above 30 percent (and often above 40 percent) during the 1950s, although most of these had a natural rate increase above 15 percent. Every one of these counties lost at least 10 percent of its population, and often 20 percent, in a decade. From 1940 to 1966 these 21 counties lost over 167,000 persons, or 27 percent of their population.[15]

Throughout southeastern Kentucky there is a steady loss of population—persons of working age, particularly the younger generation, who have given up hope of finding employment. Harry Caudill, in *Night Comes to the Cumberlands,* quotes a high school principal in one southeastern Kentucky county as saying that not a single member of the last three graduating classes has remained in the county.[16] Those who stay behind are the children and the members of the older generation who are unable or unwilling to adapt to new jobs and a new way of life in another county or another state. These losses in population have obvious implications for the vitality of

[15] Population data are from a publication of the Department of Rural Sociology, University of Kentucky, "Provisional Population Estimates for Kentucky Counties as of January 1, 1966" (mimeographed); Willis A. Sutton, Jr., and Jerry Russell, *The Social Dimensions of Kentucky Counties* (Lexington: University of Kentucky Bureau of Community Service, 1964).

[16] Harry M. Caudill, *Night Comes to the Cumberlands* (Boston: Little, Brown, and Co., 1962), 334. Caudill's volume provides an excellent introductory study for an understanding of eastern Kentucky.

political systems in the southeastern counties. The counties that are losing population rapidly include almost all of the traditional Republican counties in the southeast. They also include traditional Democratic counties in the northern part of the region and the major coal-mining counties that have been more closely competitive.

Although the heaviest and most consistent population losses have occurred in the southeast, it should be emphasized that most of the nonurban counties, except in the Bluegrass region, have been losing population and within these counties there has been a steady movement from the farms to the smaller cities. Only those counties that have succeeded in attracting industry have been able to slow down the exodus of population. The Democrats in western Kentucky, like the Republicans in the southeast, are gradually losing voters in their areas of traditional support simply as a result of population trends.

There were 33 counties that gained population from 1950 to 1960, 7 of them by more than 25 percent. During the decade the proportion of Kentuckians living in urban areas grew from 36.8 to 44.5 percent. From 1940 to 1966 there were 11 counties that gained 509,000 persons, or an increase of 62 percent. The greatest gain occurred in Jefferson County (279,000) and in two small suburban counties nearby. The greatest percentage gain (100 percent) occurred in Fayette County. Three counties—Campbell, Kenton, and Boone—that form part of the suburbs of Cincinnati gained 36 percent in 25 years. The most notable gains in western Kentucky were in Christian, Daviess, and McCracken counties, with an average of 41 percent. Franklin County, containing the state capital, gained 45 percent. (The large gains in Hardin County, 160 percent in 25 years, result largely from the growing number of military personnel and their dependents at Fort Knox.)

From population statistics the metropolitan and urban voters are obviously becoming more important in Kentucky politics. Although it is less obvious from statistical data, it is the suburban areas that are gaining most rapidly in population. About half of these new voters come from other parts of Kentucky and half from out of state. Many of them have probably come from areas of traditional Republican or Democratic allegiance, but in the suburbs traditional loyalties may gradually weaken. The suburban voter in Kentucky today is both mobile and unpredictable, and the fact that he constitutes a rapidly increasing part of the electorate is a major reason why

Kentucky politics is changing, why the traditional voting patterns are becoming less significant and less useful as predictors of voting trends in the state. Kentucky generally lags behind in urban and suburban growth, but in a few areas of the state this growth is occurring at a rapid rate, and it is these areas that will set the pattern for Kentucky's political future.

2 | Democratic Party Organization

In Kentucky, as in most states, there is a difference between the formal party structure and the informal power structure within the party. The regulations that describe the organization of the Democratic party define both the arena and the rules for the contest to control Democratic political power in the state. Although the struggle for power often occurs outside the confines of the formal party organization, the contestants usually seek to control the party machinery as well. There is incentive for politicians to gain dominant positions in the state and county party organizations not only because such victories are a matter of prestige but also because, under state law, the party committees have authority to fill vacancies for nominations and to recommend the party's members for state and local election boards and Democratic election officials in the precincts. In the contest at the state level the governor and his supporters have such an advantage that they are rarely denied a controlling position in the party organization, and during a Republican administration there may be a power vacuum within the Democratic organization. In the individual counties, however, there is no certainty that the governor's power will be sufficient to guarantee his supporters control over the organization.

State and county officers in the Democratic party are selected by different means and at separate times, although both are chosen during presidential election years. Several weeks prior to the national convention, mass meetings of Democratic voters are held in each county (and in each legislative district in Jefferson County) to elect delegates to the state convention. A county's proportion of seats in the state convention is based on the number of votes cast for the Democratic candidate for president in the last election. The state convention chooses nominees for presidential elector, delegates to the national convention, members of the state central executive committee, the state chairman and vice chairman, and the national committeeman and committeewoman. It also adopts party rules.

The election of a governor foreshadows a shift in control of the party organization, since he and his allies usually dictate the convention's choices, and that shift is more drastic if the new governor is allied with a faction different from that of his predecessor. A new governor is nominated in May and elected in November of the year preceding the presidential election. By the time the state convention meets in the following summer, the governor's political machine is well oiled and he has utilized the patronage resources at his disposal. The delegates to the convention therefore usually are persons who supported him in the primary election or those who acted promptly to demonstrate their loyalty to him in the months following the primary. They are usually willing to accept his choices for seats on the central executive committee, and with some exceptions they are willing to follow his advice on the tactics to be followed by the Kentucky delegation to the national convention. On rare occasions the governor's authority to run the state convention has been challenged, party harmony has been drowned out by factional shouting, and the convention has been chaotic rather than placid. The conventions of 1948, 1952, 1960, and 1964 were examples of strong, unchallenged gubernatorial control, but in the 1956 convention the governor prevailed only after a vigorous battle with the opposing faction that started in the county mass meetings and was climaxed on the convention floor. When the governor is a Republican, there is greater likelihood of an open struggle for control of the state convention.

The rules adopted by the Democratic convention provide that the state central executive committee "shall constitute the supreme governing authority of the Democratic Party in Kentucky, and shall have control and supervision over all matters relating to or affecting party organization, and management of campaigns, unless otherwise provided by law."[1] The state central executive committee consists

[1] "Rules of the Democratic Party," adopted by the Democratic state convention, July 18, 1964.

of two men and two women from each congressional district and seven members from the state at large. Its powers include calling state conventions, employment of a secretary and staff, and final decision on contests for the election of party officials at the county or precinct level (after initial review by the committee members chosen in the appropriate congressional district). When a vacancy occurs that requires a special election or when it occurs less than 70 days before a primary or when the winner of a primary election dies or is unable to run in the general election, the central executive committee makes the nomination.

The county organizations of the party are chosen in December of presidential election years. On the first Saturday of the month registered Democrats meet at the polling places in each precinct and elect a precinct committeeman and committeewoman. On the following Saturday these precinct officials meet to elect the county officials. In most counties the precinct committeemen and committeewomen constitute the county committee and elect a county chairman and a secretary. In large counties containing more than one legislative district the precinct officials in each district elect a chairman and a secretary; and the district chairmen, who constitute the county committee, elect a chairman and a secretary for the county. The district or county chairmen and secretaries may be chosen from among those elected to the committee or from outside that group. Party rules delegate to the county committees the authority to fill vacancies in nominations for public officials who are elected at the county level. State law gives the county committees authority to recommend members for the county boards of election commissioners, and of registration and purgation; to recommend names of precinct election officers; and to select challengers at general and primary elections. Between the state and county level there are also congressional, senatorial, judicial, and legislative district committees that are authorized to fill vacancies in nominations.

COUNTY MASS MEETINGS

Attendance at the county mass meetings is usually small and is generally confined to active political workers, local officeholders, state workers, and perhaps a few interested citizens. The Democrats who gathered at the Fayette County courthouse numbered only 35 in 1948 and between 100 and 200 in 1960 and 1964, less than the number of registered Democrats in most any precinct of the metropolitan community. In 1960 attendance at the eleven district meetings in Jefferson County ranged from less than 50 to a little more than 100. That year, attendance at mass meetings in rural counties varied from a handful to several hundred, but it was often greater, in proportion to the number of registered Democratic voters, than it was in the metropolitan counties.

The county meetings are usually run smoothly and efficiently. A list of delegates is read, nominations are closed, and the crowd murmurs its approval. Occasionally, in one of the smaller counties, all of those present at the meeting are named as delegates, though few are likely to attend. Sometimes motions are adopted endorsing specific local leaders for membership on the central executive committee or on the delegation to the national convention. Frequently a motion is adopted to require that the county delegation be bound by the unit rule. This device not only maximizes the county's voting power but, perhaps more importantly, facilitates voting amid the noise and confusion on the convention floor. Reports from 33 counties in 1960 showed that the unit rule was adopted in about half of the meetings; almost half of the meetings endorsed Lyndon Johnson's presidential candidacy, and the others made no endorsement. Unanimity was not the rule in every county meeting in 1960, however. In several of the Jefferson County districts efforts were made to place supporters of Adlai Stevenson on the delegation, but were quickly defeated. In four counties local factionalism led to the convening of rump meetings and the selection of two groups of delegates to the 1960 state convention. The hottest dispute was in Woodford County, home of former Governor Chandler, where some 500 persons attended one or the other meeting. Such disputes were rare in 1960, however; Governor Combs and his allies were in firm control of most counties. It is symptomatic of the political advantage enjoyed by the incumbent governor that only a few months after Governor Chandler left office his supporters from his home county were unable to get seated at the state convention.

The county meetings held prior to the 1956 state convention contrasted sharply with the normal pattern of discipline and harmony because Senator Earle Clements and former Governor Lawrence Wetherby refused to concede control to Governor Chandler, who had defeated the Clements-Wetherby faction in the 1955 primary. Shortly before the 1956 county meetings and the state conventions, Senator Clements had won renomination in the primary over an opponent who had Chandler's support, and the central executive committee had defied Chandler and named Wetherby to run for the Senate seat recently left vacant by Alben Barkley's death.

On the last day of June 1956 Democratic voters arrived at the courthouses across the state in unprecedented numbers. They crowded into the courtrooms and overflowed into the halls and offices. In many counties the meetings were moved outside to the courthouse lawn. The Chandler administration had sent out word to state workers that they must not only come to the meetings but must bring their families and friends. Active party workers of both factions attended. In addition, it was obvious that thousands of ordinary voters attended a party meeting for the first time in their lives. Crowds numbering several hundred were common, and there were both urban and rural counties where more than 1,000 voters appeared. Attendance at the legislative district meetings in Jefferson County ranged from 300 to 600; there were roughly 2,000 at the McCracken, Henderson, and Floyd county meetings; and a throng of 5,000 gathered in Fayette County. Perhaps the most accurate way of evaluating attendance at the county meetings is to compare it with the vote cast a month earlier in the Democratic senatorial primary, a contest in which the factional conflict between Clements and Chandler was well publicized. Of 33 counties for which attendance data were available in the press, there were 22 in which attendance at county meetings was equal to at least one-fourth of the total voting in the primary; in six of these at least half as many went to the meetings as voted in the primary.

At some of these county meetings one faction had such preponderant strength that the other faction offered no dissent when the meeting was organized and a slate of delegates was elected. But in many counties a vote was taken, either on the selection of a chairman for the meeting or on the election of delegates. It was no easy matter to take an accurate count of hundreds or even thousands of voters crowded into the courthouse or milling about outside the building, and disputes over the accuracy of the vote sometimes led to rump meetings. In many counties the leaders displayed considerable ingenuity in devising counting procedures. In Madison County the voters were counted as they filed out the door of the courthouse, and the Chandler forces had a 705-513 majority. In Floyd County the large crowd went to an athletic field and then were counted as they filed out of the gate; Chandler won 977 to 825. Where the crowds were smaller or where one group clearly outnumbered the other, it was possible to get an accurate enough count by a show of hands.

In about one-fourth of the counties, and in four of the legislative districts of Jefferson County, one faction or the other left the meeting and elected another slate of delegates, although only 23 counties brought their seating disputes to the state convention. The great majority of the rump conventions were held by the supporters of Governor Chandler. In a number of counties as soon as the first vote had been taken, or the balance of forces had become obvious, the minority group simply walked out and held its own meeting. In other counties the walkout resulted from disputes over voting procedures. In Floyd County the outnumbered Clements forces charged that some of those voting for Chandler were ineligible to participate, a charge that was plausible but obviously impossible to prove in a crowd of 1,800. In several counties one faction disputed the accuracy of the vote count or claimed that some persons were going through the doors twice to inflate the total count. In some counties a walkout resulted from arbitrary procedures used by those who were presiding and who refused to permit more than one candidate for chairman or more than one slate of delegates to be nominated.

The most chaotic county meeting in 1956 was probably that held in Fayette County. A crowd of some 5,000 persons jammed the courthouse grounds, presenting a massive problem in head-counting. But the local leaders, loyal to the Clements faction, made no effort to count heads. Clustered in and around a police cruiser equipped with a loudspeaker and guarded by several policemen, they hurriedly opened the meeting, elected a chairman, read the list of delegates, declared them elected by a voice vote, and adjourned, while leaders of the Chandler faction pushed and shoved in a vain effort to get access to the microphone that would enable them to be heard in offering alternative candidates. The Chandler forces, who were apparently in the minority, then convened a separate meeting to elect their slate of delegates, who were eventually seated.

The county meeting generally is an efficient device by which the dominant political faction in a county can formalize its selection of delegates to the state convention. In 1956 the meetings were used to settle the struggle between two factions for control of the Democratic party. In some counties the meetings served this purpose very well; there was a large turnout, and one faction won a decisive majority. But too often the meetings ended in disputes. On the one hand, it was easy for one faction to run the meeting in an arbitrary fashion or to pack it with ineligible persons; on the other hand, a minority faction that had no valid complaint about the method of running the meeting was able to hold a rump meeting and gamble on its delegates' being seated if its political allies held the upper hand at the state convention. In the largest counties the sheer size of the crowds made an accurate vote difficult, and perhaps impossible if the balance was close. In some states delegates to state conventions are chosen in primary elections. In close contests like that in 1956 there is no certainty that more voters would go to the polls than went to the courthouses, but the elections would be more orderly and efficient—particularly in large counties—and less subject to dispute. Finally, it is noteworthy that the largest turnout at county meetings in recent years was inspired by a factional struggle for control of the state party and not by a dispute over the endorsement of presidential candidates. By contrast, the turnout was small and there were few disputes at the county level in 1960 when the state party was divided over the selection of a presidential candidate.

THE STATE CONVENTION

The state convention meets in two stages. The delegates assemble in the morning by congressional districts and then meet in the afternoon as the state convention. Each district convention nominates a presidential elector, subject to approval by the state convention. Each district convention also selects some of the delegates to the national convention and some members of the state central executive committee, and reports its action to the state convention. Although the district conventions appear to have considerable independent authority, the state convention is the supreme governing authority of the party and can change the rules if necessary to limit the independence of district conventions. Moreover, the governor's influence over the convention is great enough so that conflicts are not likely to arise. If there were a struggle for control over the convention and disputes arose over the seating of delegates, the convention delegates would act on the report of the credentials committee; if delegates who had constituted a majority of a district convention were unseated, as occurred in 1956, the state convention might reverse the decisions taken by that district convention.[2]

The state convention looks and acts more like a political rally than like a decision-making body. The morning sessions of the congressional district conventions are brief and are devoted to the routine business of selecting members of the central executive committee and the national convention delegation. In the afternoon 2,000 or more Democrats assemble, usually in a room too small to provide seats for all. There are no serious efforts to check the credentials of those entering the hall. Delegates may sit with their county delegation or at least with others from their congressional district, or perhaps any place where they can find a seat. The convention completes the job of ratifying lists of members for the state central executive committee and the national convention delegations and filling other offices. It adopts whatever resolutions are proposed by the committees, usually without debate and sometimes without much attention to the substance of the resolutions. The decisions of the convention are normally made by voice vote and with little or no dissent. This is perhaps fortunate, because an accurate rollcall vote would be virtually an impossibility on the crowded convention floor. Most of the time of the convention is taken up by speeches defending the record of the state Democratic party and laying the groundwork for the presidential campaign that lies ahead.

During a Democratic administration, the governor and his associates carefully prepare a list of central executive committee members, for approval by the convention, so as to give recognition to those persons who are either most prominent or who represent the most important elements in his factional coalition. Membership on the delegation to the national convention is another form of recognition and reward for those who have been loyal members of the governor's faction and who would enjoy a trip to the convention.

[2] The authors are indebted to Thomas C. Carroll, legal counsel of the state Democratic party, for providing information on rules and procedures relating to the Democratic convention.

When the 1956 state convention met, Governor Chandler had the undisputed support of a majority of delegates to the convention as well as a majority of those representing six of the eight congressional districts. This gave him control of the credentials committee, which consisted of one member elected by each of the congressional district conventions. There were disputes about the seating of approximately one-fourth of the delegates representing 23 counties. In some cases the disputes resulted from the failure of party leaders to run the county meetings in a democratic fashion according to party rules, but in other cases the minority had simply walked out of county meetings and elected their own delegates. The Chandler forces had made greater use of rump meetings than the Clements faction had. The credentials committee quickly decided most of the disputes in favor of the Chandler delegates, and the convention accepted the committee's report. After some of the Clements delegates from Jefferson County had been ousted, the remaining ones from that county walked out. Victories in the county meetings and in the credential committee gave Chandler overwhelming control of the state convention. The convention elected a central executive committee consisting almost entirely of Chandler men, even ousting two of the members who had been chosen by the Jefferson County district convention dominated by Clements. The convention urged Chandler's presidential nomination, but carefully avoided any endorsement of the senatorial candidacies of Clements and Wetherby.

The state convention is not only a device for consolidating a Democratic governor's control over the party, but is also a vehicle for committing the party to the support of the presidential candidate preferred by the governor. The usual practice has been for the state convention to instruct its national convention delegation to vote for a specific candidate and to be bound by the unit rule. In 1948 and again in 1952 the state administration endorsed Alben Barkley and the state convention enthusiastically supported this choice. The 1948 convention voted to send a delegation that was bound by the unit rule but uninstructed in order that it could support Barkley for president or vice president, as political developments dictated. The 1952 convention instructed its delegation to cast a unit vote for Barkley and to "do each and every thing necessary to secure his nomination." Although Barkley withdrew from the race before the balloting started at the national convention, his name was placed in nomination and the Kentucky delegation voted for him as a unit on all three ballots. Governor Chandler's successful struggle to win control of the 1956 state convention not only insured the election of his allies to the central committee but also guaranteed the convention's endorsement of his presidential candidacy. The convention instructed the delegation to the national convention to cast its votes as a unit for Chandler, and the delegation did so. Even after Chandler's brief but intensive campaign across the country had clearly failed, the Kentucky delegation remained loyal and provided 30 of the 36½ votes that Chandler received in the balloting at the national convention.

At the 1960 state convention Governor Bert Combs gained full control over the party organization and used this power to promote the presidential candidacy of Lyndon Johnson, but for several reasons he placed a lower priority on complete unity than his recent predecessors had. One obvious difference was that in 1960 the governor was not supporting a Kentuckian for the presidential nomination. Another important factor was that Combs and Wilson Wyatt had campaigned in 1959 on a platform that included a pledge to abolish the unit rule for the state's delegation, and Combs reaffirmed this pledge on the eve of the state convention. Another factor that affected Combs' strategy was that several of his closest political allies preferred other presidential candidates. Lieutenant Governor Wilson Wyatt was committed to Adlai Stevenson, whom he had served in previous elections as campaign manager and adviser. Several leaders of the powerful Jefferson County organization were supporters of John Kennedy. The strongest support for Lyndon Johnson came from Earle Clements, who had served as his deputy in the Senate and later as his staff assistant.

Combs and Clements shared the responsibility for preparing a list of delegates to the national convention, and whenever possible they selected persons who favored Johnson's candidacy or were willing to commit themselves to support him. This was not difficult to do because Johnson was apparently the choice of most active Democratic workers in the state. There were a few cases, and probably only a few, in which pressure was put on party leaders who wanted to serve on the delegations but who were reluctant to become committed to Johnson. The delegation included several prominent Democrats who were committed to other candidates, and at the convention only 25½ of the state's 31 votes went to Johnson. (Chandler, who voted for Kennedy, attended the convention ex officio in his capacity as outgoing national committeeman.) Although four of the eight congressional district delegations passed resolutions urging support for Lyndon Johnson, the state convention did not endorse any presidential candidate and none of the speakers at the convention, including Combs and Clements, made reference to a presidential candidate. It is clear that at the 1960 state convention Governor Combs gave highest priority to unification of his faction and consolidation of its control over the party, and he promoted the interests of Lyndon Johnson only to the extent that this did not interfere with his prime objective.[3]

In 1964 the Kentucky Democratic convention once again imposed the unit rule on its delegation, but there was no controversy over the action because it was taken in support of the incumbent president. The delegation was instructed to vote for the nomination of President Johnson and whomever the president selected as his running mate.

CENTRAL EXECUTIVE COMMITTEE

The central executive committee usually includes the governor, several of the most important leaders of the governor's faction, and a sample of local leaders who have been loyal and valuable to that faction of the party. The committee members are important leaders at the state or local level, but membership on the committee is not necessarily a measure of importance or power within the governor's faction of the party. Half of the 28 members from congressional districts must be women, and only a few of these are likely to be as powerful politically as most of the men on the committee.

The committee has only a few formal powers, but occasionally these assume importance. Between conventions it can fill vacancies for chairman, national committeeman or committeewoman, or member of the committee itself (with members representing a congressional district chosen by the remaining members from that

---

[3] For more details, see Malcolm E. Jewell, "Leadership and Party Unity: The Kentucky Democratic Delegation," in Paul Tillett, ed., *Inside Politics: The National Conventions, 1960* (Dobbs Ferry, N.Y.: Oceana Publications, 1962).

district). In making such appointments the committee would normally be guided by the governor's wishes. The committee's power to settle disputes over the organization of county parties gives it the opportunity to protect the interests of one faction in the relatively few counties where such disputes occur.

Legally and politically, the most important power of the committee is that of making nominations to fill vacancies. Because the power to make county and district nominations has been delegated to county and district organizations, the central executive committee is concerned only with the relatively rare instances of vacancies for statewide office. The importance of this power is best illustrated by the struggle over nominating a senatorial candidate to replace Alben Barkley, who died in 1956. Barkley's death occurred on April 30, after the filing deadline for the May primary, and it became necessary for the committee to nominate someone to run in the special November election. Governor Chandler had authority to appoint a senator to serve until the November election, and he also sought to influence the committee's decision. Because of the time lag between Governor Chandler's inauguration in December and the state convention in July, however, the committee remained under the firm control of Senator Clements and former Governor Wetherby. The committee met within two weeks after Barkley's death but postponed action; the strategy was to wait until the senatorial primary election in late May, when Clements' anticipated victory over a candidate endorsed by Chandler was expected to strengthen his bargaining position. After several weeks of maneuvering and rumors of compromise, the central executive committee met and unanimously nominated former Governor Wetherby, a choice as acceptable to the Clements faction as it was unacceptable to Chandler. The aftermath of this conflict was that the state convention failed to endorse Clements and Wetherby, the Chandler faction failed to support them effectively, and both were defeated in the November election.

Aside from its formal powers, the central executive committee is not an important decision-making body. It does not make important decisions on patronage, which are settled in the governor's office; it does not supervise the strategy and financing of election campaigns, duties that are delegated to campaign committees; and it does not recruit or endorse candidates for statewide, legislative, or county office. Individual members of the committee may participate in each of these activities, but the committee as a group does not. In its meetings, about three times a year, the committee serves mainly as a communications channel and a sounding board for the governor. Probably the informal discussions that are carried on over a drink on the day the committee meets are as important as most of the business conducted during the formal sessions. Only during the few months that follow a gubernatorial inauguration is the central executive committee likely to be independent of the governor, and then only if there has been a change in factional control of the governorship.

The chairman of the central executive committee does not have the influence that is associated with that position in some states, nor does he act as a public spokesman for the party. During Democratic administrations he is chosen in fact by the governor, and he is given whatever work and responsibility the governor wishes to assign. He may share in handling patronage, raising money, running election campaigns, or maintaining liaison with county organizations, but the main responsibility for these chores is likely to be in other hands. Foster Ockerman was Breathitt's campaign manager in the 1963 primary and general elections before becoming state chairman. He worked to strengthen the state party organization, participated in the 1964 presidential campaign in Kentucky, and acted as a lobbyist for the governor's office during the 1966 legislative session. He resigned as chairman to manage the 1967 primary campaign of the administration's candidate for governor. The secretary of the committee, who is normally one of the leaders of the governor's faction, is also available for whatever advice and assistance the governor wants.

The Democratic party maintains a party headquarters in Frankfort, and the small staff includes two professional persons. The staff has housekeeping rather than policy-making functions. It maintains files on county and precinct leaders and sends out literature, including a tabloid newspaper, to local party leaders across the state. It provides information and assistance for county leaders, but it does not handle patronage or other substantive questions involving local organization. It handles the arrangements for state and national conventions. One of its major jobs—and a time-consuming one—is raising money. It sends out tickets and makes arrangements for money-raising dinners. It runs the Democratic Club of Kentucky, a device for raising money—in amounts of ten dollars or more—from active party workers across the state. This recently developed technique has created a dues-paying membership of some 10,000 persons.

THE GOVERNOR AS PARTY LEADER

In Kentucky the governor is usually recognized as the most important leader in the Democratic party. The governorship is the major prize sought by the rival factions in the party, and the outcome of the gubernatorial primary and general election determines which faction will dominate the party for the next four years. When a governor takes office, he is both a factional and a party leader, and he inherits the support of three groups of Democrats. First are those who have a sense of loyalty to the faction that the governor represents and who have supported its candidates over a period of years. The extent of these factional loyalties is discussed further in chapter 4. A second group of voters consists of those who identify themselves more strongly with the party than with a faction and who tend to support any Democratic governor. A third group, consisting mainly of local politicians and officeseekers, are those who support the governor—whatever their prior allegiance—because they respect his political power and his ability to dispense various kinds of favors.

The governor has traditionally been strong in Kentucky—as a legislative leader and as a politician—even though the constitution prevents his serving two successive terms. Democratic control of the governorship has been so common in the last 35 years that party leadership has not gravitated to other elected officials or to the party chairman. There is very little modern precedent for determining who will exercise party leadership in periods of Republican gubernatorial control. It is probable that during a Republican administration no single Democratic leader can be expected to have as much influence as a Democratic governor would, although Democratic Lieutenant Governor Wendell Ford, elected in 1967 with a Republican governor, can be expected to lay a claim to party leadership.

We have noted that the modern factions had their origin in A. B. Chandler's victory over Thomas Rhea in the 1935 gubernatorial primary. Chandler was a strong governor who was able to pick Lieutenant Governor Keen Johnson as his successor, but Johnson gained a more dominant position in the state's politics after Chandler was elected to the Senate in 1940. After four years of a Republican administration, Earle Clements was elected governor in 1947. Clements was elected to the Senate in 1950, and Lawrence Wetherby succeeded him and was elected to a full term in 1951. During the period from 1951 to 1955 it is probably most accurate to describe Clements and Wetherby as sharing leadership of the group that was generally referred to as the Clements faction. It was Clements who had built and continued to maintain the strong organization at the county level, and his continuing involvement in state politics was unusual for a senator who had heavy leadership responsibilities in Washington. But Wetherby ran the Democratic party on a day-to-day basis, and most of the political decisions originated in or at least were implemented by the governor's office. Chandler's victory in 1955 resulted from an alliance with Lieutenant Governor Waterfield, but Chandler was clearly the dominant partner during his term of office. Clements was primarily responsible for selecting Bert Combs to run for governor in 1955 and 1959. Less than a year after Combs took office, however, Clements had left the administration, and the governor was establishing his authority as the party and factional leader. Combs, in turn, picked Breathitt as the faction's candidate for governor, and in the early days of the Breathitt administration there were stories in the press asserting that the governor was the prisoner of state officials and political leaders who owed primary loyalty to Combs. But as the administration progressed, Governor Breathitt acted with increasing firmness to demonstrate his growing position in the faction, though there was no split with Combs.

One of the techniques of party leadership used by the governor is organizing the forces loyal to him in order to dominate the state convention and select delegates to the national convention and members of the central executive committee. The state convention meets about six months after the governor takes office, when his prestige and power are usually high, and we have noted that the opposition faction seldom challenges his control of the convention. The constitutional ban on a second successive term for the governor tends to erode his political influence as his term progresses. To prolong his period of influence and to keep his faction in power, the governor usually tries to designate one man as that faction's gubernatorial candidate and organizes the full potential of that faction in the gubernatorial primary. Governor Chandler selected Lieutenant Governor Keen Johnson, who won the primary in 1939; and Johnson's choice, J. Lyter Donaldson, won the primary in 1943 but lost to the Republican candidate. In 1951 Lawrence Wetherby, who had succeeded to the governorship in 1950, was the obvious choice for a full term; and in 1955 the Clements-Wetherby faction picked Bert Combs from the relative obscurity of the Court of Appeals in a vain effort to defeat Chandler's comeback attempt. The governor does not have complete freedom in choosing a new factional leader to enter the primary. There may be some political ally whose popularity and organizational strength in the faction is so great that his claim to factional leadership cannot be denied. Such was the position of Lieutenant Governor Waterfield in 1959, and his endorsement by Governor Chandler was a foregone conclusion. In 1963, however, there was no member of the Combs faction with such obvious strength. Governor Combs consulted widely among the leaders of his faction; his selection of Edward T. Breathitt was criticized by many of them but it was not challenged, and Breathitt had the solid support of the Combs faction in winning the primary. Similarly, in 1967 Breathitt picked Henry Ward as the administration's candidate, and the factional organization united behind Ward in his successful bid for the nomination.

The governor's role as a legislative leader will be discussed more fully in chapter 6, but it is pertinent to his political leadership. The governor's strength as a legislative leader rests not only on constitutional powers but also on a political base. He can depend on support from some Democratic legislators because they are factional allies, and he wins voting support from other legislators—of both parties —because of his control over various kinds of patronage and his ability to influence the passage of legislation sought by these men. Governors have varied in the degree of their participation in the legislative primaries that occur in the middle of their terms of office. Some governors have supported a few legislative candidates who were particularly close political friends or key lieutenants in the legislature. In 1961 Governor Combs provided such support more extensively in those primaries where one of the legislative candidates was a political ally or had a record of voting for administration programs in the legislature. In 1965 Governor Breathitt continued the practice, and in some primaries sought definite promises of support for his legislative program from those candidates whom he was endorsing. Breathitt also made his endorsements of senatorial candidates public, a practice followed in only a few individual cases by previous governors. He used television and the press to ask the voters to support those candidates he had endorsed. The most important effect of gubernatorial endorsements is to mobilize the county political forces of the governor's faction in support of his candidates for the legislature. In some cases the governor's tactics have the effect of discouraging some other candidates from running and unifying his faction behind a single candidate.

The governor's office is the major channel of communications between the state and county party organizations. County political leaders bring their problems and their requests to the governor's office, where they are handled occasionally by the governor but more often by a member of his staff. Maintaining liaison with the leaders of 120 counties requires a vast amount of information about the personalities, rivalries, and recent political history of these counties. In Governor Breathitt's office the main responsibility was assumed by Fontaine Banks, who had served in a similar capacity during the Combs administration and consequently was able to gain familiarity with the infinite variety of county politics over a long period.

In each county the governor chooses a contact man for the administration. He is usually someone who supported the governor actively during the primary, often as his campaign manager. He is selected carefully, and once chosen he is rarely replaced during the administration except in the case of death or illness. Although the county leaders may make suggestions, the choice is the governor's. He is the man whom the administration contacts on all patronage matters and its major source of information about developments in the county. But there are other persons in each county who have access to the governor's office, including the county chairmen, some county officeholders, and others who have provided valuable support to the governor's faction. These local leaders seek various kinds of favors and assistance, and they also provide information about county politics from a variety of viewpoints. For both reasons the governor's staff must be willing to spend time with more than just a single leader from each county.

The governor may intervene in the politics of a county in order to strengthen the position of his faction or in order to win the support of politicians from the opposition faction. Rivals for leadership in the governor's faction in a county may appeal to the governor for assistance or backing. The governor may be asked to help avoid a primary fight at the county or legislative level by appointing one of the potential candidates to a state job. A number of circumstances might induce the governor to intervene in a county, and in each case the governor must weigh the alleged advantages against the risks—particularly the risk that his action will alienate political leaders who have been loyal to him in the past.

Patronage is the currency of politics in Kentucky, and to be effective as a political leader the governor must spend it widely. The most obvious, and probably still the most important, form of patronage is jobs. The comprehensive merit system law that was passed in 1960 and took effect in 1961 reduced by 12,000 the number of jobs available for patronage purposes. At present there are about 4,000 jobs out of 20,000 that are not covered by the merit system. These include policy-making positions and part-time members of various boards. The largest single group of patronage jobs are approximately 3,000 unskilled laborers and light equipment operators in the Highway Department. There are also a number of seasonal jobs under the patronage system—including both highway and park jobs. In the case of jobs that are covered by the merit system, the law provides that the job must go to one of the top three persons who are tested, and some departments get advice—or political clearance—from county leaders in choosing which person to appoint to certain positions.

The fact that the governor appoints the highway commissioner (as two-thirds of state governors do) gives him control over this important category of job patronage as well as influence over the location and improvement of highways. Roads are important to the counties, and nothing is more important to a politician than being able to claim credit for bringing new and better roads to his county. Traditionally Kentucky governors have used roads as a device for rewarding those counties and county leaders loyal to his party and his faction; however, the governor's freedom to use highway construction as a political weapon has been increasingly restricted in recent years. As federal financing of major highway projects has grown, national agencies have come to play a greater part in determining the location of such highways. Moreover, the Combs administration established a formula to be used in allocating the two-cent gasoline tax for local roads, a formula that takes the place of gubernatorial discretion.

There are other types of state projects and institutions that are sought by the counties—parks, community colleges, hospitals, and other facilities, although in each case the governor is under pressure to make his decision on the basis of criteria other than politics. The state can bestow benefits in addition to state jobs on individual politicians. The administration may assist lawyers and insurance men either by placing business directly with their firms or by encouraging other firms that have state government contracts to do so. The governor's office may help someone to get a job with a company that has or is seeking state business. Although limited by laws requiring competitive bidding, the governor may also assist businesses in seeking contracts with the state. The governor's influence through the placing of state funds in banks is only indirect because the treasurer, an elected official, has this authority, although an appointed official, the finance commissioner, must approve such actions.

Although there are many kinds of patronage available to the governor, his freedom in dispensing it has been steadily declining as a result of the merit system and state and national legislation restricting the use of governmental funds. As his resources have declined in sheer volume, however, the governor's effectiveness as a political leader has not declined. Even though he has less to offer, the favors that he can dispense continue to be valued by local politicians. A promise to conduct a feasibility study concerning a park may be worth as much as was a flat promise to build a park a few years ago. The fact that these patronage resources are declining, however, makes it all the more important that they be expended with great care and skill. Because of the amount of detail necessary, the governor is heavily dependent on his staff for the daily choices that must be made. During his primary campaign the governor may have spent some of his patronage resources in public promises to build certain facilities in specific counties or in private promises necessary to win the support of county politicians. Early in his administration he must pick a contact man for each county, and once this decision is made, the governor must go along with most of the advice on job patronage that is given by this individual. If he chooses poorly and the contact man gives bad advice, the mistake may jeopardize his popularity among the political activists in the county. Most of the patronage jobs must be given out in the first hectic months of the administration, though the ability to fire a patronage appointee gives the governor some continuing control. The governor must also save some of his patronage resources for legislators, sometimes including those in the opposing faction or Republicans whose votes he needs on an important bill. In distributing patronage the governor may have to make a hard choice between strengthening his faction in a particular county and gaining a vote necessary to pass a piece of legislation.

The distribution of all kinds of patronage is a substantial drain on the time of those in the governor's office, and it is a frustrating exercise of political leadership because it is a major source of dissension within the party and within the faction. There always seem to be more deserving Democrats than there are jobs or contracts, and those who are left out are often recruited by the opposing faction. But the centralization of patronage control in the governor's office is a fundamental reason why the governor is the preeminent leader of his party.

FACTIONALISM IN COUNTY ORGANIZATIONS

Anyone who attempts to survey 120 Democratic county parties is likely to become inundated in details and is tempted to conclude that they defy meaningful classification. County political leaders usually think that politics in their county is unique, and in a sense they are right. No two counties are identical; each party has its own history, folkways, and personalities. But the differences among the county parties fall into patterns that make comparison both possible and meaningful.

The nature of partisan competition in a county affects the basic strategy of the party's leaders. Where the competition is close, the Democratic leaders can be expected to give highest priority to winning general elections; where the party is dominant, they may be more concerned with primary contests and control over the organization; where the party is weak, elections may asume less importance than the struggle to control the distribution of state patronage. Studies in other states have suggested that many of the variables of county party organization are related to the level of party competition.[4] For these purposes the counties in Kentucky may be divided into three categories (derived from those used in chapter 5). The average percentage of the two-party vote in each county has been calculated for the Democrats and the Republicans for three types of elections—gubernatorial, senatorial, and presidential—in the period from 1946 through 1962. The median (or middle) of the three average percentages has then been used as a basis for describing the counties. There are 50 counties defined as *Democratic* where the Democrats won two-thirds of the elections and had a median average of over 55 percent. There are 33 *Republican* counties where the Republicans won by the same proportions. The remaining 37 *Marginal* counties fall in the middle. These categories will be used throughout this chapter in comparing various characteristics of county organizations.

Since the 1930s there has been a bifactional pattern of state Democratic politics affecting primary elections for governor and sometimes for other state and legislative offices. There has been a degree of continuity in the two factions, and some politicians and voters have identified themselves with the same faction for a number of years. In order to survive, each faction must have local leaders to work in primary campaigns, and each faction should be able to attract leaders in each county through the promise of patronage. Consequently we would expect to find many of those persons who are active in county organizations to be identified with one or the other state faction. County politicians and organizations are also concerned with county elections, however, and it would be possible for these races to have a greater impact on organizational structure and political rivalries than the state contests do. County politics might just as logically be based on courthouse factions as on statehouse factions. Two patterns of factionalism might coexist independently or might overlap in some fashion. Factions of some kind are characteristic of most Democratic organizations, and an

[4] See, for example, Frank J. Sorauf, *Party and Representation* (New York: Atherton Press, 1963), chap. 3.

examination of the variations in factionalism is useful as a means of finding some patterns among the 120 counties. This analysis is based primarily on interviews and studies in 40 counties, which are roughly representative of the whole state.[5]

State-Courthouse Factions. Most county organizations are characterized by factions clearly recognizable by those familiar with politics in the county. One common pattern, found in over one-third of our sample of 40 counties, is the existence of two distinct county factions, each of which is identified with one of the state factions and also plays a part in courthouse politics. It appears to be equally common among Democratic and Marginal counties, but rare in Republican counties where few Democrats hold county office. The county chairman in the majority of counties in 1965 was aligned with the Combs-Breathitt faction, but in some counties he tried to maintain a neutral position in state factionalism, and in a few he was clearly identified with the Chandler-Waterfield faction. Democratic courthouse officials usually participate actively in the factions. In some counties the factions are tightly organized with long histories, and in others they are loosely organized and are constantly changing in their alignment.

Among the factions that are involved in both state and courthouse politics, we can distinguish several patterns of relationships. In some counties, usually Democratic, there are a few courthouse officials who have held office for several terms and have built such a strong personal base of political support that they are not seriously challenged in primaries. These men publicly endorse gubernatorial candidates in the primary and they play a leading part in county factions, but they are not necessarily dependent on factional support to hold office. The county officials may support opposing candidates in gubernatorial primaries and may lead different county factions, but they are unlikely to mobilize their factions in an effort to oust each other from long-held offices in the courthouse. In Bourbon

[5] Data on county party organizations were gathered from several sources. Questionnaires were sent to the county chairmen; those returned, from 80 of 120 counties, were evenly distributed across the state and represented Democratic, Marginal, and Republican counties in almost accurate proportions. County chairmen, and in a few cases other Democratic leaders, were interviewed in 1965 in greater depth (with particular attention to factionalism) in 31 of these 80 counties, selected to represent those with a variety of partisan, geographic, and urban-rural characteristics, and data on factionalism were obtained in 9 other county organizations from student term papers.

County, for example, most courthouse officials—who usually serve several terms—are active in state factions, but the effort of some Breathitt supporters to elect a full slate of candidates for courthouse offices in the 1965 primary fell short. In Livingston County, one of the smaller counties in western Kentucky, the county chairman has been a factional leader and patronage dispenser for Governors Clements and Wetherby, Combs and Breathitt. At the same time he and a veteran leader of the Chandler faction have alternately held the offices of county judge and sheriff (a trade necessitated by the constitutional ban on successive terms for the sheriff).

Where there is greater primary competition and turnover for county offices, courthouse officials run the risk of alienating voters if they become involved in state factions, and for that reason they often remain neutral. In those counties where elected officials are active members of state factions, factional alignments are likely to be rigid, and the party chairman often gives either public or quiet support to factional allies who are running for county office in the primary. Candidates for county office do not usually run openly as a slate, although there may be some unpublicized cooperation with respect to financing or workers at the polls. An example is Caldwell County, where the chairman is a link between state and courthouse factions and where there are county races so bitterly contested that supporters of the losing candidate often provide the votes to elect a Republican in the November election. Mercer County provides an excellent example of factionalism that has deep historical roots and that pervades state and courthouse politics. Several of those active in Mercer County politics have been identified with one state faction since the 1930s. For example, the county chairman for two decades, I. C. James, was a leader of the Rhea faction in 1935 and subsequently worked for Clements, Combs, and Breathitt. He had held county office (usually county attorney) for 28 years when he retired in 1965. He was defeated for the party chairmanship in 1964 in a hotly contested race but continued to serve as contact man for the Breathitt administration. Recent county primaries have had strong factional overtones. When James retired as county attorney in 1965, he supported John Keller, a factional ally and a friend of Breathitt's, to succeed him. Eulyn Dean, who had run against James in 1961 and whose family had shared in the leadership of the Chandler faction, defeated Keller by just 28 votes. Keller had the support of state workers but not the public support of Governor Breathitt, which had been anticipated by some leaders of the faction. The Chandler faction also maintained control over the county clerk's office. The bitterness of the factional dispute became evident in November when the first Republican to run for county office in some 35 years came within 355 votes of defeating Edwin Freeman for county judge; Freeman had defeated James for party chairman and had supported Dean for county attorney.

In at least a few counties it is common for the leaders of state factions in a county to endorse a slate of candidates for county offices. In Knott County, a strongly Democratic mountain county on the edge of Republican territory, there are frequently large numbers of candidates for county office. Each of the factions endorses candidates for several—but not usually all—of the county offices. These endorsements are often crucial, and a candidate who has been endorsed by neither faction is unlikely to win a race against one who has such endorsements. The multitude of candidates obviously creates problems for factional leaders who run the risk of alienating some of their allies by endorsing others. Occasionally one of the candidates in Knott County races receives financial or organizational assistance (such as pressure on state workers) from outside the county, and sometimes county factional leaders are under pressure from factional leaders at the state level to support a specific candidate.

State Factions. In almost half of the sample of 40 counties there are two distinct county factions, each of which is identified with a state faction, but neither of which becomes involved in courthouse contests. In such counties the courthouse officials, if Democrats, seldom become actively involved in the state factions and often remain publicly neutral in gubernatorial contests. This is more characteristic of Republican and Marginal counties than of Democratic counties.

In most Republican counties there are few if any Democratic primaries for county office, and it is rare for Democratic factional leaders to become entrenched in the courthouse. Consequently the factions that exist are oriented toward state rather than courthouse politics. Even in counties where the Democrats are badly outnumbered they are likely to be divided into two factions, simply because each of the state factions recruits supporters in every county and offers patronage as an incentive. In Republican counties, because patronage is available only from state government and not at the courthouse, the faction that is allied with the state administration is more likely to be the dominant one. In some counties the dominant administration faction has swallowed up the opposition, and temporary unity has been achieved. In the mountain Republican counties patronage assumes greater importance because jobs are scarce; and because there are never enough state jobs to go around, the opposition faction can always find recruits who hope to benefit from a change in the state administration. One characteristic of mountain counties, many of which are Republican, is the importance of family in determining partisan and factional loyalties. In some of these Republican counties there are two Democratic factions identified with state factions but based primarily on family loyalties that have prevailed in the county for generations. When there is a rivalry between two powerful families in a county, the alliance of one family with a particular state faction is guaranteed to lead the other family into an alliance with the opposing faction.

In a number of Democratic counties and in Marginal counties where the Democrats usually win county office, there is an invisible wall between courthouse politics and state factionalism. Most of the counties in our sample that fit this description are in western Kentucky. In most primaries there is a vigorous competition for county office, and long tenure in office is the exception rather than the rule. As a consequence, few county officeholders acquire such security that they can take the risk of becoming involved in state factional politics. As individuals, they may support gubernatorial candidates, but they seldom work for them actively because they do not want to alienate those whose votes they will need in the next county election. Sometimes local candidates cooperate in a county primary, usually without any publicity, but the basis for this cooperation is expediency rather than allegiance to the same state faction. The factional leaders remain neutral in courthouse races. They cannot afford to jeopardize the position of their faction by supporting one candidate in a county race and alienating the supporters of others. One party chairman said, in describing court-house races in a small county, "I have to stay away from the candidates. If I'm just seen talking to one of them, people get the wrong impression." Sometimes the backers of a county candidate will try to enlist factional support for him or even support from the administration. One party chairman, a leader of the Breathitt faction, described his unsuccessful efforts to keep the governor from making telephone calls in behalf of a candidate for sheriff.

The party chairman is usually the leader of the administration faction; he is likely to be a banker or businessman or a state legislator, but not a county officeholder. In western and central Kentucky, family ties are less likely to be a basis for factionalism than in the mountains, but in some counties it is possible to identify some local base for the factions. In Calloway County the Breathitt factional leadership consists primarily of younger business and professional men, while the older generation of leaders are men who have been associated with Chandler and Waterfield. In Graves County, on the other hand, a new generation of political leaders that has gradually been winning power in the last few years consists of persons who are identified with both state factions. Although gubernatorial primaries are often bitterly contested in Graves, leaders of both factions in the "new guard" cooperate rather closely in running the county Democratic organization.

Two counties, Harrison and Daviess, may be used to illustrate the division between courthouse and state factional politics. The dominant party figure in strongly Democratic Harrison County, since he won the chairmanship in 1960, has been Wilson Palmer, one of the Combs-Breathitt administration supporters in the Senate. Since 1960, under Palmer's leadership, the administration faction has gradually consolidated its control over the party. There is a well-defined Chandler faction, but it has been weakened and divided during its years in opposition. Palmer and the other state factional leaders have not become involved in courthouse politics; and in the courthouse, where there is substantial primary competition and turnover, the officeholders usually do not become involved in state factional politics. In Daviess County, an urban county in western Kentucky, the Democratic party is deeply divided along state factional lines. Since 1959 the administration leader and contact man has been Wendell Ford, who became chairman in 1964; he was elected to the Senate in 1965 after a bitter primary fight with Casper "Cap" Gardner, the incumbent, who had long been identified prominently with the Chandler and Waterfield forces.

He was elected lieutenant governor in 1967. The deep factional division has persisted in the face of growing Republican strength in state and national elections. The state factional leaders usually stay out of courthouse primaries, where there is considerable competition and frequent turnover for some of the offices. Although the county officeholders usually have factional loyalties, they do not often become active in state factionalism.

County Courthouse Factions. In a few counties (five in our sample) there are local factions that have a long history and relatively stable membership but have only very loose ties to the state factions. Many of those who are active in the local factions also participate in state factional politics. At a given time each local faction may be roughly identified with a different state faction, but over a period of years there are likely to be shifts in the alliances with state leaders. The differences between this type of factionalism and the state-courthouse factions described earlier are not great, and it may be difficult to classify a particular county precisely. The question is whether allegiances to state factions or local factions are more stable over a period of time. In these counties, courthouse officials and other politicians who are primarily interested in courthouse politics tend to dominate the factional organizations.

An example of a county where the factions are primarily local is Taylor, a rural county that is Republican in national and state politics but is dominated by Democrats at the courthouse level. There are two strong local factions in which courthouse officials are active and which concentrate their efforts on local races. Antagonisms between the two groups are sharp, and supporters of the loser in a primary often vote Republican in November. The priority given by factional leaders to local politics is illustrated by the willingness of some of them to make deals that sacrifice state candidates in order to gain votes for local candidates. The dominant faction was friendly to Chandler in the 1963 primary but was able to make patronage accommodations with the Breathitt administration. Lincoln County, a Marginal county that is usually Democratic in county races, provides another example of local factions that are based on family ties and rivalries between personalities. The allegiance of local leaders to state factions seems to be less durable and less important than the loyalties to local factions.

A Dominant County Faction. There are a few counties in which the party organization is dominated by a single faction which, though occasionally challenged, succeeds in defeating its opponents and retaining control for years and even generations. The factional leadership picks friends and allies for county office and mobilizes the votes necessary to assure their success in the primaries. It may establish a firm alliance with one of the state factions, or it may bargain with whichever faction wins the governorship. The number of Kentucky counties dominated by a single factional organization is declining, either because of the death of a strong leader or because a new generation of politicians has defeated the entrenched organization. Democratic politics in Clark County, for example, was dominated for half a century until the early 1950s by one man; now two factions are contesting for power. Similarly the Mason County party was run by one man for almost 30 years and is now divided between two factions. Morgan County politics had long been dominated by one leader, who served as party chairman for 24 years, but a new faction has arisen that challenged the established group and defeated the son of the veteran leader in the 1964 contest for party chairman. Among the other counties where the Democratic party is no longer dominated by a single leader or faction are Nelson, Casey, and Estill.

One of the few remaining political organizations that dominate a county, and one of the most famous, is the Beauchamp organization in Logan, a solidly Democratic county in western Kentucky on the Tennessee border. Emerson "Doc" Beauchamp, who has served as lieutenant governor and in a variety of other elected and appointed state positions, is one of the Democratic party's most colorful leaders, with a loyal following across the state. Alben Barkley once said that he knew of no one who was "more intimately associated with the grass roots of politics than Emerson Beauchamp." The organization that Beauchamp runs in Logan County was inherited from Tom Rhea, who gained power early in the century and whose candidates lost county office only once over a period of 30 years until Rhea's death in 1951. Rhea's power in Logan County was not shaken when he lost the gubernatorial primary to A. B. Chandler in 1935. Beauchamp, who was one of Rhea's lieutenants, has succeeded in maintaining his control of the county organization while holding state office. He has been allied with Clements and Wetherby and in recent years with Combs and Breathitt. The power of the Rhea and Beauchamp organizations is illustrated by their ability to deliver the votes in crucial state primary elections. Logan County delivered the largest percentage of any county for Rhea in his 1935 race against Chandler and for Clements in the 1947 gubernatorial primary (in each case 92 percent). Under Beauchamp's leadership the county voted for Combs in 1955 and 1959 and for Clements in 1956 by percentages ranging from 70 to 81, which in each case was the second highest county percentage in the state.

Beauchamp, while in Frankfort, runs the organization through several lieutenants. Although he makes final decisions on patronage and the endorsement of candidates, Beauchamp consults widely with his leaders and tries to achieve consensus. He has controlled not only patronage jobs in Logan County but a number of others at the state level in agencies which he has headed or in which he has political contacts. The Beauchamp organization has paid attention to Negro needs in the county and has been able to count on strong support from Negro voters. Beauchamp's candidates have won most county offices in recent years, but there have been frequent primary contests. The opposition has come from dissident members of the Beauchamp organization, sometimes in alliance with the relatively weak Chandler forces; it reached a high point with two primary victories over Beauchamp-endorsed candidates in 1961. Despite these challenges, the Beauchamp faction continues to maintain a dominant position in the county through skillful use of time-tested organizational techniques and a generous supply of patronage.

In Breathitt County, a Democratic stronghold in the southeastern mountains, the Turner family has dominated the Democratic party and county politics since 1938. The Turner family won its first election in 1913, then battled other families and factions for 25 years before achieving control. The leaders of the political clan are Circuit Judge Ervine Turner and his wife Marie, school superintendent (since 1931) and vice chairman of the Democratic state central executive committee. Other members of the family include the state senator, county judge, and sheriff. The Turner family is allied with the state administration faction of the party. Their political power is built on their persistence in getting federal and state aid and services for the poverty-stricken county and jobs for their constituents. In a county like Breathitt, where jobs are scarce, the school system is one of the most important sources of employment. Some member of the Turner family has been school superintendent since 1913, and the teachers and other employees in the system have become valuable workers in the Turner organization.

The Pattern of Factionalism.   With few exceptions the Democratic county organizations are divided into two clearly recognizable factions. Among the exceptions are the declining number in which a single strong faction has long been dominant. In a few Republican counties the administration faction appears to have temporarily unified the party. There also are a few Republican counties in which the Democratic organization is so weak as to be barely visible, and consequently its internal structure has little form or substance. In the vast majority of counties having two factions, most leaders and active members of each faction identify themselves with a different state faction. In most Republican and many Marginal counties these factions stay out of courthouse politics, and where Democrats win county office, these officials usually play a minimal role in state-oriented factions. In another category of Democratic and Marginal counties each of the factions is deeply involved in both courthouse and state politics, and county officials play active and often dominating roles in the factions. In eastern Kentucky (in counties dominated by either party) the factions often are rooted in family allegiances and rivalries.

The goal of political parties is often defined as gaining political power by winning elective office, and the local party has the dual task of winning local elections and helping the state and national parties to win elections at those levels. It is obvious that pervasive factionalism within a county party is disruptive of these purposes. In most Kentucky counties, except for the highly urbanized ones, however, the Democratic party either is so strong that it need not fear defeat in county elections or is so weak that its county electoral chances are negligible. In the few closely competitive counties the Democrats usually seem willing to take the risks of defeat that accompany factionalism. The growth of Republican competition in national and state politics has not yet affected the interests of local political organizations sufficiently to force any change in factional practices.

One function of factions within county organizations is purely local. Those who hold office may be organized in order to hold power, and outgroups may be organized by those who are seeking office. We have seen that factions in some counties have an orientation that is principally or partly local, but local factionalism does not seem to be an inevitable feature of county politics. The most widespread and important function of factions within county parties is to serve the needs of the state factional system. County factions provide statewide candidates with the necessary manpower and organizational assistance, they provide the voters with voting cues in state primaries, and they provide a means of access for local persons who are seeking tangible help from state political leaders. For these reasons, most county Democratic organizations are likely to remain split into two factions paralleling those at the state level as long as the state party remains sharply divided into factions.

THE COUNTY CHAIRMAN

Patterns of Selection. Democratic party chairmen come predominantly from a few occupational backgrounds.[6] Almost half of them are businessmen, particularly in banking, real estate, and insurance. Another 21 percent are lawyers, and 11 percent are in teaching and other professions. Almost 10 percent are farmers, although many others in rural areas list farming in addition to a business. Seven percent have a state job or public office as their only occupation.[7] Two-thirds of the chairmen are in their forties and fifties. Two-thirds of them have attended college, but little more than one-third are college graduates. Sixty-one percent of the party chairmen have run for a public office, and 54 percent have done so successfully; these percentages do not vary much among Democratic, Marginal, and Republican counties. In Democratic and Marginal counties the chairmen are most likely to run either for county or legislative office; only a few run for city or school board offices. Because there are nonpartisan elections always for the school board and often for city office, Democratic chairmen in Republican counties are as likely to seek these offices as to run for county or legislative office.

---

6 Data on chairmen come from the 80 who returned questionnaires.

7 In a comparable state, North Carolina, only one-fourth of the Democratic chairmen are businessmen, over one-third are lawyers, and the percentages of farmers and government officials, teachers, and other professionals are about the same as in Kentucky. William J. Crotty, "The Social Attributes of Party Organizational Activists in a Transitional Political System," *Western Political Quarterly*, XX (1967), 669-81.

There is no well-established ladder of party offices leading to the chairmanship. About one-fourth of the chairmen have served as county secretary, chairman of the Young Democrats, or as a campaign chairman in a primary; and about one-seventh have served as precinct chairman. According to the questionnaire (which may not have been fully answered in this respect), over 60 percent came to the chairmanship without having held any party office. One reason for this may be that when one faction controls the party, it monopolizes party office, and when a factional turnover occurs, the chairman must be drawn from outside the formal party organization. Often the new chairman has served as chairman—or in some other post—of the county campaign for the newly elected governor.[8] Public office appears to be more important than formal party office as a steppingstone to the chairmanship. Forty-one percent of the chairmen (most of whom had held no other party office) had been elected to public office prior to winning the chairmanship. In 1964, 44 percent of the chairmen were elected for a first term and 41 percent for a second term; the others had served up to 25 or 30 years.

The circumstances surrounding the selection of a chairman are important because they shed light on his role and particularly his relationship to state and local factions. He is formally elected by the precinct committeemen and committeewomen in December of presidential years, or in the larger counties by the legislative district chairmen previously chosen by the committeemen and committeewomen. When asked to describe the circumstances of their initial election, 59 percent said they had no opposition, 20 percent had limited opposition, and only 21 percent described the competition as serious. Among those who had served more than one term, 79 percent had no opposition in their most recent election, and only 7 percent had serious opposition.

One reason why close contests are unusual is that in many of the counties it is customary for the party chairmanship to change hands the year after there is a change in factional control of the state party. Occasionally the county faction that is in power will offer resistance, but usually it makes no effort to oppose the faction that has supported the winning gubernatorial candidate. The chairmanship often goes to the campaign manager of the newly elected governor; if not, the choice will be someone who is completely acceptable to the gover-

[8] Some chairmen apparently did not mention such experience in answering the questionnaire, which referred to "party offices."

nor's faction. In 1960 a large majority of chairmanships changed hands as men loyal to the Combs administration were elected; despite the factional continuity in administrations, some of these men stepped aside in 1964 to give the job to persons who had managed Breathitt's campaign. In addition, supporters of the Breathitt administration in some counties won control from some of the Chandler supporters who had remained in power in 1960. Some counties have a long-established custom of electing a new chairman who is loyal to the administration. The reason usually given for this practice is that the county has a better chance to gain benefits from the state administration if there are no doubts in Frankfort about the chairman's loyalty. In other counties the practice may be less a matter of custom than a recognition of political reality—the ability of the administration faction to organize the county party through the use of state workers and active political workers who want to demonstrate their loyalty. Adequate information on the circumstances of the chairman's election was available from most of the counties in the sample of 80; in 65 percent of these a new chairman was chosen when state factional control shifted, and in most of these the administration candidates won with little or no opposition. This pattern is most likely to be found in counties where the Democratic factions are identified primarily with state factions rather than with courthouse politics.

In 13 percent of the sample of counties, the present chairman was elected as a result of a contest among local factions and not because he was a leader of the administration faction; in most cases he was identified with the Chandler faction. Most of these are counties in which the Democratic factions are oriented, at least in part, toward courthouse politics. The circumstances of the chairman's election varied. Several chairmen in 1960 or 1964 defeated long-entrenched political machines, with or without the help of the administration faction. In one county the supporters of the administration elected a Chandler-Waterfield man in 1960 and reelected him in 1964, apparently for local political reasons. In one county in 1964 the Chandler faction defeated a veteran party chairman who was closely identified with the administration. In a few counties (4 percent of the sample) the present chairman was chosen as a compromise by the two dominant factions, who apparently viewed the chairman's primary duty as unification of the party.

In 17 percent of the counties in our sample the chairman serves a prolonged term, usually without opposition. There are at least seven party chairman in Kentucky who have been in office more than 20 years, and a number of others who have served during both the Chandler and Combs-Breathitt administrations. A few such chairmen have shifted their allegiance with changes in factional control of the state Democratic party. Others have been able to retain their chairmanship despite their occasional opposition to the administration faction. In most of these cases the chairmen belonged to the Clements and Combs factions but were able to stay in office during the Chandler administration. They are likely to be in counties where the factions are oriented toward courthouse politics, but not necessarily where state factional ties are weak.

Responsibility for Patronage. The administration's contact man in the county, who is responsible for patronage, is not necessarily the county chairman. The contact man is likely to be the campaign manager for the successful gubernatorial candidate in the preceding primary election, although the administration may decide that some other political leader in the county would be more effective. Half of the county chairmen (in the sample of 80 counties) report that patronage appointments are usually cleared with them, and another 17 percent indicate that they are usually consulted on patronage questions. In those counties where a change in the chairmanship results from a change in state factional control, the chairman is almost always consulted about patronage and usually he is the man primarily responsible for it. Some of the chairmen who are allied with the administration faction prefer to yield the responsibility for patronage to another leader of the faction in the county. The chairman is more likely to be consulted about patronage in Republican than in Democratic or Marginal counties.

In those counties where one man has held the chairmanship for a prolonged period, and where he is allied with the administration party, he is usually responsible for patronage; presumably such chairmen are so well entrenched that the administration considers it wise to work through them. In those counties where the chairman was selected after a local factional contest, or as a compromise candidate, someone else—more closely allied with the administration—handles patronage. Some of these chairmen are consulted individually, or as part of a committee on patronage; but others are left out of the patronage process completely, and this is often a source of resentment and conflict in these counties.

In only about one-fourth of the counties does the chairman have any significant voice in the distribution of courthouse patronage, and only a few say that they are consulted regularly. This is usually left in the hands of the individual officeholders, even in those counties where the local factions—and the chairman—are active in courthouse politics. The amount of courthouse patronage that is available in some of the smaller, poorer counties is relatively little. In most of the Republican counties there are few if any Democratic office-holders, although one chairman asserts that he is sometimes consulted about patronage by Republicans holding office in the courthouse.

Participation in State and Local Primaries. Although some county chairmen owe their election to the strength of state factions and others to a dominant local faction, nearly all chairmen take sides in primaries for governor and other statewide offices. In the sample of 80 counties, 95 percent of the chairmen support candidates in state primaries frequently or always, 70 percent usually make this support public, and the rest do so more quietly. Most of those who owe their election to local factions, as well as those elected by state factions, endorse state candidates publicly.

County chairmen do not play such a consistently large part in nominations for county office. More than a third of them frequently encourage candidates to run for local office, and another one-half do so occasionally. Such encouragement is less frequent, and less necessary, in heavily Democratic counties. Several reasons are given for recruiting candidates: to find someone who is more capable than a candidate who is already running, to support a candidate of a particular faction, or simply to make sure that there is at least one Democrat running. In Republican counties the chairmen are often more concerned about the quality than the quantity of candidates. They sometimes deliberately avoid recruiting a full slate of candidates because doing so may arouse the Republicans to run a more vigorous campaign in the fall. They sometimes discourage candidates who are unlikely to make an effective race, and in particular they try to prevent primary contests because it may deter better candidates from running and may undermine the unity that is absolutely necessary if any of the candidates are to win the general election. A candidate may be persuaded to run for a lesser office if he would have a better chance of winning at that level.

Chairmen were asked whether they gave either public or behind-the-scenes support to candidates in local (county or legislative) primaries, and the answers varied with the nature of factionalism in the county. Fifty-seven percent reported that they supported local candidates publicly at least occasionally, and another 34 percent gave only behind-the-scenes support; 9 percent never supported local candidates in any fashion. Most chairmen in Republican counties, a majority in Marginal counties, and less than half in Democratic counties took a public stand in local primaries. Almost all chairmen took a public stand in those counties where the factions are oriented toward courthouse politics, but a minority did so in the counties where the factions have an exclusively state orientation. Similarly, those chairmen who were elected in strictly local factional battles or who had held the post for many years were more likely to become publicly involved in county races than were the chairmen who owed their jobs to their participation in the state administration faction. It is clear that those chairmen whose main interest is strengthening the position of a state faction in the county usually either stay out of local primaries completely or exercise great caution when they become involved. Those chairmen who are most deeply involved in local primaries are likely to be either those who lead a faction that is closely allied with courthouse officeholders or those in Republican counties who find it necessary to recruit candidates and continue to support such candidates if they run into opposition in the primary. Although individual chairmen have considerable freedom in determining their role during local primaries, the choice they make is influenced by the factional situation and the level of primary competition in the county.

We can gain some perspective on the participation of county chairmen in the nominating process by looking at data from other states. In North Carolina, which has a two-party system very similar to that in Kentucky, roughly 40 percent of the Democratic chairmen play no part in the recruiting of candidates for local and legislative office. Democratic chairmen in that state are ordinarily expected

to remain neutral in the primary contests that occur in their county.[9]
A study of county chairmen in five plains states showed that at least
80 percent of the Democrats were active in the recruitment process,
trying to find qualified candidates and sometimes persuading persons
to run in the primary even though someone else had already filed
for the office. Approximately 60 percent of the Democratic chairmen
in these five states said that they usually or sometimes openly
supported candidates who had opposition in primary elections.[10]

FUNCTIONS OF THE COUNTY DEMOCRATIC ORGANIZATION

Precinct committeemen and committeewomen are elected at mass
meetings held in each precinct on the first Saturday in December
of presidential election years. Unless there is a well-publicized factional contest in the county, these precinct meetings—like the county
meetings already described—are poorly attended. It is not unusual
for three or four voters to find that they are the only participants
in the meeting and to elect two of their members on the spur of
the moment. Usually the leaders of the dominant faction draw up
a list of precinct leaders and make sure that enough persons attend
precinct meetings to elect the persons on the list. When possible,
these should be men and women who are loyal to the dominant
faction, but in some precincts it may be expedient to reelect veteran
precinct leaders whatever their factional affiliation. In some counties
the precinct committeemen and committeewomen may be virtually
identical with the leaders who work for the dominant faction at the
precinct level in primary elections.

One-third of the county chairmen say that all precincts have
chairmen who can be counted on to work actively in most campaigns;
another one-half say that at least half of the precincts have active
chairmen. Almost half of the Democratic counties have active
leaders in all precincts; only one-third of the Republican counties
and one-fifth of the Marginal counties are that well organized.
Only a very few counties in any category have active leaders in less

[9] William J. Crotty, "The Party Organization and Its Activities," in William J.
Crotty, ed., *Approaches to the Study of Party Organization* (Boston: Allyn and Bacon,
1967).
[10] Marvin Harder and Thomas Ungs, "Notes toward a Functional Analysis of Local
Party Organizations," unpublished paper presented at 1963 annual meeting of Midwest
Conference of Political Scientists.

than half of the precincts, however. These estimates by county chairmen appear to be optimistic, particularly in the Republican counties; definitions of an "active" precinct leader may vary from county to county, and it is possible that some chairmen are thinking particularly of activity in primary campaigns. The county committee, in most counties consisting of the precinct leaders, meets more than once a year in 40 percent of the counties and at least annually in another 29 percent. During campaigns the meetings are more frequent—at least monthly in over half of the counties. The committee is more likely to meet frequently in Marginal counties than in either Democratic or Republican ones.

Functions in a Campaign. In general elections the Democratic candidates for statewide office rely on the regular party organization in most counties, although this is less likely to be true if members of the local organization have supported other candidates in the primary election. In county races there is very little work for the organization to do in those Democratic counties where there are rarely Republican candidates or in Republican counties where Democrats seldom run for office. County chairmen were asked to specify the most important support given by the party organization to local candidates. Some did not answer the question because of the absence of Republican opposition in races for offices in their counties, and others did not distinguish among several types of support. Among those who did indicate priorities, over 60 percent listed getting out the vote on election day, 25 percent listed financial assistance, and a few emphasized the maintenance of a campaign headquarters or the organization of rallies.

According to the chairmen, 92 percent of the county organizations work to get out the vote in county general elections; 82 percent assist in financing; 78 percent provide advertising assistance; 72 percent organize rallies; and 60 percent maintain a campaign headquarters. (Eight Democratic counties where there is rarely any Republican opposition are excluded from these calculations.) In Marginal counties most party organizations engage in all of these activities, although only three-quarters maintain party organizations. In those Democratic counties that have some Republican candidates, the party is just as active in most respects; only two-thirds maintain headquarters, and two-thirds conduct rallies. In Republican counties most organizations get out the vote and provide financial aid, but in other respects the organizations are less active than in the other counties. Candidates for county office work closely with the party organization in most Democratic and Marginal counties, but in almost half of the Republican counties the candidates usually set up their own organizations—presumably because the existing party organizations are relatively ineffective.

The Local Party and Campaign Financing. There are no reliable figures on the costs of primary and general election campaigns at the county level. Until 1966, state law set a limit, for either primary or general election, of $1,000 for state Senate candidates and $750 for House candidates; the limit for county offices ranged from $1,000 to $2,500, depending on population. It is apparent that actual expenditures have often exceeded that level. The 1966 campaign financing law, repealing these limits and requiring stricter reporting of expenditures, may make possible more accurate descriptions. In many counties, particularly strong Democratic ones, much more is spent on primary campaigns than on general elections. In urban counties such as Fayette, Warren, and Daviess, a candidate may have to spend from $10,000 to $20,000 in a close contest for a major county office. In one of the urban counties there were estimates of $25,000 to $30,000 spent by each of the candidates in a recent state senatorial primary. In the less urbanized, smaller counties party chairmen who were interviewed estimated the cost of running for county judge or sheriff at anywhere from $1,000 to $8,000. One way to put these figures into perspective is to estimate the amount a candidate spent in comparison to the total number of voters (in a primary or general election, as the case may be). These estimates range from 25 or 50 cents in some counties to $1.50 or $2.00 per voter in others.

The variation in costs from county to county can be explained in part by the different techniques of campaigning. In large cities it is almost essential to use television, and the costs are high. In Lexington, for example, a single fifteen-minute telecast early in the evening costs about $100 plus the cost of facilities such as taping. In many of the rural counties it is a common practice for candidates to run large advertisements in the local newspapers. A full-page advertisement is likely to cost between $100 and $200.

Interviews with party chairmen lead to the conclusion that the costs of campaigning vary in rough proportion to the prevalence of vote buying in the counties. The buying of votes is common in many low-income precincts, both urban and rural, but it is not a common practice in every county. Some counties have gained notoriety because the buying of votes has become a custom; there are hundreds of voters who expect to be paid (sometimes as many as 10 to 20 percent of the electorate), and the politicians are resigned to this practice as a necessary evil. There are other counties where, as several chairmen described it, "we don't spoil the voters," and the buying of votes is rare. There is no obvious pattern to explain the differences in custom, and it is not simply a contrast between poorer and more prosperous counties. The contrasting practices can be illustrated by two counties in western Kentucky, in each of which the chairman estimated that it would cost about $3,000 to run for county office in the primary. One county has about 12,000 Democratic voters, and the chairmen says, "We don't waste money by giving it out to haul voters to the polls." The other county has only a little more than 3,000 Democratic voters, and half of the amount spent in a campaign goes to buy votes, though the practice is declining.

Vote buying takes several forms. In some of the low-income city precincts, including a few of those in the largest cities, it is common to see precinct leaders bringing voters to the polls and then taking them around the corner to be paid. Probably the most common practice is that of paying political "workers" $25 to $50 to haul voters to the polls. The worker may pocket the money and drive one or two carloads of his family and relatives to the polls, or he may hand out the funds in small amounts to a larger number of voters as an inducement to get them to the polls. Under this decentralized plan it is easy for the money to be wasted, and the shrewd politician is one who knows how to give out money without throwing it away. The inefficiency and unreliability of this technique appear to be reasons for its gradual decline.

In a primary campaign the candidate cannot rely on the party organization for financial assistance, although he may be able to get help in fund raising from individuals who are party leaders. Primary candidates sometimes pool their funds for election-day expenses. In the general election campaign some candidates receive substantial help from the party, but others are expected to finance their own campaign and even to contribute money to the party for such expenses as hiring workers and maintaining a headquarters. In some counties the candidates are assessed a fixed percentage of their anticipated salary to pay for common campaign expenses. When chairmen were asked whether county candidates supplied funds to, or received funds from, the party organization in a general election campaign, 44 percent said the candidates supplied funds, 20 percent said the organization did, and 36 were unable to make such a clearcut generalization. It is rather surprising to find that the candidates are most likely to be counted on to supply funds in Marginal counties.

The chairmen were asked to describe each of five potential sources of funds as having major, minor, or no importance in fund raising.

TABLE 2.1

*Sources of Campaign Funds in Counties as Ranked in
Importance by Party Chairmen (in percentages)*

Source	Major	Minor	No Importance
Local officeholders and jobholders	48½	37½	14
Candidates for local office	41	26	33
Fund-raising dinners	39	35	26
Businessmen	16	50	34
A few relatively wealthy persons	12½	40	47½

Table 2.1 shows how heavily the parties depend on persons who hold county office or are candidates for office and those who hold jobs, either in the courthouse or with the state. These are particularly important sources of funds in Marginal counties. Fund-raising dinners are common in many counties, and local businessmen are at least a minor source of funds, though they are of little importance in Republican counties. Relatively few chairmen said that the party relied on a few wealthy individuals for the bulk of their funds.

Even though the parties usually rely heavily on the men who are running for, or have won, local office, most of them (the 82 percent noted earlier) claim that they provide some financial assistance to local candidates. They rarely receive any aid from the state party for this purpose. Twenty percent of the chairmen describe fund raising as the most important function of the county party organization, and another 59 percent describe it as an important job carried out in each campaign; at the other extreme only 5 percent say that the local party never engages in fund raising.

Data from North Carolina show that the county Democratic parties in that state relied on similar major local sources for funds: officeholders and jobholders, local candidates, businessmen and professional people, although the reliance on officeholders and jobholders was not so heavy as in Kentucky. The North Carolina county Democratic parties differed in one important respect, however, from their counterparts in Kentucky; they received about half of their funds from sources outside the county, generally the state Democratic party.[11] Although local parties in Kentucky get some help from the state party for state and national elections, and the exact proportion is difficult to specify, the state party does not appear to contribute so substantially to the local party treasuries.

PATRONAGE AT THE COUNTY LEVEL

Most of the state patronage jobs in the average Kentucky county are found in the highway department. In a county with 14,000 population (the median size) there are likely to be 20 or 25 patronage employees of the highway department. Although each county is likely to have a few other patronage appointees, the distribution among the counties is uneven. Those counties near a state park, for example, benefit from large numbers of summer jobs that are filled on the basis of patronage. If a state institution, such as a hospital, prison, or mental institution, is in the county, the party leaders may have a chance to give political clearance to those persons who score high on examinations under the merit system, but usually the politicians are not at all concerned with filling the professional positions of such institutions.

Traditionally patronage has been considered the lifeblood of a political organization, the incentive that is essential for recruiting, rewarding, and disciplining workers in the organization. This assumption has been challenged in recent years by several political scientists who have studied the question. Sorauf, for example, has expressed doubts that the unskilled jobs currently available as

[11] Crotty, "The Party Organization and Its Activities."

patronage will attract persons who have the ability needed to make them useful to the party, and he has also questioned whether patronage is consistently used as a disciplinary technique or whether persons are kept on the state payroll long after they have become ineffective or unreliable as political workers.[12]

Democratic party chairmen in Kentucky who answered the questionnaire generally stressed the importance of patronage. Eighty-six percent agree that patronage is essential for creating an effective political organization, and two-thirds accept the proposition that a major factor in the state administration's popularity in the county is its handling of patronage. But it is somewhat surprising to find that less than half of the chairmen (44 percent) believe that the decline in the amount of state patronage available since the expansion of the merit system has hurt the party organization in their party. Another question raises further doubts about importance of patronage: Do most active party workers remain active because they expect to receive some kind of patronage? Just over half (56 percent) of the county chairmen believe that this is true. The viewpoints of chairmen vary with the partisan competitiveness of their counties. The chairmen from Republican counties are most likely to view patronage as an incentive for party workers and an important criterion of the administration's popularity; and chairmen from Democratic counties are least likely to share these views. In Republican counties the Democratic party is more heavily dependent on state patronage because it has little chance of electing men to county office.

When some of these chairmen were interviewed in greater depth, it became evident how much disagreement there was about the value of patronage to the party organization. Several chairman described practices in their counties that reduced the value of patronage as an incentive. A few said that there was relatively little turnover in patronage jobs when there was a change in factional control of the state administration. In one county a number of Chandler supporters were kept on the payroll in 1959 as a means of uniting the party behind the Combs administration. Another chairman commented that many of the patronage jobs had been given to supporters of courthouse officials in order to strengthen their

12 Frank J. Sorauf, "Patronage and Party," *Midwest Journal of Political Science,* III (1959), 115-26.

political position, and consequently these workers could not be counted on to work in statewide primaries.

Most chairmen agreed that those workers who are under the merit system are of little value as political workers; some chairmen commented scornfully that these persons would "hide behind the merit system" when they were asked to do any political work. How useful are the patronage workers, most of whom are in unskilled and semiskilled highway jobs? In relatively few cases the state workers are the key men in most of the precincts, with responsibility for getting out the vote and advising the voters on how to cast their ballots. State workers are more likely to have this function in lower income precincts. More often they are used to do such routine jobs as hauling voters to the polls and distributing literature. One county chairman said that in the past state workers supporting the Chandler administration had alienated voters by their loud promises about what the administration would do; he used the workers for political purposes, but kept them quiet. Obviously some state workers holding patronage jobs are more articulate, skillful, and influential than others, but in general they seem to be declining in importance as active workers who can be depended on to swing votes and to carry a precinct.

Many of the chairmen who described patronage workers as a potent political force meant only that they could be depended on to come to the polls, to bring their families, and to vote the right way. How can the votes of 30 patronage workers and their families be significant in a county where 3,000 to 5,000 votes are cast in a primary or general election? The answer depends in part on the size of the workers' families. One county chairman estimated that the average patronage worker was worth about five votes. Some of the counties where chairmen placed the greatest emphasis on the value of patronage were those—often in the mountains—where families are large and family loyalties are politically important. A state job in such a county might be worth ten votes or even more. In the mountain Republican counties where families are large and turnout in the Democratic primary is small, patronage may be a particularly important factor in state primary elections. The high rate of unemployment in the mountain counties makes state jobs, however unskilled and poorly paid, more attractive than they would be elsewhere and probably makes state workers more receptive to requests that they engage in political activity. In one western Republican county, which has highway and parkway toll jobs as well as up to 150 summer park jobs, the chairman estimated that most of the Democrats had relatives on the state payroll year round or part time. In the urban and metropolitan counties, where there are proportionately fewer patronage jobs and where family ties are weaker, the number of votes controlled by state patronage workers is relatively small and insignificant. Several chairmen, including those who were dubious about the political usefulness of state workers, emphasized that the lure of state jobs was important in the recruitment of workers by the faction out of power. They described this as one of the major obstacles to factional unity in their counties; there were always persons looking for state jobs— particularly where unemployment was high—who could be persuaded to engage in factional politics.

Generalizations about patronage in 120 counties are difficult if not meaningless. In the poorer, more rural counties patronage continues to be important to the party organization, mostly because patronage workers can be depended on to bring their relatives and friends to the polls in large numbers and to perform routine organizational chores. Patronage is one of the factors that perpetuates factionalism because it assures a nucleus of political workers who have a stake in the election of the out-faction. In some counties the mishandling of patronage by the administration's contact man undermines the administration's prestige and causes dissension even among those politicians who are identified with the administration faction. The impression persists that state patronage is declining in importance in most counties and is relatively unimportant in the urban counties. There are fewer and poorer jobs; those who hold them do little more than drive their families to the polls; and in most counties voters are more likely to be influenced by the administration's policies and projects that affect them directly rather than a job given to a distant relative.

DEMOCRATIC ORGANIZATIONS IN THE METROPOLITAN AREAS

Jefferson County. The decline of the political machine is a familiar story in American cities. The abrupt drop in immigration and the migration of ethnic groups to the suburbs have deprived the urban organizations of loyal voters; the social-welfare functions of the party have been taken over by governmental agencies; the patronage system has been eroded by the expansion of civil service; and candidates have grown independent of the organization because of their ability to reach the voter through radio and television. The Democratic party organization in Jefferson County and Louisville has suffered from all of these trends, but it has also been afflicted by old age, complacency, and the trauma of electoral defeat.

At one time the "regular organization" in Jefferson County had achieved a degree of political control that was unmatched in the urban parties of Kentucky. The Jefferson County organization was built by Michael J. Brennan, who nurtured the party while it was out of power during the 1920s and developed it into an effective machine from 1933, when the Democrats captured office in Louisville, until his death in 1938. He was an old-fashioned boss who used patronage and assessments from patronage appointees as the means of welding a cohesive and powerful organization. After Brennan's death, the organization was dominated by the mayor of Louisville for several years. In 1943 the Democrats lost control of the city board of aldermen and lost some seats on the county commission; in 1945 the Democrats narrowly elected the mayor but failed to win any seats on the board of aldermen and lost county offices, including the judgeship. As a result of these defeats there was an upheaval in the party organization. McKay Reed became Democratic county chairman in 1944; in 1947 Mrs. Lennie McLaughlin became executive secretary and John Crimmins became organizational chairman. Mrs. McLaughlin had worked closely with Brennan but had been ousted from power after his death by the mayor, and Crimmins had been associated with both Brennan and—at the time of his appointment—the mayor. In 1949 the Democrats regained complete control of city and county offices.

From 1947 until the early 1960s the Jefferson County Democratic organization was run by the triumvirate of Reed, Mrs. McLaughlin, and Crimmins. The chairman, McKay Reed, was a highly conservative man whose views affected the endorsement of candidates for the party nomination and the positions taken by Democratic officials in the county on local and state legislation. Mrs. McLaughlin (always referred to as "Miss Lennie") worked full time at the party headquarters, and over the years she built an efficient organization of precinct workers who were personally loyal to her. She also had much of the responsibility for making decisions regarding patronage. More than anyone else she personified the party organization in Jefferson County, and those who were familiar with that organization gave her much of the credit for its continuing effectiveness in an age when many urban political machines had become outmoded and ineffective. Crimmins' role at party headquarters, if not subordinate to hers, was less publicized. Because she was so often credited with the organization's success, it was inevitable that the Democratic party's defeat in the 1961 city and county elections would lead to demands for her ouster, but she continued to serve as secretary of the party until the end of 1965.

Although a number of jobs, including the police and fire departments, are under civil service, there are enough patronage appointments in both the city and county governments to give the party in power a great advantage. In 1961 it was estimated that the number of city patronage jobs was 1,500 and the number in the county was about 700. In addition to local jobs, the party organization handled patronage appointments in state government from Jefferson County. The patronage jobs were valuable to the party organization not only as a means of rewarding Democratic workers but as a continuing source of revenue for the organization. Since the 1930s it had been the custom to assess those persons holding patronage jobs 2 percent of their salaries. Even if only imperfectly implemented, this policy would be a major source of revenue. One party official estimated in 1957 that the assessments produced about $60,000 annually. At least half of that amount was used to maintain the party headquarters, with its elaborate files of voters and precinct workers, and to pay the professional and secretarial staff at the headquarters. The remainder was used, together with funds raised from other sources, for election campaigns. These jobs and the assessments from city workers were abruptly cut off when the Republicans swept into city offices in 1961, and the Democrats lost county jobs more gradually as the Republican party won these offices in two stages, the 1961 and 1963 elections. The leaders of the Democratic organization not only became the scapegoats as a result of the election defeats, but they lost the weapons of jobs and money that were essential to defend their position in the party.

The relationship between the Democratic organization and the

Democratic mayor of Louisville was not always smooth. As the most prominent local official, with the most jobs at his disposal, the mayor sometimes sought a greater voice in running the organization or clashed with it on questions of patronage and other policies. In 1948 Mayor Charles Farnsley tried to add some of his supporters to the Democratic county committee. He had been elected to fill a vacancy by the board of aldermen despite the organization's opposition. He appealed to rank-and-file voters as well as city employees to support him at the December precinct meetings, but he succeeded in electing only two of the four persons that he was trying to place on the eleven-man committee. Eventually he gave up his challenge of the disputed elections, and the organization agreed to endorse him in the 1949 primary for a full term. One of the bargaining tools occasionally used by a mayor in dealing with the organization was the threat to withhold the assessments of city workers from the organization. Despite occasional friction, the alliance of the organization and the mayor usually remained strong. The organization endorsed and elected a loyal ally as mayor; it provided help in the off-year elections for the board of aldermen, and the mayor handled patronage through the organization and channeled assessments to it.

For many years the Jefferson County Democratic organization has endorsed candidates for office at the state, legislative, county, and city levels. The endorsement is made by the county executive committee after extensive consultation with party leaders and in some cases after preliminary screening by an advisory committee. As long as she was active at party headquarters, Mrs. McLaughlin played an important part in the endorsements. The local candidates endorsed by the organization usually win in the primaries, and its candidates for state office usually carry Jefferson County. Frequently, Democratic candidates decide not to run if they fail to get the organization's endorsement, and as a consequence the proportion of contested local primaries is relatively low. The Democratic precinct workers keep the voters informed about primary endorsements, making extensive use of sample ballots, which are essential when the ballot is long. As long as there were 2,200 Democrats holding patronage jobs, the organization had a solid nucleus of persons who would work at the polls and who would bring family and friends to vote the right way in primary elections, but the loss of these workers and the defeats in general elections have not yet undermined the organization's ability to secure the nomination for most of the candidates it endorses.

The Democratic organization in Jefferson County developed a firm alliance with the Clements faction of the state party, and a prominent figure in the Clements faction—Lawrence Wetherby—served for a time as a member of the county committee. It delivered majorities—usually large ones—for the Clements faction in the important gubernatorial primaries of 1947, 1955, and 1959 and in Clements' battle for the senatorial nomination in 1956. In 1959 Bert Combs owed his majority in the primary almost entirely to his margin in Jefferson County. The Jefferson County organization fought A. B. Chandler in the 1955 primary and the 1956 state convention. It defeated his efforts to take over the county executive committee in the 1956 precinct and district meetings, and throughout the remainder of Chandler's term there was open hostility between his administration and the Jefferson County organization. For many years the Democratic organization controlled the legislative delegation from Jefferson County, which it had selected through its endorsement procedures. The delegation held binding caucuses and voted in a disciplined fashion on local issues and on the governor's measures. The Democratic organization was able to provide those governors whom it supported with a reliable block of legislative votes, and in return it could expect favorable treatment from the governor. The sharp Republican gains in 1961, however, drastically reduced the size and importance of the Democratic delegation from Jefferson County.

In the 1961 local elections many labor union and Negro leaders deserted the Democratic ticket in protest against the increasingly conservative policies of the city and county administrations. These losses, and the growing suburban vote, were fatal, despite the two-to-one Democratic lead in registered voters in the county. As one prominent Democrat said after the defeat, "If we don't have the poor people, the Negroes, and the labor unions on our side, what have we got left?"[13] As liberal Democrats became increasingly critical of the "old guard," McKay Reed was replaced by Raymond Bossmeyer, and John Crimmins left to take a federal job, but Mrs. McLaughlin held onto her post as party secretary.

In 1963 the party organization informed precinct leaders that it

[13] Louisville *Times*, Nov. 8, 1961.

would take no stand in the gubernatorial primary and that they could support whichever candidate they chose; the organization endorsed Harry Lee Waterfield against John Breckinridge for lieutenant governor. Some have attributed this break with the Combs administration to Mrs. McLaughlin's long political friendship with Clements; others think the leaders did not want to back the man—Breathitt—whom they expected to be the loser. The organization described this strategy publicly as an effort to unify the party, but the consequence was further disunity within the party. Breathitt carried Jefferson County (as did Breckinridge), and those who had organized his campaign in Jefferson County challenged the regular organization by establishing their own independent Democratic group. For about a year this group, which was regarded scornfully by the regular organization as a collection of amateurs, handled state patronage. As the 1964 precinct elections approached, the two groups prepared for a showdown. The precinct meetings attracted unusually large numbers, ranging from 50 to 150 in most precincts, and when the county executive committee was elected, it contained a close balance of organization men and amateurs. Before the struggle for control of the county party reached a decisive phase, Governor Breathitt stepped in and persuaded both sides to accept the appointment of Thomas Carroll as chairman. (A year later Mrs. McLaughlin stepped down.) Carroll had not been identified with any particular faction or clique in the party organization, but he was closely identified with the Combs-Breathitt faction, was a close friend of Breathitt, and had acquired organizational experience in several state campaigns. Once again the organization was allied with the state administration, but it had lost some of its independence and bargaining power. In 1967 the organization supported the administration candidate, Henry Ward, with considerable effectiveness in the gubernatorial primary.

The governor succeeded in imposing leadership, but not unity, on the Jefferson County Democrats. The fragmented party consists of at least five elements:

(1) The old-line precinct workers are growing old and many of them have lost interest in political work since the doors to patronage closed and since Mrs. McLaughlin stepped down (after the 1965 election). There is a decline in the proportion of precincts where a strong organization could be built on patronage and favors.

(2) The political amateurs, who are the most effective workers in the increasingly important suburbs, have gained power on the county executive committee, which they share uneasily with the politicians who have been allied with the old organization. The amateurs, allied with the Combs-Breathitt faction, often show more interest in state and national elections than in county and city politics. Like political amateurs elsewhere, they have had difficulty in translating their voting strength into political power.

(3) The Chandler and Waterfield factions have been weakened by their isolation from both state and local sources of power and patronage, but there is a substantial political underground of political workers who share these loyalties.

(4) The labor unions in Jefferson County, which split away from the old Democratic organization, have been cautious about reestablishing the alliance. Their political effectiveness has been hampered by disunity and by the personal identification of individual leaders with different state factions of the Democratic party.

(5) The Negro leadership, which had also been alienated by the old organization, remains independent, but its bargaining position is weakened by serious divisions among the individual leaders.

Other Metropolitan Counties. From the turn of the century until his death in 1937, Fayette County and Lexington had a political boss, William "Billy" Klair. He used the traditional tools of patronage, favors, and a strong precinct organization to maintain his power, and he developed into one of the powerful leaders in state politics. Within a few years after Klair's death, R. P. "Dick" Moloney became the dominant figure in Fayette County, while he served the Clements, Wetherby, and Combs administrations as a highly effective legislative leader until his death in 1963. Today there is neither a dominant Democratic leader nor a strong party organization in the county. The lower income precincts in the center of the city, which were the base of the Klair and Moloney organizations, have become heavily outnumbered in this rapidly growing county by the suburban precincts, which defy the efforts of politicians to create strong and durable organizations. State patronage has been handled by the administration's contact man, and county patronage is controlled by individual officeholders in the courthouse; a system of nonpartisan elections isolates the city government from the

Democratic party. The county executive committee lacks finances and patronage; it makes no endorsements in primary elections; and as a result, control of the committee is not hotly contested.

Except for the tradition of a dominant organization, the Fayette County party shares many of the characteristics of that in Jefferson— state factions, the clash between an old guard and the amateurs, and the erosion of Democratic power resulting in part from suburbanization. The party in Fayette County, however, has become even more fractionized than its counterpart in Louisville. The Chandler and/or Waterfield forces carried Fayette County in the gubernatorial primaries in 1955, 1959, 1963, and 1967, but since 1960 the formal party organization and most of the prominent party leaders have been allied with the Combs-Breathitt faction. The county's Democratic legislators have played prominent roles in support of the Combs and Breathitt administrations, several Demo- crats from the county have served in these administrations, and Foster Ockerman served as state chairman from 1963 to 1966. But political campaigns in Fayette County are individual efforts. The courthouse officials, some of whom have served several terms, usually run independently in the primary, and candidates for legislative office seldom make any reference to their factional allegiance. One of the most independent figures in Kentucky politics is John Y. Brown, who has run a number of statewide campaigns but whose most frequent victories have been in Fayette County legislative races. Another political figure who has been independent in county and sometimes in state politics is John Breckinridge; he was attorney general in the Combs administration, ran without factional affiliation against Waterfield for lieutenant governor in 1963, and was nomi- nated for attorney general in 1967 on the administration ticket.

The fractionization of Fayette County politics was best illustrated in the 1965 primary for county judge. The incumbent, Bart Peak, had some support from Chandler supporters and from residents of older sections of the city. The winner, Sheriff Ed Hahn, was supported by many of the party professionals and veteran precinct workers, as well as by most of the political leaders who were identified with the Combs-Breathitt faction. Dick Moloney, Jr., son of the late county leader, had strong support from the political amateurs, who were critical of the conservatism and business orientation of the local party leadership, but Moloney finished third. The party disunity generated by this race contributed to a Republican victory in the November race for county judge, but not for the other county offices. The Fayette County party continues to be more of a holding company for individual politicians than a powerful or cohesive organization.

The two metropolitan counties of northern Kentucky—Kenton and Campbell—are suburbs of Cincinnati. Most of the residents work in Cincinnati, and they often take greater interest in the political issues of that city than they do in Kentucky politics. Among the many varied components in the Kentucky electorate, northern Kentuckians have been among the most isolated from the mainstream of state politics. Neither Kenton nor Campbell County has had a strong Democratic party organization, probably because these are predominantly suburban counties. In both there has been a factional division among politicians paralleling the state factions. Northern Kentucky was one of the strongholds of the Chandler forces, and some of the legislators from this area provided support and leadership for the Chandler administration. During the Combs and Breathitt administrations, the balance of factional power shifted. In Kenton County a younger generation of political leaders allied with Combs and Breathitt has gradually been assuming leadership within the party and in elective office. In Campbell County both political parties were shaken in 1961 by the victory of an independent reform candidate for sheriff, who was pledged to eliminate the gambling that had made the county notorious. At the same time the Combs administration was using the resources of the state against gambling in Campbell County. These events brought about changes in the Democratic party leadership that gave the Combs-Breathitt forces greater, though not unchallenged, influence within the party. Of the two counties, Campbell County has had closer partisan competition, with both Republicans and Democrats holding courthouse positions. This used to be the result of trading agreements between leaders of the two parties, but it has persisted because of the personal popularity of individual officeholders.

3 | Republican Party Organization

ORGANIZATION AT THE STATEWIDE LEVEL

Standing at the apex of the formal Republican party organization in Kentucky is the state central committee (scc). Party rules delineating the role of the scc in the party organization are as follows: The scc "shall have immediate charge and full control of the political affairs and subordinate organizations of the Republican party in the state, the management of its campaigns, the collections and disbursements of funds; shall adopt such measures as may best promote the success of the Republican party and the election of its nominees"; it shall cause the various electoral districts of the state "to be thoroughly organized for political purposes by proper campaign committees which it shall constitute for all elections general to the state, and which shall at all times be subordinate to and under the control" of it.[1] Rule 24 gives it the power to fix the place and date of the state convention; to fix the day and hour of the county conventions to select delegates to the congressional district and state conventions (such county conventions are to be "mass" conventions, unless otherwise provided by the scc, according to Rule 27); and to apportion the number of delegates each county may send to the state convention. Rule 14 gives the scc the authority to select a replacement for a delegate-at-large (or alternate-at-large) to the Republican national convention "in the event of the death, resignation, or inability to act." Party rules also give the scc authority over the lower organizational levels in the party.[2]

State conventions are held each spring of presidential election years. Delegates are chosen at the county mass meetings. The state central committee determines the number of delegates per county, the usual criterion being the number of votes cast for the Republican presidential candidate four years earlier. The main importance of the state convention is the selection of delegates-at-large to the Republican national convention. The other delegates are chosen at the conventions at the congressional district level.

Membership on the scc is for a term of four years. Rule 9 stipulates that "each member shall be a Republican in good party standing." A rule adopted in 1964 provides that scc members must contribute $100 per year and may be dropped from membership for failure to do so.[3] Membership is composed of the chairmen and chairwomen of the congressional district committees, one person from each of the state's seven congressional districts (elected at the congressional district conventions), a Young Republican member from each congressional district, the chairmen of the Young Republican clubs of Kentucky, and a number of persons (sixteen in 1964) appointed by the permanent chairman of the quadrennial state convention of the party. Officers of the scc are a chairman, vice chairman, a secretary, and a treasurer.[4]

Party rules prescribe that the chairman of the scc shall "preside at all meetings of the scc." He is to "carry into effect the views and orders of the scc, he being hereby vested with such discretionary powers, in the absence of specific instructions, as may be necessary to the discharge of his duties." During political campaigns occurring while in office he is to attend at the headquarters of the state campaign committee and "by and with the advice of the said campaign committee shall have the supervision and management of such campaigns." He is to call meetings of the scc, and is to call to order the state convention and preside over it during the election of a temporary chairman.

The formal status of the scc and its chairman in the hierarchy

[1] Rules of Republican State Central Committee, July 12, 1944. Some amendments (applying to certain metropolitan counties) have been adopted since 1944.

[2] *Infra*, pp. 100-102.

[3] Interview with T. H. Hardwick, chairman of the state central committee. In 1966, Hardwick reported that no expulsions under this rule had been necessary.

[4] Rule 6; Louisville *Courier-Journal*, April 12, 1964. No precise, detailed occupational-social breakdown of scc membership was made. "Attorneys, insurance men, bankers, farmers, doctors, and businessmen" were said to be the occupations of the great majority of members.

of party organization can be ascertained by simply reading the rules. To explain the actual role that the scc and its chairman play in the Kentucky Republican party as a functioning organization is less easy. Some insight into this may be obtained by considering the views that various elements in the party hold about the proper role of the scc and its chairman.[5] The general concept is some form of leadership (variously phrased as "organizing," "keeping in contact with the county chairmen on party affairs," or "coordination"). Many persons who were polled thought the scc, led by the chairman, should be more vigorous in "ferreting out paper organizations" at the county level, as one person expressed it, while others thought there should not be "dictation" from the state level, or anything "undemocratic" in its activities.

Interviews with the men who have held the position of state chairman elicited basically the same views on their conception of their roles. This can be expressed as general supervision of the various committees of the party. Dewey Daniel said he felt his duty was to "build up a good organization." W. A. Stanfill said he called meetings of the scc when necessary, presided over them, and tried to maintain as much harmony as possible in the county organizations. T. H. Hardwick, the present state chairman, said he views his duties as "seeing that the organization functions well at all times, especially during campaigns"; trying to settle or conciliate factional disputes

[5] A brief note on methodology is in order. Much of the information on which this chapter is based was obtained from questionnaires sent to Republican county chairmen and chairwomen and from interviews with many members of the party holding various positions. Many persons stipulated anonymity, and, of course, this request has been respected. The questionnaires were first sent out in 1963 to both chairmen and chairwomen. In 1966, questionnaires were sent to chairmen from counties not heard from in 1963 and also to chairmen who had been elected in 1964. As a result, a total of 68 of the 120 counties in Kentucky were heard from. Sixty-eight chairmen replied in one or both years, from a total of 62 counties. (This was because of hearing from pre-1964 and post-1964 chairmen in the same six counties.) Eighteen chairwomen replied, of which six were in counties from which no chairmen answered. The questionnaires received from these 68 counties are fairly representative of the entire state. Of the 120 counties in Kentucky, 38 percent are classified as Strongly Democratic; 38 percent of the counties heard from were Strongly Democratic. Comparable figures for the other classifications of counties, and the percentage of counties from which questionnaires were returned, are: Democratic, 10 and 9 percent; Democratically Inclined, 11 and 13 percent; Marginal, 10 and 9 percent; Republican Inclined, 5 and 5 percent; Republican, 8 and 6 percent; Strongly Republican, 17 and 21 percent. The counties from which the questionnaires were received are widely spread over the state, and thus the geographical representation is considered to be sufficient. Because the problems of the two parties differ, no attempt was made to include the same items in the questionnaires submitted to Democratic and Republican leaders.

in the county organizations; directing the scc as something of a liaison between Republican candidates, between sections of the state, and between ideological elements in the party. He also believes that the scc can be an important instrument of raising money, and hopes that by contributing to the election of more Republicans in Kentucky it can increase the quality of the party's county organizations.

The scc has no regular schedule of meetings. It meets some four to six times annually, the attendance of members being approximately two-thirds. It is most active, of course, during the period preceding elections.[6] Except for a finance committee (with a state finance chairman and regional vice chairmen at Louisville and Lexington), there is no particular division of labor within it; ad hoc committees are appointed as the occasion arises.

How effective is the scc in party affairs? How well does it perform in coordinating and supervising the constituent organizations in the performance of that crucial function of a political party—getting its nominees elected to office? For many years in the past it has been weak and ineffective, a judgment confirmed by Republican gubernatorial candidates. One said that "there was just no state organization" when he ran for governor. He said he had to devote a great deal of time to building up "something resembling a state-wide organization" during his campaign. Another gubernatorial candidate said that during his race "the organization at the state level didn't amount to a hill of beans." There was no money and no staff in the state headquarters, and the situation there often was one of "chaos and confusion." Another told of the great burden upon his time and energy because of the weakness of the state central committee. Even by the time the election was held, he said, "We never got a truly functioning state-wide organization established." Another gubernatorial candidate said that his campaign organization was his own and that his contacts with the scc were few. "Most of the persons on the state committee weren't happy about my nomination," he declared.

The appointment of a full-time executive director, and the

---

[6] During the Eisenhower administration, many meetings were concerned with federal patronage. During the 1943-1947 administration of Simeon S. Willis, state patronage was a frequent cause of scc meetings. The administration controlled the scc and many factional disputes within county organizations were resolved, nearly always in favor of the administration.

activities he has performed, should contribute to the strengthening of the scc and of the Republican party in the state. Warren Schweder, a former reporter for the Lexington *Leader*, was appointed to this position in December 1964. He is also editor of the *Kentucky Republican*, a monthly newspaper published by the scc in conjunction with its sustaining membership program. This newspaper contains news about party affairs as well as the expected propaganda. Its subscription cost is $2 per year, but its chief function is to serve as one inducement for individuals to become a "sustaining member" at $12 annually and thereby contribute money to the Kentucky GOP. The first effort at the establishment of this program obtained some $11,000, about $1,000 more than expected, which indicates, according to one party official, "that there are some sources for building a stronger Republican party in Kentucky" if there is the will and effort to capitalize upon them. Names of potential members were obtained from the Republican national committee, from the lists of those who had attended fund-raising dinners in the past, from names suggested by scc members, county chairmen, etc. A letter soliciting membership was sent out, and a follow-up letter was sent to those who did not respond to the first one. The overall response was about 20 percent. With some 5,000 to 6,000 names now on the list of potential members, it is hoped that about $30,000 annually can be obtained from this source. Added to the money raised from private contributors, fund-raising dinners, and from the county organizations, the scc hopes to have about $50,000 per year available for its activities.

A good percentage of these funds will go to finance an important activity of a political party—the recruitment of candidates. Much effort in this direction was expended under scc auspices in the 1965 "off-year" local and state legislative elections. Schweder and Marge Cruse (a vice chairman of the scc), working with various local or regional officials—such as county chairmen and state legislators— "started in the west" of the state and worked eastward to recruit candidates for the state legislature.[7] These efforts were to a large degree responsible for the fact that there were 71 Republican candidates in the 120 state legislative races that year, the largest number since 1947. In about 45 of these legislative districts, where

[7] Their efforts were mainly in areas of weak Republicanism, because, of course, in strongly Republican areas there is no problem finding GOP candidates.

it was considered that there was a reasonable chance of a Republican victory, Schweder and Cruse concentrated their efforts: holding workshops for workers at which they discussed voting laws, hauling voters to polls, and encouraging registration efforts, for example. In the 1965 legislative elections, the Republicans retained essentially the same number of seats they had won in 1963, when their legislative representation increased substantially because of the near-victory of the Republican candidate for governor. This fairly good showing in 1965 must be attributed in part, at least, to these efforts of the scc.[8]

The central organization of the Republican party in Kentucky has in the past been generally weak and ineffective.[9] Its prolonged minority party status has contributed to this weakness. With a larger supply of funds and a full-time worker to attend to party affairs, however, the scc should be able to help make the party more influential in state politics. But the extent of its influence will be limited by its relationship to the essential element of any state political party—the local organizations.[10]

ORGANIZATION AT THE CONGRESSIONAL DISTRICT LEVEL

The intermediate level in the formal organization of the Kentucky Republican party is at the congressional district.[11] The congressional district committee is composed of the chairmen and chairwomen of the counties embraced within the district. A chairman is elected

[8] There was also some effort at recruiting Republican candidates for county offices. Hardwick said that after the 1965 elections there were more Republican county officials than ever before in Kentucky history. In years prior to 1965, there was some recruitment effort by the scc, but not on the scope of 1965. Lack of funds and interest by the state leadership appears to be the main reason.

[9] One of the most prominent men in the party, who has long been active in party affairs at various levels, said in 1963 that the scc was a "weak and lackluster organization." He said it was too large, and that too many members of it were interested only in the prestige that membership brought and did very little in active party work. He also said that lack of finances was a serious drawback, and indicated that this could be alleviated by more aggressive action on the part of the scc. "Fewer and better people" was his brief prescription for increasing the effectiveness of the scc. In 1963 a man who has had occasion to observe the operation of Republican state committees in several other states declared that the scc of the Kentucky GOP, along with the Kentucky Republican organization in general, rated in the lowest 10 percent of those he had observed.

[10] Infra, pp. 100-102.

[11] For multicounty districts other than the congressional district, the Republican district committee is composed of the county chairmen and chairwomen of the counties embraced within the district. Rule 7.

by these persons at the congressional district conventions. These conventions are usually held within a week or two after the county conventions in March of presidential election years. The term of office of the congressional district chairmen is four years.

Duties of the CDC chairmen are delineated in the party rules. They are "specifically charged with the duty of organizing the several counties in their several districts at an early date preceding each state and congressional campaign, and of visiting each county when necessary during the canvass for purpose of encouraging greater efficiency and activity in political work." The chairman is to call the CDC "together at some convenient and central point in the district as often as may be necessary for the general welfare of the party and the success of the Republican ticket; and shall aid, by counsel, and in every other proper way, the party nominees." Reports of these meetings are to be sent to the state central committee upon request. The chairman "is also charged with the proper conduct of each Congressional campaign." Under the supervision of the state central committee, the CDC "may provide a campaign and other subordinate committees."

The role played by the CDC depends largely upon the activities and personal qualities of the CDC chairmen. Most are relatively experienced in party affairs or in public office (or both, in some cases), and thus the influence they wield is based upon personal relationships established over a period of time. Chairmen view their main function as "organizing." One said he saw his duty as "supervising the county organizations, seeing that they are as well built-up as possible." He added that an important function he performed during the Eisenhower administration was handling patronage matters in his district. Another man said that "acting as a sort of conveyor belt" between the state and county levels was one of the main things he did. Another said he considered his main role to "act as a liaison with the SCC" and to manage the holding of the district conventions each four years.

Meetings of the CDC tend to be infrequent, and most of them are held in the period preceding elections. One man said the CDC met rarely except during the period of three to four months preceding the November elections. He said that about 30 percent of the chairmen and chairwomen would diligently attend these meetings, about 50 percent would usually do so, while the others would rarely or never be present. Another said frequency of meetings of the CDC "depends upon the campaign." Three chairmen said there were several counties in their district with "hacks" or the "deadwood" type in the county organizations.

Two chairmen said they had solicited campaign funds, one reporting many contributions of $25, $50, and $100. Two said they had not solicited contributions, leaving it up to the county organizations to do so. The men reported that they had received money from the state level for allocation to the counties in their district. One said he saw the state chairman about six times a year, another two said "quite often," another said "it depends upon campaigns and upon district business," and the other said "not too often." Three chairmen said they had made efforts at, or had been involved in, soliciting Republican candidates for United States House of Representatives races. One in the traditionally Republican district in southeastern Kentucky observed "that is no problem here," adding that he had been engaged in primary elections for the House nomination.

How do county chairmen view the chief functions of the CDC chairmen? In descending order of frequency of replies to this question, the answers were as follows: "provide organization" (or "leadership"); "coordinate county chairmen"; "keep county chairmen informed"; "promote harmony in the party"; "pass on information from, or to, the state committee"; "promote candidates for district office"; "hold regular district meetings"; and "take care of the general interest of the district."

Thus we have some general, if not exhaustive, picture of the operations of the congressional district chairmen in the Republican party. The general impression we get concerning their role is that the influence and authority they exercise depend basically upon the personal attributes of the individuals who hold these positions. A chairman possessing leadership qualities (the "right" personality, knowledge, ability, and aggressiveness) could be of considerable influence in party affairs in his district. The actual influence of the chairman varies widely. One man described a chairman with great influence in his district: "If we had had a primary for governor, he could have lined up most of the county organizations in his district behind the man he supported." This particular chairman has long been active in party affairs, has a wide circle of friends in the county organizations in the district, courteously listens to the people from the county organizations when they come to him, and has helped a lot of people in patronage matters. "So—he can swing a lot of weight." William O. Cowger, former mayor of Louisville and member of the United States House of Representatives since January 1967, exerts considerable influence in party affairs, but very little of this is due to his position as chairman for his district. Some persons interviewed said that some chairmen were detrimental to the party and should be replaced by more active and aggressive persons. "Firing some of the chairmen" was the recommendation for strengthening the party by a man prominent in party affairs.

THE COUNTY ORGANIZATIONS

Structure. The basic unit of organization of the Republican party in Kentucky as in most of the United States is at the county level. Kentucky is one of the states where the organization of political parties is not extensively prescribed by the statutes. Hence, the rules adopted by the party govern its organization at the county level.

Organization at the county level is based upon the precinct, the basic unit for the conduct of elections. On the third Saturday in March of each presidential election year at 2:00 p.m. standard time, precinct chairmen and chairwomen are elected by the registered Republicans of those precincts. These elections may be held within the precinct, or if the county committee so decides, they may be held at the county seat during a "county mass convention." Generally, the latter procedure is followed. Voting may be *viva voce* or by the use of ballots. The *viva voce* procedure is apparently more common.[12]

These precinct chairmen and chairwomen collectively constitute the Republican county executive committee (more commonly known as the county committee). They elect the officers of the county committee—chairman, chairwoman, secretary, and treasurer—who are not necessarily chosen from those present at the meeting. If new precincts are created within the county, the county committee appoints the chairman and chairwoman therein. The term of office

---

[12] ". . . with few, if any exceptions, county meetings are held," instead of precinct meetings. J. E. Reeves and William C. Brafford, "Method of Choosing Delegates and Officials of Political Parties," *Kentucky Law Journal*, XLV (1957), 462.

for these positions is four years, except that in some of the urban counties the county chairmen and chairwomen hold office for one year only.

In some of the urban counties of the state, the rules regarding the county committees differ from the above. In Fayette County, the precinct chairmen and chairwomen elect a 12-man county executive committee. This executive committee in turn elects the county chairman and chairwoman. In Kenton County, the county committee is limited to 40. This committee is to be elected as the state central committee may direct. Because of the heavily Democratic registration in the county (approximately 8 to 1), most precinct chairmen are usually persons who have volunteered for the job, after having been screened and accepted by the county committee. Area captains (or chairmen) are elected by the precinct chairmen, with an area comprising 4 to 5 precincts. These area captains select a district leader (i.e., a Kentucky legislative district), who is directly responsible to the county committee. Campbell County, adjacent to Kenton, has also recently been permitted by the state central committee to adopt special rules. These rules are essentially the same as in Kenton County. Precinct committeemen and committeewomen are appointed by the county chairman and chairwoman. Subchairmen for different parts of the county may also be appointed if deemed desirable.

During the spring in presidential election years, usually in April, county mass meetings are held to choose delegates to attend the congressional district conventions and, in turn, the state convention, which is the supreme organ of the party. The most important function of the state convention is choosing the at-large delegates to the Republican national convention. The other delegates are chosen at the congressional district conventions.

Thus, it is seen that, in an indirect way, the ultimate formal authority in the party flows from the quadrennial mass meetings at the county level; *de jure*, the rank-and-file party members enjoy the final power of decision. In reality, the Kentucky Republican party, like nearly all state political parties, is effectively controlled by a small number of "political activists." The meetings are usually attended by only a small number of party members. In some counties there may be a fairly large turnout of the rank and file, usually as a result of conflicts between cliques in the county who want to control the county committee. A sharply contested presidential nomination in the Republican party may also stimulate an unusually large attendance at the meetings. This happened in 1952, during the Eisenhower-Taft contest for the nomination. Typically, however, a small number of persons interested and active in party affairs choose the county committee and the delegates to the higher conventions. This means that a fairly small number of persons active in party affairs can "deliver" the Kentucky delegates' votes at the Republican national convention to whomever they want. As one prominent party official said: "We have solid men, men of substance, who could certainly exert considerable influence in the choice of delegates. If they got behind one man, it is probable that he would get our votes at the National Convention." A former state chairman, asked if he thought it would help strengthen the party if the precinct chairmen and the county chairmen and chairwomen were elected by formal secret ballot in voting machines, answered in the negative, adding that "your leaders ought to have influence. They do the party work, and it seems only fair that some benefits should flow to them. Leaders shouldn't be hamstrung." A congressional district chairman in a district with many strongly Democratic counties said that usually "only a handful" of persons showed up at the county mass meetings. "A good many of the precinct chairmen are appointed by the county chairmen." In Jefferson County the selection of the county executive committee clearly indicates oligarchical control. Contests for seats on the county executive committee or for delegates to the state convention would occur only if some faction within the party organized for such contests and furnished the necessary funds for the election.[13]

One indication of the type of leadership and its oligarchical nature may be gained by a consideration of certain data about county chairmen and chairwomen. Of a total of 86 persons polled, 19 had been in office for over 12 years (40 years was the longest; 2 were in their thirtieth year; 7 had been in office from 20 to 30 years); 8 had been in office from 8 to 12 years; 21 had been in office

[13] "The Edwin G. Middleton–George W. Norton–Archie P. Cochran faction of the Republican party here yesterday elected its slate of county committeemen and delegates and alternates to the state convention without opposition. . . . It had been thought for a while that a slate would be submitted by that faction of the party in Jefferson County with which Edward C. Black and certain leaders of the Third District Republican Club are identified." Louisville *Courier-Journal*, March 3, 1960.

from 4 to 8 years; and 38 had served less than 4 years. Nearly all the last reported being elected at the latest quadrennial election, but a few had gained office since that time as a result of the death of their elected predecessor. Of the 56 persons who replied in 1963, 30 were still in office after the 1964 reorganization elections.

To the question, "Is there generally competition for the chairmanship?" there were negative replies from 56 persons, while 25 persons said there was competition. These answers indicate that in some 47 of the 68 counties there was no competition for the chairmanship. There might be two explanations for an absence of competition. One is that a tightly organized clique or faction has such control over the party in their county that opposition would be futile and pointless. One prominent Republican stated that he had observed this situation in certain counties. "You have these little cliques in some counties who are interested only in controlling patronage. They are so entrenched and so skilled" that it is a practical impossibility to get rid of them. He added that, in some cases, such situations had hurt the Republican candidates in statewide races. "Many of them do little more in party work than vote," and keep out of the organization many persons who would be willing actively to work for the party. The other explanation would be that the position of county chairman is not deemed sufficiently attractive or important to justify any struggle for its possession. The situation undoubtedly varies in different areas, but it would seem that the second reason applies in a majority of cases. One chairman said that he had no particular desire for the job, but that he was prevailed upon to accept it. "If we could find some other good man to take my place, I would gladly relinquish it." Another chairman said there were "no takers" for the job, and thus he was still holding it. A congressional district chairman of a predominantly Democratic district said in an interview that there was generally little competition for the county chairmanship in the counties of his district. "It's a job" to get someone to take the position in the heavily Democratic counties, he added. Another district chairman indicated that much the same prevailed in his district. One chairman reported, however, that his election as chairman "was bitterly fought by the only county newspaper, the state senator and county officials, but I received the overwhelming support from the rank-and-file of workers and voters."

Information worthy of mention in regard to county chairmen and chairwomen concerns their education and occupation. Thirty-three persons reported possessing a college degree. Many of these indicated additional college work, and five reported a master's degree. Fifteen persons reported they had done some college work short of a degree. Twenty-four stated a high school education, five reported an eighth grade education, and the remainder omitted mentioning their level of education. Thus it can be seen that these people in leadership positions are in the upper educational levels, as the median number of school years completed by Kentuckians of 25 years of age or over is only 8.7 according to census data.

Persons in leadership positions at the county level lean toward business occupations. By far the highest number (38) of these chairmen and chairwomen reported they gained their livelihood (or had gained it, as eight persons said they had retired) from some sort of business enterprise. Merchants, realtors, savings-and-loan-association operators, salesmen, lumber dealers, coal operators, retailers, and advertising directors are among the list of businesses so reported. Nine persons (mostly chairwomen) reported occupations as teachers, while seven reported they were housewives. Nine farmers, eight professionals (five lawyers, one engineer, one physician, and one chiropractor), four county officials, one publisher, one news editor, one steamfitter, one sheet metal worker, and one railroad conductor round out the list of occupations reported.

Functions and Operations. Rules of the Republican party place important responsibilities on the county organizations. As they are on "the front lines of combat"—most directly in touch with that ultimate target of the party, the voter—they are of critical importance. Among the duties of the county committees prescribed by party rules are the following: "By itself, or through the county campaign committee," it "shall have entire control of the county and district campaigns for districts embraced in such county and provide ways and means for conducting the canvass; distribute all supplies received from the state central committee in accordance with instructions"; send a list of precinct chairmen to the state central committee; poll the county and report thereon to the state central committee; "meet with committeemen in every precinct and see that they are instructed as to their duties; supervise the polling and other campaign work therein and arrange the times and places of all political meetings in the county." The county chairman is to see that each precinct chairman procures a copy of registered voters for his precinct and sends a duplicate copy to the state central committee.

These rules provide, in a general way, a conception of the duties of the county organizations. How do the chairmen, ostensibly the most important person in the county organization, conceive their roles? Chairmen were asked: "What do you think should be the chief function(s) of the county chairman?" The most frequent response (from 59 persons) was to "provide organization" or "leadership." Eight persons answered "work for harmony within the party," an apparent indication of factional struggles in their counties. Six persons viewed their functions as simply "to preside at meetings of the county committee." Various other replies were received, such as "to get good candidates"; "to produce enthusiasm"; "to coordinate all party business"; "keep in touch with the voters"; "help build up the party." Other replies included one each of the following: "correct false propaganda"; "know election laws"; "work"; "educate the rank-and-file on party principle"; "carry out the wishes of the party members"; "inform elected officials of the desires of the electorate"; "know the issues"; and "get publicity for the GOP."

How often do the county committees meet? Prima facie, one would assume that fairly frequent meetings would be an indication of an effective organization, although this would not necessarily be so. Party rules specify "regular meetings for the transaction of any business that may come before the body to enable members to exchange ideas about party affairs." Monthly meetings are the rule in the urban counties of Jefferson, Fayette, Kenton, and Campbell. In the other counties, information from chairmen indicates wide variation in frequency of county committee meetings. As might be expected, nearly all meet at least once during the campaign period prior to the November election. Only 10 percent of the chairmen reported meeting weekly; the other replies suggest that two meetings during the campaign is the approximate average. During the approximately ten months per year when no campaign is in progress, the chairmen report meetings of the committee ranging from "none," to once a year, to "occasionally," and "for special business." One congressional district chairman said that about the only meetings of county committees in his district, aside from those near the election, were held to discuss matters concerning patronage during the presidency of Eisenhower. Another district chairman estimated that county committees in his district averaged one meeting per year. "In some of the strong Democratic counties the county committee exists only on paper," said another man. "Some of them don't even meet during years of state-wide elections, although there is some informal consultation among the members of the committee."

There is a wide variation in the frequency with which the county chairmen report contacts with the upper echelons of the party (the congressional district chairmen and the state central committee chairman). One county chairman with an eight-year tenure of office, another with a six-year tenure, and another with a three-year tenure said they had never been in contact with either the congressional district chairman or the state chairman, formally or informally. Eleven persons (with tenure ranging from 2 to 40 years) replied "seldom" or "rarely." Twenty-four persons reported contact on the average of once or twice a year with the congressional district chairman; eleven reported three to four contacts a year; four reported five to six contacts annually; the remainder reported more frequent contacts (two persons reported monthly, or almost monthly, contacts with the congressional district chairman, who resided in their county or nearby), or said "several," "often," "not often," "during the active part of the campaign," or words to that effect. Reports of frequency of contact with the state chairman ranged as follows: 17 persons said once a year; 17 said two to three times a year; 8 said four to six times annually; the remainder said more often (10-12, 8-10, 6-12, etc.) or "several," "often as necessary," or "only during campaigns."

Communication between the various levels of the party appears to be somewhat haphazard. Present and past chairmen of the state central committee indicated there was no formalized procedure for communicating with the county chairmen. "I did it on an *ad hoc* basis," said Dewey Daniel, state chairman from 1955 to 1960. Congressional district chairmen indicated the same. "As a rule," said one, "about the only time I ever see the chairmen in this district is in the three to four months before the election." Another one said that usually the only matter the county chairmen contacted him about was money. "When Ike was president, though, I had a lot of contacts about patronage."

The county chairmen were asked in the questionnaire if they believed that they and/or the county committee had any influence with the upper echelons in the party. Fifty-three replied "yes," and 21 said "no." The remainder either did not answer the question or said "very little," "some," or "not much." No discernible pattern appeared in the type of counties classified according to Republican strength, nor were all the "no" answers received from chairmen who had been in office only a short time. Nearly the same proportion of chairmen reported that their views on party affairs had been solicited by either the state central committee or the congressional district chairmen. The following comments shed some light on contrasting attitudes toward the higher echelons held by county personnel. A chairwoman from a Strongly Republican[14] county said: "We trust the higher echelons; our views are sometimes solicited, but they are usually better informed of the better candidates, procedures, etc." A chairwoman from a Strongly Democratic county reported that "I don't think we have much influence with them. They usually want us to send money to their headquarters and we always need money in our county." A chairman from an urban county remarked: "We are always asked our opinion on all party matters." A chairman from a Strongly Democratic county said it was his experience that the "state committee does not solicit views until they are ready to submit [sic] for approval." Saying he thought his county organization had "very little" influence with the higher levels, a chairman in office since 1960 in a Strongly Democratic county added: "Incidentally, I do not feel particularly obligated to the state or district committees. They have never helped us one way or another. If I felt called to go against their desires, I would not hesitate." A chairwoman from a Strongly Democratic county said: "We don't seem to have any trouble getting through to our party leaders; they are always on the alert for new ideas, are never aloof." A chairman from a Marginal county said that "suggestions are always welcome. However, it is well recognized that the officers in state headquarters are generally more experienced and devote more of their time to their work than do county officers." A chairman in a

---

[14] See, *infra*, pp. 185-187, for an explanation of this classification.

Republican county suggested that county chairmen have little influence "and are seldom consulted on campaign strategy, but are always asked to raise funds and to contribute." A chairman in another Republican county said the higher echelons "set the policy and the rank-and-file fall in; this is not democracy and we believe this is one reason why the Republican party in Kentucky is a minority party." One old gentleman of 76 who had over 20 years experience as chairman in a Democratically Inclined county lamented that "a county chairman in a county which is two and three times outnumbered has a very difficult job and I don't believe that the Big Boys appreciate our work as much as they should."

In order to obtain some impression of the role of the county organizations in the nominating process of Republican candidates for statewide and multicounty constituencies, this question was included in the questionnaire: "Have you been consulted about, or participated in, any 'pre-primary' activities regarding the nominee of the party for such races as governor, U. S. Senator, U. S. House of Representatives, or the state legislature?" Eighty persons replied, 52 in the affirmative, 23 in the negative. Of those answering "no," 22 had been in office since 1960 or later, and the other 4 had been in office from 8 to 40 years. Seventeen were in predominantly Democratic counties, and 11 were in predominantly Republican counties.

How effective are the county organizations in performing their main function—doing the things which culminate, on election day, in the highest possible vote for the Republican nominee? Nearly all chairmen report that the county organization makes some effort to locate and register potential Republican voters. In many counties, however, this is not a vigorous effort. Two chairmen acknowledged only a "token effort" in this direction; one said "not nearly as much as we should"; one reported "some" effort along these lines; and another reported only "a feeble effort." One chairman said: "Very little—our county is rural in nature and voters and prospects are scattered over a large area. We do make an effort in each small town." Another remarked: "Yes for the good voter. But no if we believe he is a floater for we never have enough money to buy him on election day." A chairman in an urban county said: "Yes, through periodic polls and registration drives." A chairwoman in an urban county said: "Yes, last year by a huge phone campaign; this year through precinct organization."

Some systematic effort to raise campaign funds was reported from more than 90 percent of the counties. Again, there is much variation in the vigor and success of these efforts. One party official said that although some chairmen lament about the scarcity of campaign money in their counties, "it wouldn't be scarce if they would look for it a little harder." A few chairmen admitted that "only occasionally" did they try to raise money. One chairwoman said very few efforts were made at raising funds, adding that "a few of us carry the expenses." Another chairwoman said that "elected officials put up most of the money." One chairwoman commented: "Yes, we send letters to all registered Republicans. We believe the smallest donation makes a person feel more a part of the party. We solicit large sums in person or by phone." The main source is individual contributions, and the bulk of the money probably comes from businessmen and officeholders. The comment of the chairman in a Strongly Democratic county appears typical for most counties: "A half dozen provide all or most of the funds." Barbecues, fish-fries, picnics, and fund-raising dinners seem to be a major source of funds in relatively few (probably not over 10 percent) of the counties. In the larger urban counties the general rule is that a finance committee is appointed for this purpose.[15]

Evaluation. What is the general evaluation of the county organizations by persons who have been in a position to observe them and to work with them? The broad impression conveyed by such people is that the county organizations could be improved considerably. Every gubernatorial candidate interviewed commented on the large number of counties in which the county committee was little more than a paper organization. One said he virtually had to build up his own organization in about one-half of the counties. He estimated that the regular county organizations were "on paper only" in about one-third of the counties. In the remaining counties, the organizations ranged in effectiveness from "poor" to "excellent." In many counties, he said, there was no one to meet him when he arrived to

[15] In 1948, the Jefferson County chairman directed that the finance committee was not to solicit funds from gamblers and other persons on the shady side of the law. Louisville *Courier-Journal*, April 13, 1948.

campaign, and no one to schedule meetings and speeches for him. "In a lot of the counties I never saw the county chairman. About all I did by way of campaigning was to shake hands in the main town" of the county.

Another gubernatorial candidate observed that in many counties the organization was composed of "provincial-minded" people whose main interest was in county politics. He cited one Strongly Republican county in which, during his race, the local organization was more interested in a school board contest than any other. "The county committee was split wide-open on this race, and had no interest at all in the gubernatorial race." Another gubernatorial candidate said that in many counties, especially the Strongly Democratic counties in the western part of the state, Republican organizations were "just non-existent." Another who has had contact with nearly every county organization used the word "weak" in describing the quality of "nearly all" of the county organizations. This is not surprising, he explained, when it is kept in mind that the party had no state patronage for twenty years after the end of the Willis administration in 1947. "It's hard to keep up enthusiasm" after continually losing gubernatorial elections, he acknowledged. All these men, as well as others, told of many counties in which there were many precincts with no precinct chairmen or chairwomen.[16]

One high-ranking Republican referred to many chairmen in many counties, especially Strongly Democratic counties, as "Alabama-type chairmen": interested in controlling the local organization so as to be in a position to dispense any federal patronage which might be available under a Republican president. "They want to keep the party in the county as small as possible in order to control it more easily." He added that "perhaps to the surprise of many, you will find these types in some of the Republican counties," mentioning some counties in the southeastern part of the state. A former state chairman said the greatest single thing that could be done to strengthen the GOP in Kentucky would be to "fire half of the county chairmen." "We need a lot more younger people in as

---

[16] In 1966, almost one-fourth of the chairmen reported that there were active precinct workers in all the precincts in the county. In one-fifth of the counties, there were active workers in about three-fourths of the precincts. Not quite half of the chairmen said that such was the case in about half of their counties' precincts. The remainder of the chairmen estimated that in one-third or fewer of the precincts in their counties were there active workers. One chairman in a Strongly Democratic county said there was only one precinct in his county with an active worker.

chairmen," said another person.[17] One man cited the Republican county organizations in two mountain counties which are heavily Democratic. "They won't provide enough Republican challengers there to cover anything like all the precincts," with the result that much fraudulent voting occurs—"enough to carry the state for the Democrats in a real close election."

Senator Thruston B. Morton won reelection in 1962 apparently by forming what amounted to his own organization. Mrs. W. C. Cruse, vice chairman of the state central committee told of extensive organizational efforts which began in the latter half of 1961, more than one year before the election.[18] In a great many counties she and others had to bypass the county chairmen because they were unenergetic (too old, in many instances) or lackadaisical. She believed that this special, extensive, and lengthy organizational work on behalf of Senator Morton's race was of considerable importance in his reelection. Senator Morton concurred in the evaluation of the importance of this work. A prominent Republican, with extensive knowledge about this campaign, said Senator Morton was not reelected by "a Republican organization; it was by a Morton organization."

County chairmen were asked: "In state-wide races, do the party's nominees rely chiefly upon the regular county committee for the conduct of the campaign in your county, or do they (all or some of them) more or less build up their own campaign staffs?" Sixty-four persons replied that the nominees relied upon the regular committees, though many qualified their answers by using words such as "usually," "most of the time," or "generally." Thirteen persons answered that it was a combination of using the regulars and special committees in their counties; only two persons (in a Strongly Democratic and Marginal county, respectively) answered that the nominees used their own campaign staffs. In statewide campaigns, of course, it is usually the practice to appoint campaign committees in each county. In counties where the regular county organization is largely a paper organization the campaign committees perform what efforts are exerted on behalf of the Republican candi-

17 The 1966 survey showed the median age of the chairmen to be 48. There were seven under 35, four between 35 and 40, six between 41 and 50, six between 51 and 60, and seven over 60. The oldest was 76. No ages were obtained in the 1963 survey.

18 In a talk before the Young Republican Club at the University of Kentucky, May 2, 1963.

date in that county, and these committees are, in effect, part of the ad hoc organization built up by the candidate in the particular race.[19]

A substantial number (from one-third to one-half) of the county organizations are clearly ineffective. The chairmen devote a minimum of time to party affairs and make no serious efforts to fashion an effective organization which will deliver the maximum number of votes to the party's nominee on election day. Many would appear to be holding party positions in order to handle patronage matters when there is a Republican president. Some are also apparently motivated to gain or retain party office so as to exert influence in local politics. In many Strongly Democratic counties one gets the impression that some chairmen serve out of a sense of duty; no one else wants the post, and so they retain it because they feel it should not go unfilled. An overwhelmed minority locally, and in the minority on the state level (though not so overwhelmingly), their activity is very limited indeed.

In other counties, the Republican organizations vary from the mediocre to the efficient and effective. In several counties, party officials are capable, articulate, with a "civic-minded" interest in politics, and devote considerable time and effort (and probably a not small amount of money) to party affairs. They operate an organization which can, on election day, turn out a respectable Republican vote. In most of the urban counties, the local Republican organizations appear to be quite effective. Republican strength in urban areas is one indication of this. Also, the only counties in the state in which there are permanent Republican headquarters are in the urban areas: Louisville, Lexington, Covington, and Ashland. Full-time party workers are in these counties also. A man with considerable experience in Republican affairs averred that "some of the highest-caliber" people in the county organizations were in the urban areas.

One of the significant features of the Republican party in Kentucky is its decentralization. As a practical matter, the county

[19] The state campaign manager for Senator John Sherman Cooper's campaign in 1966 said he worked through the regular county organizations in waging the campaign. In those counties (the number unspecified) where the regular organization was "not too energetic" he saw to it that capable people were put on the campaign committee. This could be easily done, he said, since "I have a knowledge of working Republicans" as a result of lifelong work in the Kentucky GOP.

organizations exercise a high degree of autonomy. Operating authority does not flow in a unified channel in the party, either up or down.

Formal rules of the party give the appearance of a highly centralized organization, or at least provide the formal authority for centralization. Rule 3 gives the state central committee "at any time, after charges filed against the precinct chairman or the county committee of any county and a hearing on said charges" the authority to "order a reorganization of the precinct chairman and county committee of such county. . . ." Rule 5 provides that any officer or member of a county committee "may be removed by the state central committee for malfeasance, nonfeasance or misfeasance in office" after due procedural action. Rule 15 further bolsters the authority of the state central committee: it is "empowered to create such new committees and abolish such existing committees and make such rules for the organization and government of the Republican Party as are in its judgment necessary to the best interests of the party." Rule 31 gives it the authority to remove any member of a subordinate committee when he fails to give proper attention to communications from the state central committee. Rule 35 gives it the final authority on appeals from the actions of subordinate committees concerning party positions or nominations. Rule 37 provides that all party rules "may be altered, amended or repealed by" majority vote of the state central committee. In short, as T. H. Hardwick, the present chairman of the state central committee, put it: "On paper, the state central committee has all the power."

As a practical matter, however, the state central committee does not have such power. Dewey Daniel, chairman of the state central committee during the 1956 state convention, said in a speech that the committee was going to "eliminate every inactive official in the Republican party and replace him with someone who is going to work." He asserted that in many counties the required meetings were not being held and the required reports were not being submitted to the state central committee. "County and precinct chairmen who have not been doing the work prescribed in the state committee's rules must be ousted," he declared.[20] Not much was done, however. Daniel said that "you just can't go in and fire them

[20] Louisville *Courier-Journal*, April 15, 1956.

left and right. It is just not expected that this sort of thing is to be done; there are just not enough people who will support this kind of action." He did indicate that, in a relatively few cases, some chairmen and party workers were prodded into more effective activity through the use of patronage.[21] Hardwick echoes this view of the limits of the effective authority of the state central committee over the local organizations. If the state central committee tried to implement the authority given to it by party rules to remove the lethargic and incompetent, he said, there would be too much ill will and recrimination. This sort of action by the state central committee is "just not done." A change in party rules to permit annual reorganization (instead of the present quadrennial reorganization) would be one way to improve the caliber of the local organizations, and he is hoping to bring about such a change.

Another man with extensive experience in working with the county organizations said, regarding the status of the county organizations in the hierarchy of the party, that "persuasion" was the method by which the county organizations could be induced to support the wishes of the upper echelons and the party's nominees in statewide races. "They can't be ordered" to go along. He indicated that what influence and authority was exercised by the people on the state central committee and the congressional district committees was primarily because of such things as ability, personality, and knowledge, and secondarily because of the formal authority they possess. "Good people" in the higher echelons were the essential factor in the influence exerted from there, he said.

Other persons who had held (or hold) positions on the state central committee expressed similar views. One man said that "in the absence of all state patronage being funnelled through the state committee," there was little to be done to make the county committees "go along." Even if there were a Republican governor, he continued, "he would probably use patronage to build up his own following. That's about what happened during Willis' administration." He then referred to the factional struggles in the Democratic party in the state.

<hr>

[21] Interview with Dewey Daniel. Another person who was on the state central committee at the time said of Daniel's warning: "Dewey was just talking; he didn't do much" in implementing the warning. Another person, longtime active in the party, was asked if Daniel had any success in this campaign to chop away the deadwood. He replied: "No."

It is seen that, de facto, the county organizations in the Kentucky Republican party are subject to little control by the higher echelons in the party. Cooperation by them with the wishes of those holding these high party positions is largely voluntary. Effective and aggressive action on their part in support of policies or nominees must be induced, for whatever reason (personal affection for the candidate, ideological affinity with him, or hope of patronage). Such action cannot be commanded.

In this respect, the Kentucky Republican party is similar to most parties throughout the United States. Loose organization is a prevalent feature of state parties. Hinderaker points out that "generally it is possible to draw a horizontal line on the state and local party organization chart between the county committees and chairmen and the state central committees and their chairmen. This line can be used to indicate the state central committee does not often exercise much if any control over county party activities. County committees generally go their own way, cooperating with the state organization of the party when it suits the county's fancy or interest and not doing so when it does not."[22]

The Jefferson County Republican Organization. Since Jefferson County (containing Louisville) is the metropolitan center of the state (with some 20 percent of Kentucky's population), and since its population will probably continue to increase for some time to come, a strong Republican organization here will be of great significance in the prospects of the GOP in statewide political races. The ability to win votes in Jefferson County will be of crucial importance in winning statewide races. Therefore, it is pertinent to give some extensive consideration to the Republican organization in Jefferson County.

The Republicans have long done well in obtaining votes in Jefferson County. In the competitive political situation existing there, where traditional partisan preferences do not make the name "Republican" a great handicap, a capable political organization able to turn out a large vote on election day may constitute the difference

22 Ivan Hinderaker, *Party Politics* (New York: Henry Holt, 1956), 129. V. O. Key, Jr., observes: "County, state, and national party organs are each to a degree autonomous"; and elsewhere he says: "County organizations go their own way and may or may not be well geared into state headquarters." *Politics, Parties, and Pressure Groups* (New York: Thomas Y. Crowell, 1964), 360 and 370.

between victory and defeat. In turn, control of the city and county governments with the consequent control of patronage contributes to the maintenance of a strong party organization. In 1961, the GOP won control of the city and county governments for the first time since 1933, and retained control by winning the 1965 elections.

Formal party organization in the Jefferson County GOP is based upon a city-county executive committee, presently composed of 37 persons. Six of these 37 members are holders of public office in Jefferson County. They are chosen by the other Republican elected public officials, and their terms are subject to review every two years. This executive committee appoints ward chairmen (called district or area chairmen outside the city limits of Louisville) and the precinct chairmen (or captains). The executive committee determines the procedure to be followed in the selection of the new executive committee in March of presidential election years. In recent years, the procedure followed for the selection of the new executive committee has been as follows: Any Republican so desiring may present a slate or list of persons as candidates for membership on the executive committee. When the list is presented, however, it must be accompanied by funds sufficient to defray the cost of conducting an election in each of the precincts in the county. The result has been that only one slate, the "organization" or "regular" slate, has been presented at the prescribed date, and this slate was, of course, declared elected.[23]

The executive committee consists of something of a cross section of the rank-and-file Republicans of Jefferson County, in terms of geography, wealth, religion, occupation (including two or three members of labor unions), race (including four or five Negroes), and ideology (liberals, conservatives, "middle-of-the-roaders," and the "unideological"). The executive committee meets at least once a month to consider any outstanding business. It has no standing subcommittees; when such are needed, they are formed on ad hoc basis.

One of the more important activities of the executive committee is the choosing of candidates to be supported by the organization in the primary elections. Each December a candidate selection committee is appointed by the executive committee. In turn, the candidate selection committee is often divided into subcommittees

[23] The amount in 1960 was $8,000, and in 1964 it was substantially the same.

dealing with specific types of offices: aldermanic, state legislative, judicial, etc. The committee sends a letter to each ward chairman and each precinct chairman asking them for recommendations. Usually, by February the candidate selection committee submits to the city-county executive committee a list of candidates which it recommends be endorsed by the executive committee for the forthcoming primary elections in May. The organization runs a credit check and a police check on aspiring candidates, and these checks must, of course, be satisfactory before the aspirants will be endorsed. Generally, about 90 percent of the individuals recommended by the candidate selection committee are given endorsement by the executive committee.

Endorsement by the organization is an effective step along the road to nomination (and therefore public office) by those persons with such aspiration. From 1947 through 1967, 96 of 139 GOP candidacies for the Kentucky House of Representatives from Jefferson County have been uncontested in primary elections; for the Kentucky Senate 19 candidacies have been uncontested, while 10 were decided in primaries. In local (county and city) elections, the regular organization has nominated its choices, with only occasional setbacks. In 1965, the organization-backed candidates easily won in those contested primaries (a total of 12) for nominations for local office. In the most important of these contests—that of mayor—the organization candidate won by over three to one. Of the 20 legislative seats, there were contested primaries in four House of Representatives districts, and the organization candidates won three of them. In 1961, "the regular Republican organization candidates turned back with ease yesterday a bid by rebel Republicans to gain control of the party." The winning margin was approximately three to one. In 1957, the organization candidates in the three top races (mayor, county judge, and sheriff) were unopposed in the primary. Its candidates "swept past scattered opposition in other races." In 1953, the organization lost in the primary contest to nominate the candidate for county judge. The remainder of its slate, except for one person in a Kentucky House of Representatives race, was nominated. The decisive element in defeating the organization candidate for county judge was the use, by the nonorganization faction, of counterfeit sample ballots. With one exception, the ballots were identical to the "Official Sample

Ballot—Regular Republican Organization Candidates" circulated by the regulars. The exception was the name of the man aspiring to be the nominee for county judge. In 1949 the regular organization won without great difficulty in the face of a concerted effort against it.[24]

The foregoing illustrates the potency of an effective organization, which makes direct primary elections almost superfluous. It approximates that conception of political party as a small group of activists who perform one of the basic functions of political parties: determining who is to run under the party label in the general election. With a network of capable precinct organizations turning out a good vote for the "official" party man, the challengers (lone wolves, mavericks, or whatever) have a formidable obstacle to overcome.[25]

Data on the nomination of Republican candidates for the United States House of Representatives from the legislative district which encompassed Jefferson County until 1966 (when urban Louisville became a separate district and suburban eastern Jefferson County became part of another House district) buttress the above conclusion. In the 23 elections held since 1920, there have been only 5 primary elections for the Republican nomination. Four of these primaries were only "nominal"; the ultimate nominee won the primary by more than 60 percent of the vote. The only "real" primary occurred in 1966, when the city-county executive committee refused, in effect,[26] to make an endorsement of either of the two main

[24] Louisville *Courier-Journal*, May 26, 1965; May 24, 1961; May 29, 1957; Aug. 2, 1953; Aug. 7, 1949. In the other years, nominations for Kentucky legislative seats were completely uncontested (1947, 1951, 1955, 1959, and 1967 for Senate seats, and 1959 for House seats) or contests were very few (one Senate seat in 1963; one House seat in 1963 and 1947; two House seats in 1951 and 1955; and eight House seats in 1967). Scrutiny of the *Courier-Journal* indicates the organization candidates won.

[25] In an interview, William O. Cowger said there were good precinct workers in all precincts. There had been no necessity for removing any for incompetence. Replacements of precinct captains had been ncessitated by deaths, retirements, moving away, etc.

[26] It actually endorsed both men. Louisville *Courier-Journal*, April 6, 1966. Before the state legislature divided Jefferson County in the 1966 redistricting act, the Republican executive committee endorsed William O. Cowger, former mayor of Louisville, for the House seat, over Snyder. Snyder was undecided about running in the primary against Cowger when the redistricting occurred. Cowger got over 90 percent in the primary, with only token opposition. In 1962, Snyder received the organization's endorsement and was elected in November. Snyder told the authors in 1963 that he would not have sought the nomination in 1962 without preprimary endorsement by the organization, as a candidacy under such circumstances was considered futile. Both Cowger and Snyder were elected to the United States House in November 1966.

contenders from Jefferson County, former Congressman M. G. Snyder and James Thompson.

The Jefferson County Republican organization has permanent headquarters in the Sherwyn Hotel in downtown Louisville, operating on a year-round basis. There are nine salaried workers here, directing the work of voter registration, transportation, etc. This is also the headquarters of the finance committee, which implements the year-round financing appeals of the Jefferson County GOP. The party headquarters also acts as a clearinghouse for the dispensation of the approximate 2,000 patronage jobs available in the city and county governments. Generally, the precinct captains must endorse applicants for patronage positions, and then the final recommendation for appointment is made from the party headquarters. Patronage also provides a source of revenue for the party. Workers are assessed at a rate of 2 percent of their salary. These funds, plus those of other contributors, assure the organization of adequate revenue for the general elections in November. In fact, the Jefferson County party provides a good deal of funds for statewide races.[27]

The Republican party in Jefferson County has attracted the support of Negroes, who are estimated to be about 15 percent of the population of Jefferson County. While Negroes here, as elsewhere, are predominantly Democratic, the GOP has not written them off as irrevocably so, and receives a respectable percentage of their vote. Negro Republican candidates have been elected aldermen and members of the state legislature. The Republican administration in the city of Louisville includes a Negro prosecuting attorney and a Negro police judge. There are about 60 Negro Republican precinct captains, and from one-fifth to one-fourth of the patronage jobs in the city and county governments are held by Negroes. W. O. Cowger, mayor of Louisville from 1961 to 1965, said that one reason the Republicans have done so well with Negroes was because the GOP "opened doors to Negroes to run for public office." Also, under the Cowger administration, a public-accommodations ordinance was passed in 1963.

The top leadership of the Jefferson County GOP has been an important factor in the success and effectiveness of that organization.

[27] One man said that about 70 percent—another man estimated 75 percent—of the money obtained by the state central committee came from Jefferson County, and much of this via the Jefferson County Republican organization.

Cowger, County Judge Marlow Cook, and Mayor Kenneth Schmied exemplify that type of the pragmatic politician who flourish in the American political environment. Their "image" as such has undoubtedly been an important factor in their electoral triumphs. Perhaps the most appropriate political label to apply to them, and to the Jefferson County organization as a whole, would be "moderately conservative" or "moderately liberal." There are both more conservative and more liberal elements in the organization, but no persistent factionalism has resulted from this.[28] The general party consensus has been pragmatic—obtaining and supporting candidates who have a favorable prospect in the general election.

STATEWIDE NOMINATING AND ELECTORAL PRACTICES

For statewide offices, most Republican candidates are nominated without primary competition. This is a consequence of the party's minority status. There have been only three genuine (as distinguished from nominal) primary elections for major statewide offices in the period since the end of World War II: for governor in 1947, 1951, and 1967. A brief consideration of these nominations may throw some light on the Kentucky Republican party.

The 1947 primary was fought when the Kentucky Republican party was most nearly divided into two fairly well defined factions. The Republican governor was finishing his term of office that year, and the party was divided into pro- and anti-administration factions. The factions resulted from a clash of personalities and a struggle for power and influence within the party. There was no clearcut division on ideology or on substantive issues. Simeon S. Willis, the incumbent governor, had created considerable antipathy among many party officials over the handling of patronage. He had not worked his way to prominence in the party through the regular organizational channels. He had a long and prominent background

[28] The most dramatic instance of this difference in viewpoints in the Jefferson County GOP is illustrated by the electoral career of M. G. Snyder. He is a Goldwater-type conservative, elected to the United States House in 1962, defeated in his reelection bid in 1964, and winner of the 1966 primary for nomination in the new House district which includes the suburban (and most wealthy) part of Jefferson County. Snyder won 63 percent of the Jefferson County vote in the primary, while the more liberal Thompson won 35 percent. The remaining 2 percent went to the five other candidates who were not from Jefferson County. Cook, Cowger, and Schmied were not happy at Snyder's victory, but promised support in November. Such support helped Snyder win in November.

in the judiciary when he was chosen as the Republican gubernatorial candidate in 1943.[29] Because of his background, "he did not 'play ball' with the professional politicians in his own party as he probably would have had he come from the organization itself."[30] There was also considerable personal dislike between Willis and Jouett Ross Todd, leader of the GOP in Jefferson County, and John M. Robsion, United States representative from the heavily Republican congressional district in southeastern Kentucky.

In late March 1947, Thruston B. Morton, United States representative from the Jefferson County congressional district, announced his candidacy for the Republican nomination for governor. A few days later Willis announced his support of Morton. Had he remained a candidate, it appears that Morton would have been unopposed. On May 5, however, he announced his withdrawal. Soon thereafter, Eldon S. Dummit, the incumbent attorney general, entered the race. Todd and Robsion supported him, but Willis refused to do so.[31] Willis was able, after much importunity and very close to the deadline for filing, to persuade John F. Williams, the incumbent superintendent of public instruction, to enter the primary.

Each candidate formed a slate for the other statewide offices, and the ensuing campaign in the primary became heated and bitter. Indeed, a few scars inflicted then probably have never completely healed. Dummit won the nomination (but lost the general election to Earle Clements), and carried all his slate to victory except the aspirant for lieutenant governor. Dummit won by 8,410 votes in a turnout of 129,100 (plus 3,175 votes for a minor third candidate). The ninth congressional district (Robsion's) cast over one-fourth of the total vote, and Robsion was unable to carry it for Dummit; Williams had a 191 vote majority in a total vote there of 33,475.[32] The decisive factor in the primary was Dummit's support by the organization in Jefferson County. He won there by a margin of 11,378 votes, in a total vote of 17,574.

Dummit acknowledged that the support of Robsion and Todd

[29] He was so well known and respected that when he was persuaded to become the Republican candidate, others who were contemplating making the race withdrew.
[30] William C. Spragens, "The 1947 Kentucky Gubernatorial Election" (M.A. thesis, University of Kentucky, 1951).
[31] Eldon S. Dummit said in an interview that Governor Willis probably would have supported him if Todd and Robsion had not done so. Personal antipathy was the apparent reason.
[32] This was described as "the first defeat Robsion has suffered in his district since he first went to Washington in 1918." Louisville *Courier-Journal*, Aug. 5, 1947.

was decisive in his victory. Without the support of these two men, he could never have defeated the candidate backed by an incumbent governor, who used all the resources of his position in the struggle. He also considered that his own personal following in the party was of considerable aid in his victory. He attributed the success of the Williams-slated aspirant for lieutenant governor to that individual's network of friendships and acquaintances. "He worked with our faction in some counties, and the other faction in the other counties." Dummit further expressed the opinion that the strenuous and hard-fought primary that year was of some significance in his defeat by the Democratic candidate in the November election. "We are the minority party in Kentucky, and party unity is indispensable" if the Republican nominee is to have a realistic hope of being elected governor. He said a good many people in the Willis-Williams faction were restrained in their support of him in the general election.

The Republican nominating process in 1951 was the last until 1967 in which a primary election was used to reach the decision. Eugene Siler, a native of the Republican southeastern part of the state with service on the Court of Appeals (the highest appellate state court), was the first man to announce his intention to seek the Republican gubernatorial nomination. Siler's candidacy would have faded into insignificance if the generally acknowledged strongest man, John Sherman Cooper, had desired to become a candidate. Cooper had been elected United States senator in 1946, proving his potency as a votegetter. Though defeated in his bid for reelection in 1948, he had run far ahead of the rest of the Republican ticket that year. Party leaders were hopeful of inducing him to become a candidate for governor, and he was on the verge of announcing his candidacy when Virgil Chapman, the Democratic senator from Kentucky, was killed in an automobile accident in Washington.[33] This meant that an election would be held in 1952 to fill his unexpired term, and Cooper decided that he would accordingly bypass the gubernatorial race in 1951. His decision disappointed most party officials, and incidentally pleased most Democrats, who felt he would have been a formidable opponent.

The next man to announce was W. Howes Meade, from far-eastern

[33] "There is no doubt that Cooper's decision not to run for governor represented a complete change of mind within a week. On the day Chapman died, Cooper was known to have been ready to be the gubernatorial candidate." *Ibid.*, March 18, 1951.

Kentucky, who had served in the United States House from that area in 1947-1948. Hoping to avoid a possibly divisive primary, Republican leaders (on the state central committee and elsewhere) tried to induce James S. Golden, incumbent United States representative from the southeastern Republican district, to become the candidate. Meade then announced his withdrawal, but Siler did not. "I thought that if I were elected governor, I could do some good things," he said in an interview. It was irrelevant whether he had to fight a primary, and therefore he remained in the race. Golden declined to become a candidate, however, and Meade then announced that he was reentering the race.

The resulting primary became largely a personal struggle between the two aspirants. The state central committee exerted no efforts in either direction, and its members were rather evenly divided in personal support. The regular organization in Jefferson County remained neutral, an agreement reached unanimously by the county executive committee and the local candidates. Several prominent Louisville Republicans supported either candidate as individuals. Thruston B. Morton, then in the United States House, supported Meade, as did Jouett Ross Todd of Louisville, who was then Republican national committeeman. Charles I. Dawson of Louisville, the Republican candidate for the United States Senate in 1950, announced his support of Siler, as did James S. Golden.

There were no slates for the remainder of the statewide offices; aspirants for seven of these offices were unopposed.[34] Most, if not all, of the other statewide candidates were aligned with Meade in the primary. Siler said his failure to select a slate and get it nominated probably had detrimental effects upon his campaign in the general election.

Siler won the primary handily, getting 58.4 percent of a total vote of 106,355, but he lost the general election to Lawrence Wetherby. He carried by substantial margins most of the Republican counties, the real area of decision in a party primary. Most of the Republican counties carried by Meade were in the area of his home, indicating a certain amount of "friends-and-neighbors" appeal. Meade carried Jefferson County by 1,130 votes, obtaining 55.9 percent of a total vote of 9,500 there. He also carried Campbell

[34] Allan Trout observed in this regard: "As a footnote to 1951 politics in Kentucky, the conclusion is inescapable that potential candidates thought these nominations were not worth the money and effort of a race." *Ibid.,* July 29, 1951.

County substantially (57.4 percent). Turnout in the other urban counties was small, reflective of the small Republican registration therein. Siler carried them, 3,457 to 3,001 (53.5 percent).

Siler stressed his support among the rank-and-file Republicans as of considerable significance in his victory. He said he carried many counties, and made a respectable showing in others, where the local party officials and leaders were opposed to him or, in some instances, were only nominally in his favor.

Only a token primary occurred in 1955. Many party officials hoped to persuade former Senator John Sherman Cooper or former Representative Thruston B. Morton to become the party's candidate for governor. When they indicated a lack of interest, several persons in the party organization indicated a preference for Edwin R. Denney, a man who had long been active in party affairs. He had been a circuit judge, had served in the Kentucky legislature, and had been minority floor leader in the Kentucky House in the 1947-1948 legislative session. In 1947, Governor Willis had asked him to run for governor in the primary election. He declined because he felt he was not ready to do so. In 1951 he was state campaign manager for Eugene Siler, and was chairman of the state central committee in 1952-1954. He had been appointed a United States attorney under the Eisenhower administration. Because of turmoil in the ranks of the Democratic party occasioned by the reentry into state politics of former Governor A. B. "Happy" Chandler after a decade's absence, 1955 appeared to be a good year for Republicans. Thus, Denney let it be known that he was interested in becoming a gubernatorial candidate and discussed the matter with various party officials and others concerned with party affairs. No significant opposition to his candidacy was encountered, and he won the nomination without real opposition in the primary election.

There were no Republican primary races in three of the eight other statewide offices, a token one in two, and genuine competition in the three others. Denney said he did very little about choosing his running mates, observing that it was "difficult to get men of stature to run" for these offices, since the chance for victory in November was usually small.

In 1959 the Republican gubernatorial candidate was selected in a manner reminiscent of the days when the convention system was used for this purpose. A meeting of the state central committee was held in the last days of 1958 for the purpose of discussing potential Republican gubernatorial candidates for the coming year. It was generally thought that the best candidate would be John M. Robsion, Jr., who had served in the United States House from the third (Jefferson County) congressional district from 1953 through 1958 (he had been defeated in November 1958). Robsion, however, had evinced little interest in becoming a candidate. It was decided that the county organizations would take soundings at the grassroots to determine who would be the strongest candidate. Louie B. Nunn, who had been the state campaign manager for the successful Republican ticket in 1956, filed as a candidate on January 2, 1959. The general consensus at the state central committee meeting held a few days earlier had been that Nunn was too young (35) and unknown to be a strong candidate. Nunn said, when filing, that a primary was the best way to choose the nominee and made the routine remarks about the virtue of choice by the rank-and-file membership instead of by men in a smoke-filled room.

Robsion indicated on January 3 that he would be amenable to a draft. He had promised Nunn that he would not enter the race if Nunn became a candidate, but he said that consenting to be drafted would not mean a breaking of that promise. He presumed that if he accepted a draft, the state central committee would persuade Nunn not to force a decision in a primary. On January 6, Nunn offered to withdraw if Senators Cooper and Morton would say they favored Robsion. "What spurred Nunn to the attack was a letter from William O. Cowger, Congressional District Chairman of the Third District, in which he gave the impression that both senators were actively engaged in the Republican draft."[35] Cooper and Morton expressed the opinion that Robsion would be a strong candidate, but said they were not trying to draft anyone.

On January 9, the day before the congressional district committees were scheduled to meet for the report by county chairmen on the strongest candidate, Nunn announced his withdrawal as a contender "in the interests of party harmony." He had traveled around in various areas of the state, making soundings, and acted accordingly.

[35] *Ibid.*, Jan. 7, 1951. One gathers that Cooper and Morton favored Robsion. One person said that Cooper and Morton felt that "Louie was in too big a hurry" to run for governor; he was still young and could try later.

On January 10 the congressional district committees met.[36] All formally endorsed Robsion. In the first district, however, where it was said "they believed John M. Robsion, Jr. would make a strong candidate," most chairmen and chairwomen expressed disappointment at Nunn's withdrawal. Some of the congressional district committees also endorsed candidates for other offices; for lieutenant governor, three favored men from their district.[37]

At the meeting of the state central committee on January 18, when the reports of the results of the meetings of the congressional district committees were received, "the state central committee took no formal action to endorse Robsion or any other candidate. Instead, it appointed an eight-man subcommittee to notify Robsion that he was the party's grassroots choice and urge him to make the race."[38] Robsion thereupon agreed.

A slate was chosen for the remaining statewide offices. It was not easy to persuade capable candidates to offer themselves. One member of the state central committee said he "drove all over this state" soliciting candidates, and "spent a hell of a lot of my own money" in the process. There were no primary races in two of the offices, and token contests in all of the remainder except for the office of lieutenant governor. This position was won by the unslated candidate, Pleaz Mobley, in the primary.[39] Mobley, who enlivens his appeal to the electorate by playing the guitar and singing "hillbilly and country" music, was thus the only nonorganization candidate to win, and not to the joy of his running mates in the general election.[40]

[36] Except in the fourth district, where inclement weather prevented it, and in the third district, where Congressional District Chairman Cowger said that he had discussed the matter with many people and that Robsion "has the full endorsement of the Republican workers and voters. . . ."

[37] The congressional district committee in the eighth district also took ballots on candidates for the rest of the statewide offices. Louisville *Courier-Journal*, Jan. 11, 1959.

[38] *Ibid.*, Jan. 18, 1959. There are genuine drafts and the spurious variety. This was genuine. Robsion had attempted to get an appointment to the United States Court of Claims after his defeat for reelection to the House in 1958. In an interview he said: "I was drafted. I had no illusions about my prospects of being elected governor."

[39] Mobley carried Jefferson County by a small majority. The county organization endorsed J. Phil Smith, the slated candidate, while the executive committee of the Third Congressional District Republican Club endorsed Mobley. *Ibid.*, May 25, 27, 1959.

[40] Robsion confined himself to saying on this matter: "Pleaz is a good Republican." Campaign appearances of the two men together were relatively rare.

In 1963, no primary was required to determine the GOP gubernatorial candidate. Contacts and queries among the prominent persons in the party resulted in Louie B. Nunn being unchallenged by serious opposition in the primary election. Since 1959, he had again managed successful Republican campaigns—in the presidential and senatorial races of 1960 and in the senatorial race of 1962—and his stature in the party was correspondingly enhanced. By early January 1963, three of the four Republicans from Kentucky in Congress (Morton, Siler, and Snyder) announced that Nunn could have the nomination if he wanted it; they foresaw no serious opposition to him. Siler said he might become a candidate for the nomination if Nunn declined. Commenting on the possibility that the county judge of Jefferson County, Marlow Cook, a Catholic, might become a candidate, Siler observed that his religious affiliation would be a severe handicap to him, especially in eastern Kentucky. These comments from Morton, Snyder, and Siler provoked comments from Cook and the Louisville mayor, William O. Cowger, that the "Republican candidate for governor will not be chosen from Washington by Senator Morton, Congressman Snyder, or Congressman Siler." They also chided Siler for his remarks concerning Cook's religion and announced their strong opposition to him as a gubernatorial candidate.[41] Cowger and Cook shortly thereafter announced their strong support of Nunn for governor and Bemis Lawrence, county commissioner in Jefferson County, for lieutenant governor, as did the chairman and members of the Jefferson County Republican executive committee. The only other significant development occurred on January 31, when 20 of the 35 Republican members of the state legislature signed a resolution calling upon Siler to become the candidate for governor. Only two of the Jefferson County members (both in the House) were among the signers. Siler declined, saying that he did not request or instigate the endorsement. "And while I deeply appreciate the expression of confidence from people who know me best, the senators and representatives from rural areas and the smaller Kentucky cities," he reiterated his support for Nunn. The prime mover behind the resolution was state Senator H. Nick Johnson of Harlan County, which is located in Siler's congressional district.

[41] *Ibid.*, Jan. 13, 1963.

Johnson "has long nursed a desire to run for Congress from Siler's district."[42]

Nunn thus became the unopposed (aside from a minor opponent) nominee for governor. Talks with party officials convey the impression that no other individual was seriously interested in the candidacy. Senator Morton said in an interview that if there had been a primary, he would have felt obligated to support Nunn because of Nunn's services to him as campaign manager in his races for senator in 1956 and 1962. Another person said that, as far as he knew, no others were interested in the nomination, as the GOP was a minority. He then commented on the difficulties involved in getting top-caliber candidates to offer themselves. "More often than not they are sacrifical victims." Did not the prospects of a bitter Democratic primary with a consequent split in the Democratic party, and therefore a better prospect of a Republican victory in November, make the Republican nomination more attractive in 1963? "Not to the point that it encouraged more people to seek it. Everybody thought 'Happy' Chandler would win the primary, and that he could never be beaten in the fall."[43]

A slate was agreed upon for the remaining statewide offices. There were no primary contests for three of the positions. In the remaining positions, the primary contests were nominal, and all slated candidates won. It was basically a matter of persuading these candidates to run.[44]

Manuevering for the 1967 gubernatorial primary began the day after the 1966 election. On that day Jefferson County Judge Marlow Cook announced his intention to be a candidate for governor. The next day, Louie B. Nunn, the 1963 Republican gubernatorial nominee, announced he would not be a candidate in 1967 if Senator Thruston B. Morton could be persuaded to become the Republican candidate. Nunn apparently expected to be Morton's running mate for lieutenant governor. A Morton candidacy also would avoid the possibility of a divisive primary. Morton gave consideration to pleas that he accept a "draft," but announced on November 14

[42] *Ibid.*, Feb. 1, 1963.

[43] Prospects of a split Democracy was, however, one factor in Nunn's decision to become a candidate. After some hesitation in declaring, according to one person, Nunn phoned him and said he had decided to run: "It looks too good to turn down this year," in an allusion to the situation in the Democratic party.

[44] One of these men said he was "requested and consented to become" a candidate.

that he preferred to remain in the Senate. On November 23, Nunn formally filed as gubernatorial candidate. Cook waited until January 16 to file formally. Each man slated running mates for the other statewide offices from various areas of the state, hoping to widen their support.

The primary campaign was devoid of any significant issues and became essentially a matter of personalities. Cook asserted that Nunn's conservative image would hurt the party, especially in the urban areas. His campaign stressed his ability to win, citing the fact that he had never been defeated in a political contest. Cook, a Roman Catholic, also endeavored to neutralize any anti-Catholic sentiment by declaring his belief in the "absolute" separation of church and state and saying that religion was irrelevant in the campaign.

Nunn's campaign featured charges that Cook had not been sufficiently active in support of the Republican ticket in 1963, thereby reducing the number of votes it received in Jefferson County and thus causing Nunn to lose. Cook denied this charge, citing statistics to substantiate his support. Nunn's campaign manager also called Cook a "dictatorial, autocratic, tricky and evasive politician," and there were charges that crime had flourished in Jefferson County during Cook's tenure as county judge. This "sin city" ploy was doubtless an effort to win rural votes, and was supplemented by Nunn's charge against Cook that "the former New Yorker made fun of the way that the people of Eastern Kentucky talked" and "poked fun at the hill country courthouses and local political organizations. . . ."[45]

The two candidates did not take clear and contrasting stands on major issues; both men, for example, opposed any compulsory open-housing laws, although Nunn was the more unequivocal in his opposition. Nevertheless, the contest had liberal-conservative ramifications. Nunn received the support of most of the conservative elements in the party, while Cook received the support of most of the liberal elements. Nearly all the activists who favored Goldwater in 1964 supported Nunn, while those who supported Scranton were for Cook. The most conservative officeholder from Kentucky, Representative M. G. Snyder, was a Nunn supporter (although largely inactive), while the more liberal Representative W. O.

45 *Ibid.*, May 12, 1967.

Cowger actively supported Cook. Cook also received the support of Senator John Sherman Cooper and Congressman Tim Lee Carter late in the campaign. Both had intended to remain neutral, but changed their minds because, said Cooper, "I think Nunn's campaign, whether with his approval or denunciation, has the purpose of stirring up religious prejudice." Carter said Nunn had injected "racism, religious bigotry, and mudslinging" into the campaign. Nunn issued a denial and said he had instructed his workers to refrain from such activity. He added: "I repudiate any such appeals to prejudice and bigotry."[46] Senator Morton remained neutral throughout the campaign.

Nunn won the primary by a narrow margin, 90,216 to 86,397 (51.1 percent of the two-candidate vote; a third candidate polled 2,949 votes). Cook's best showing was in Jefferson County, where the strong Republican organization worked vigorously in his support; he won over 77 percent of the vote (39,295 to 11,732). He also carried Fayette County, but only by 53.8 percent (2,838 to 2,437). But Nunn carried each of the other six counties classified as urban (Boyd, Campbell, Daviess, Kenton, McCracken, and Warren), with a majority of 62.1 percent for these six (8,452 to 5,146). In the fifth congressional district in southeastern Kentucky, the major rural area of Republican strength, Nunn won 63.9 percent of the vote (33,963 to 19,189). In all of the 35 counties in the state classified as Strongly Republican, Republican, and Republican Inclined (all of which are rural), Nunn received 62.1 percent of the vote (44,331 to 26,998). In the remainder of Kentucky (the nonurban counties classified as Marginal, Democratic Inclined, Democratic, and Strongly Democratic) Nunn had 60.9 percent of the relatively small number of votes (22,260 to 14,261). Nunn carried 94 of the 120 counties in the state.

It is clear from these statistics that the Cook-Nunn contest was not simply an urban-rural battle. Aside from a narrow victory in Fayette County, Cook's only urban triumph was in his own county, Jefferson. Nunn's percentage in the other urban counties was identical to that in the 35 rural Republican counties. Moreover, though an urban, Catholic candidate, Marlow Cook won almost four out of every ten votes cast in the rural counties. It is obvious that many of the voters did not perceive the race as an urban-rural

46 *Ibid.*, May 17, 22, 1967.

contest, but it is impossible to determine from aggregate data whether or not a large proportion of the electorate perceived it as a liberal-conservative contest. There is no way to determine, of course, if a substantial increase in the number of registered Republicans in the cities would result in a more liberal voting pattern in Republican primaries.

There seems to be little doubt that the religious issue was important in the 1967 primary, though it is impossible to estimate its importance with any precision in the absence of survey data. Newspaper reports indicated that, as in the 1960 presidential election, there was a substantial amount of anti-Catholic sentiment in rural Kentucky and particularly in the heavily Republican fifth congressional district. Rural Kentucky is part of the fundamentalist Protestant "Bible Belt," where many of the voters are apparently unwilling to vote for a Roman Catholic for any major elective office. Because the outcome of the election was so close, it seems safe to speculate that the religious issue was important enough to have been decisive in this election. In this connection, it is noteworthy that every other one of the statewide candidates slated with Cook was nominated.

One factor that was clearly not decisive was the level of campaign expenditures. A new law requiring comprehensive reporting of expenditures showed that Cook spent $152,542 and Nunn spent $89,388. Both candidates obviously had extensive resources at their disposal, and the five-to-three advantage that Cook enjoyed in financing did not produce victory at the polls.

Nominations for Republican candidates for the United States Senate are even less determined by primary elections than is the case for gubernatorial nominees. There have been several nominal primaries, but their significance can be illustrated by the fact that the lowest percentage of the primary vote received by the nominee in the last twenty years was 70, in 1956.[47] One explanation for this state of affairs is, again, the minority status of the Kentucky Republicans. Another is the fact that incumbent senators ordinarily face no serious opposition, and incumbent Republican senators were running in Kentucky in 1966, 1962, 1960, 1954, and 1948.

The basic fact about nominations of senatorial candidates in the

---

[47] Since 1920, only one quasi-serious primary for senatorial nominations has occurred. This was in 1942, when the nominee received 50.8 percent of the vote. Of the other three aspirants, the high vote was 25.4 percent.

Kentucky Republican party has been the problem of obtaining excellent men who have a reasonable chance of winning in a state where most voters are Democrats. A good illustration of this occurred in 1956 upon the death of the incumbent Democratic senator, Alben W. Barkley, on April 30. John Sherman Cooper, then serving as American ambassador to India, was considered to be the one Republican with the best chance of winning in November. The state central committee quickly began trying to persuade Cooper to accept its designation of him as the Republican candidate. After about one month of contacts and persuasion, Cooper decided he would not become the candidate.

At the state central committee meeting at which this news was revealed, Chairman Dewey Daniel asked the committee members to make surveys in their areas regarding the strongest Republican candidate. Pressure was again exerted on Cooper when it appeared that no other formidable Republican candidate could be found. At a meeting of the state central committee held in late June it was decided to defer selecting a candidate in the hope that Cooper could be induced to accept the nomination. Daniel, in an interview, told of two trips to Washington and numerous phone calls made by him for the purpose of gaining Cooper's consent to accept the party's nomination. Talks were held with Leonard Hall, Republican national chairman, Sherman Adams, assistant to the president, and Herbert Brownell, the attorney general. Through these men (principally Brownell, said Daniel), President Eisenhower was persuaded to request Cooper to become the candidate. In early July, Cooper told the state central committee that, at Eisenhower's request, he would become the Republican candidate for the Senate.[48]

This survey of the Republican nominating process for statewide offices shows that the nomination of the party's candidates is usually decided without resort to a primary election. The basic cause of this appears to be the fact that the party is the minority in the state. Since the outlook for victory in elections for state office is usually dim, gaining the nomination is not so desirable a prize as it would be under contrary circumstances. If an aspirant finds that a primary election campaign is necessary, he may conclude that

[48] *Ibid.*, July 8, 1956. There was evidently a lot of mail from the rank and file to administration officials urging them to induce Cooper to become the candidate. Dewey Daniel mentioned this when he announced Cooper's acceptance. This was not "inspired" mail, either, he said. *Ibid.*

the labor and expense involved outweigh the prospective rewards. Doubtless also, the fact that a divisive primary would further decrease the chances of victory acts as a deterrent in some cases.[49] Agreement and unity among the party leadership (both organization and elected officials) can be of substantial, probably decisive, influence in preventing a real, as distinguished from a nominal, primary. Such was the case in 1959. The conclusion suggesting itself is that a relatively small group of party activists exert paramount influence in the nominating process.[50] Though pro forma, the primary election is the place where the Republican nomination is bestowed upon those aspiring to win it; in practice the party activists make the decision.

LOCAL NOMINATIONS AND ELECTIONS

United States House of Representatives. In the politics of Kentucky's representation in the United States House of Representatives, tradition is the important conditioning factor. The state's political configuration is such that there is one safely Republican House seat, two marginal seats,[51] and four safely Democratic seats. Two of these Democratic districts (in the far-western part of Kentucky) are overwhelmingly so, and Republican victories here will, in the foreseeable future, be something of a miracle.[52] In the two other Democratic districts (in central and northeastern Kentucky), Republican prospects are not much brighter.[53]

In these safely Democratic districts, serious Republican primaries

[49] Whether or not more genuine primaries would help the Kentucky GOP is a question which cannot be answered conclusively. There is the ever-present possibility that the disunity engendered in the primary might have detrimental effects in the general election campaign, as witness the Kentucky Democrats. On the other hand, many party officials believed that the publicity for the GOP nominee created by the primary would more than outweigh this possibility. "Too many of our gubernatorial candidates are relatively unknown when the fall campaign starts," said one man.

[50] A man who has served as state chairman thought that unity among the leadership, or agreement among the more important elements of it (he mentioned Cooper and Morton, the Jefferson and Fayette organizations, and "most of the state central committee," though these were not meant to be exhaustive), would probably suffice to assure the nomination to the individual supported. "I doubt if a primary in such a case would make any difference."

[51] The Louisville district, and the district of which the remainder of Jefferson County is a part.

[52] Since World War II, Republicans have contested these seats from one-fourth to one-third of the time, and the average GOP percentage of the vote has been around 30 to 35.

[53] Since World War II, Republicans have contested these seats from four-fifths to all of the time, and the average GOP percentage of the vote has been around 42 to 44.

are rare (about 15 to 20 percent of the time), for obvious reasons. Candidates recruit themselves mainly, with some encouragement from the state central committee, the congressional district chairmen, and other prominent Republicans in the district. It is basically personalized politics.

In the safely Republican district (in the southeast), the situation is essentially that described by Key in his comments on congressional districts in general: "Outside of those areas in which strong city or county organizations incidentally encompass congressional districts, the organization tends to be more an informal and personal organization of the incumbent Representatives than a party organization. When the incumbent dies or retires, his organization falls to pieces and a free-for-all contest for the nomination may ensue."[54] Precisely this happened in this district the last two times the incumbent did not run (in 1954 and 1964). In both these years, the victors in the primaries (Eugene Siler in 1954 and Tim Lee Carter in 1964) defeated four serious contenders, and won with a plurality of about one-third of the total vote. Here, too, the politics tends to be personalized; the victorious congressman builds up his own organization. It contains some, but not all, of the county chairmen, public officeholders, personal friends, and persons prominent in Republican affairs who are not party officers. In essence, this individual organization is the network of personal relations formed over a period of time. Being reasonably efficient in performing errands for his constituents and voting "reasonably right" makes the incumbent virtually invulnerable; he can be renominated as long as he wishes.[55]

Legislative and County Offices. Nominations of Republicans for the state legislature are gained more often than not without a contest in a primary. Table 3.1 shows that, since 1947, 58 percent of the GOP nominees for the Kentucky House of Representatives have been unopposed, while the figure for the Senate is 59 percent.[56]

[54] Key, *Politics, Parties, and Pressure Groups*, 490.

[55] Siler had no serious opposition after his initial nomination. Carter was renominated in 1966 by a majority of nearly two to one.

[56] Based upon the classification of the county or counties (within which it is comprised or which it comprises) in statewide races, 1946-1962. In some of the urban counties, of course, legislative seats are only part of the county, and this means they may be more (or less) inclined toward one party than the county as a whole. This accounts for the lack of Republican candidates in some of the SR-R and RI legislative districts.

TABLE 3.1

Republican Legislative Primary Elections, 1947-1967

Type of District	Total GOP Primaries	Number of Primaries Contested	Percent	Number of Primaries Uncontested	Percent	No Republican Candidate
			HOUSE OF REPRESENTATIVES			
SR-R	194	145	75	49	25	5
RI	192	59	31	133	69	8
M	102	43	42	59	58	86
DI	72	9	12	63	88	80
SD-D	57	8	14	49	86	304
Totals	617	264	42	353	58	483
			SENATE			
SR-R	37	25	67	12	33	0
RI	37	11	30	26	70	3
M	24	11	46	13	54	5
DI	10	2	20	8	80	19
SD-D	16	2	12	14	88	58
Totals	124	51	41	73	59	85

The table shows also, as one would expect, that the greatest frequency of competition occurs in the safely Republican districts. The expectation of going to Frankfort as an elected legislator induces more competition in primaries.

The nominating process for these legislative seats (as well as for the county offices) varies greatly, making generalizations hazardous. In the strongly Democratic areas, of course, running for office as a Republican is normally unaccompanied by any realistic hope of success. The Republican organizations in those areas may persuade some uneager soul to permit his name to appear on the ballot; or perhaps some individual with a yen for seeing his name in print or with hopes of a miracle may file registration papers on his own initiative. Nearly all chairmen from counties where Democrats predominate indicated that they made some effort (most said "occasionally"; only a very few said "frequently") to encourage Republican candidates to offer themselves for these offices. The insignificance of this, however, is suggested by the reply of one such chairman that "registration is so heavily Democratic that no Republicans ever run."

In the counties where the partisan division is closer, variation is again common. Many chairmen in such counties reported that the county organization would often agree on a slate of candidates to support. Some chairmen reported that the organization would remain neutral if at least two "good men" offered themselves as candidates for a particular office. In other instances it was reported that individual members of the county committee would support some candidates, while others would support different candidates.

In most of the predominantly Republican counties contests for legislative and county office follow a pattern of individualistic politics. Primary nomination is almost always tantamount to election, and the competition for office is more fierce. An individual seeks the office entirely on his own, or, in some areas at some times, a slate of candidates forms for the various offices. Because candidates draw most votes from friends and neighbors in rural primaries, such mutual backscratching may be of considerable importance in winning the nomination.

In some rural counties, the county organization may be of considerable influence in affecting the nominations of these local officials. Just how important or effective county organization support can be in local races would depend a great deal upon the situation locally. In most rural areas, endorsement by the county committee per se amounts to very little. This is because of the effective limitations placed upon the county organizations by the existence of the direct primary election. Any capable, popular, or colorful individual who can favorably impress the voters can wage his own campaign for the party's nomination, and if he has the time and money, and "projects a favorable image," he has a good chance of winning. The potency of the county organization in local politics depends, more than anything else, upon the influence its members possess as individuals. If they are well known, personable, and able to influence others, they may very well be powerful in their county. Lacking such attributes, their significance will be limited. One prominent Republican with nearly 20 years of experience in party affairs said that in some predominantly Republican counties the county committee could, to a large extent, control the results of the primaries for the local offices. In fact, he added, in some such counties the organization cares little about any other elections and often makes only a token effort in statewide races.

In many counties most persons who constitute the regular

Republican organization are more figureheads than real sources of influence and leadership. Talks with elected officials convey the impression that they (individually or in groups, sometimes antagonistic groups) are the persons of power and influence in Republican affairs in their counties. "I won my election by myself," said one such official. "The county chairman doesn't have a very high reputation for integrity, and he can't swing many votes any longer." The former editor of a county newspaper in a Strongly Democratic county said, not in a tone of boasting, that he and another person (a businessman not on the county committee) were the "real Republican Party" in the county. "When Chandler was governor, the Democrats in this county and in an adjoining county" (which constituted a district in the Kentucky House of Representatives) "got so badly split that my friend and I worked with one of the Democratic factions in the Kentucky House race. We were able to get our man elected."

Most county chairmen and chairwomen acknowledged that non-committee members exerted power in Republican party affairs in their counties. Sixty-three answered "yes" to this question: "Do you believe that there is any person in the county, who, though not a member of the county committee, is influential in party affairs in your county or on the state level?" Nineteen persons answered in the negative. A chairwoman in a Strongly Republican county commented: "Yes. Lumbermen or businessmen who employ a lot of men. They usually express their own views and 90 percent or more of the employees adopt the employers' views. County School Superintendent—the teachers and employees wish to go as their superintendent goes."[57] A chairwoman in a Republican Inclined county said: "A teacher—through his working in and out of school with young people." Others mentioned frequently were a variety of elected officials (county and legislative), farmers, insurance agents, lawyers, physicians, bankers, real estate brokers, a radio station owner, businessmen in general, and employees of business concerns. Influence was reportedly exerted by financial contributions, prestige, and knowledge.

[57] In many rural counties, because of the money and the jobs at his disposal, the county school superintendent is the closest thing to a "boss" in the local politics. Many persons interviewed made reference to this fact, stating that in many counties the school board elections (where control of the county educational system is determined) were the most fiercely fought.

In the larger urban counties, the regular organizations probably exert more influence on the nominating process than in most rural counties. The impersonal nature of urban life is probably of considerable importance in this regard. In urban areas an individual finds it more difficult to develop the personal contacts which often are decisive in political races in rural areas.[58]

Campaign practices for the general election vary considerably from place to place and from time to time, but a high degree of individualistic campaigning is usually the rule. In the safely Republican areas, of course, the autumn election campaign is usually a token affair, the actual electoral choice having been made in the primary. On occasion, a bitter primary may cause the defeated faction to support the Democratic nominee in November (or, at times, a write-in campaign may be waged if there is no Democratic nominee).

In the more competitive counties or legislative districts there may be a more unified, less individualistic campaign effort for the November election. Practice here is so varied that a more generalized statement cannot be made. In the Democratic areas, the campaign of the GOP nominee is usually lackluster or nonexistent. The basic exception to this generalization would be when a split in Democratic ranks would give the Republican some realistic hopes of winning.

FACTIONALISM IN THE KENTUCKY GOP?

The Kentucky Republican party is like most state political parties in the United States: it contains heterogeneous elements. The areas of strongest rank-and-file party support are in the more wealthy urban areas and in the generally poorest counties in the state. Is there a division among the activists—the "party" in the more restricted sense? Is there a wide diversity in the viewpoints of activists across the state, like that already described in the Jefferson County Republican organization?

Divisions within the party are shown by the actions of the state delegation to the Republican national convention in the past two

[58] Data to demonstrate this assertion of organization influence is meager, since the Democrats predominate in these counties in state and local races. Primaries are rare in these counties, and an important reason for this is the minority status of the Republicans.

decades. In 1948, the state convention proceeded harmoniously, and 23 of the 25 delegates were sent to the national convention uninstructed; the two delegates from the Republican congressional district in southeastern Kentucky were instructed for Dewey. In the voting at the national convention there was an almost equal division of votes for Taft and Dewey. In 1952, a struggle did ensue between the Taft and Eisenhower supporters in the Kentucky party. The result was that the state convention instructed 19 of the 20 delegates to the national convention to vote for Taft.[59] The 1956 and 1960 Kentucky delegates were solidly behind Eisenhower and Nixon, respectively. In 1964, when the national GOP was racked with the struggle between Goldwater's supporters and opponents, the Kentucky party did not undergo a similar struggle. Had Senator Thruston B. Morton been an aspirant for the presidential nomination, the Kentucky GOP delegation would have supported him overwhelmingly. In fact, however, the state convention sent the delegates to the national convention uninstructed, and the delegates voted 21-3 for Goldwater.

Most of the party activists can be described as moderately conservative on substantive issues. Although there are those in the party both to the left and to the right of this "middle of the road," this is the party's center of gravity. Senator Morton fairly accurately reflects the consensus of the party in this respect. He is the more conservative of the two Kentucky Republican senators,[60] and the impression is strong that the great majority of party activists find his views more congenial than those of Cooper.[61] The bulk of the party leadership would prefer governmental policies more in line

[59] A detailed account is in Jasper B. Shannon, *Presidential Politics In Kentucky 1952* (Lexington: University of Kentucky Bureau of Government Research, 1954).

[60] At the end of the session of Congress in 1966, the Americans for Constitutional Action, a conservative group which issues a rating of the conservatism of members of Congress, gave Morton a cumulative rating of 63, and Cooper a cumulative rating of 35. This cumulative rating was based upon their entire period in Congress. Louisville *Courier-Journal*, Oct. 27, 1966.

[61] An undoubtedly widespread notion was manifested in the remarks of one person interviewed. He said Cooper was probably too liberal for most people in the organization, "but he is our best vote-getter, and that is what counts in the final analysis." Another man said Cooper "isn't too damned liberal after all," citing some action by Cooper aiding certain businesses, while another man said Cooper "isn't as liberal as he is painted up to be" by the news media. Senator Morton said, "There are no Cooper and Morton factions" in the Kentucky GOP. He did say that, among the electorate at large, there were different elements of support for him and for Cooper, "but there is considerable over-lapping" of them.

with the traditional Republican policy of minimum governmental activities, but they are aware of the contemporary political realities. They are, as several of them put it, "practical politicians" and "responsible"; the clock cannot be turned back to pre-New Deal days. The Goldwater debacle in 1964 reinforced this conviction on the part of many and perhaps persuaded some of this fact for the first time.[62]

In the past there has been no persistent, coherent urban-rural factionalism in the party. There have been differences between these two elements of the party, but they have been of minor significance. In the 1951 gubernatorial primary, there was an inchoate factionalism along urban-rural lines related to the wet-dry issue. Siler, unabashedly dry, advocated changes in the local-option laws detrimental to the wets. He believed that the rural components of the party were more enthusiastic about him, while his opponent in the primary was the choice of most of the organization members in the urban areas. In the primary election, Siler did best in the rural Republican counties, while losing in the urban counties. In the general election, Siler said, the rural Republican leaders tended to be more active in supporting him than did the urban leaders. In the 1963 gubernatorial election, the rural Republicans were generally more enthusiastic about the candidacy of Louie B. Nunn (from a rural county) than were the urban Republicans. Many of the rural people grumbled about the level of support given Nunn by the Republican organization in Jefferson County and said that more vigorous support there might have given him the governorship. In 1966, there was some urban-rural conflict over selecting the Republican leadership in the state legislature. The Republican urban representation was higher that year than at any previous time, and the urban members demanded a larger voice in the leadership. After some squabbling, their wishes were met. In the state central committee, no important rural-urban cleavage appears to exist. One member said that there were some manifestations of slight hostility or resentment toward Louisville (a sort of "hayseed suspicion of city slickers") by some persons from rural areas, but he said it was of no significance. Another man said that he had observed

[62] At the 1966 state convention of the Kentucky Young Republicans, the "moderates" elected their candidate for chairman over a more conservative candidate, by a vote of 279 to 179. *Ibid.*, June 26, 1966.

a greater respect for Jefferson County's influence in state party affairs since the GOP victory in the 1961 local elections in Jefferson County.

Although these urban-rural differences have been of limited importance in the past, they may take on greater significance in the future. As the traditional rural Republican counties decline in population and in influence, the urban Republicans will become a more important element in the party as a result of population shifts and a higher proportion of urban residents being registered as Republicans. Some of these urban Republicans, of course, will continue to be recent migrants from rural counties whose political attitudes have changed very little as a result of moving. This factor contributes to minimizing the differences between urban and rural Republicans, but such differences are likely to increase, and they could become crystallized along rather definite factional lines.

The 1967 gubernatorial primary provided some evidence that such a factional split is developing, but the split was not so much an urban-rural one as a split between Jefferson County and, to a lesser extent, Fayette County on the one hand and most of the other counties—both urban and rural—on the other. It remains to be seen whether greater unity develops among the urban Republican counties than was evident in the 1967 primary. Another possibility is that a factional division will emerge in the Republican party that is more distinctly along liberal-conservative than along urban-rural lines.

The most important factionalism in the Kentucky GOP, according to party officials at the upper levels, is at the county level. Some counties are divided between different cliques struggling to obtain control of the county committee. While Eisenhower was president, an important drive behind these struggles was the desire to have a voice in the disposition of federal patronage. Dewey Daniel, state chairman from 1955 to 1960, said there were local factions in nearly every county and thought that patronage was the main cause of them. Thomas F. Manby, state campaign organization chairman in 1963, said there were factions in "about half" of the counties in 1963. An important cause of factionalism that year was the anticipation of a Republican victory in the gubernatorial election and a consequent acquisition of state patronage. In many counties the factionalism is doubtless based upon local personalities. Antagonism between different individuals is carried over into the struggles for control of the local organization. In some counties, age (the young versus the old) is probably a factor; in others, it is probably liberalism versus conservatism. In many counties, the contests over local elective offices are carried over into the county organization.

Summary. Loose organization characterizes the Republican party in Kentucky. Contact between the higher echelons and the county organizations is limited and sporadic, occurring mostly just before elections. Lack of finances to provide the personnel and facilities for regular contacts has been one of the main reasons for this situation, which is indicative of a basic weakness in party organization. It should improve, however, as a result of the recent appointment of a full-time executive director and the steps taken in an effort to provide permanent financing of the state central committee.

The party is a collection of county organizations of varying effectiveness, of cliques and factions within these counties, and of the personal followings and organizations built up by Republican elected officials. Power and influence within the party are based upon the complex, nebulous, and shifting network of personal relationships and have been rather widespread and diffused. No one person or small clique of persons has "bossed" the party, although the two United State senators undoubtedly have considerable influence within party ranks. They have built up personal followings which transcend party lines, an important fact in a state in which the party has been a minority.

The election of a Republican governor in 1967 should contribute to the concentration of power within the party. We have described the dominant role that the Democratic governor has played in his party. Because of the tradition of strong gubernatorial leadership and the patronage available to him, a Republican governor may be expected to attain a comparable position of strength as a party leader.

A major weakness in the Kentucky Republican party is in the county organizations. Far too many of them appear to be paper organizations only. In many counties little is done in the way of obtaining the maximum vote for the party's candidate on election day. A great many individuals hold county committee positions apparently in the hope of being able to dispense patronage, and do very little of the humdrum campaign chores. Replacement by more energetic and aggressive persons would be desirable in such cases, but as a practical matter this is not feasible. The "unwritten constitution" governing intraparty relationships precludes such action.

The state central committee is not the head of an efficiently operating statewide organization. Such an organization, when it does exist, comes into being essentially as the personal creation of the candidate campaigning for statewide office. Senator Morton had essentially such an organization in his campaign for reelection in 1962. The state central committee has played an important role in the selection of candidates for governor and the other statewide offices. As the formal center of authority of a minority party, it (or its more active members) has been instrumental in the task of filling out the slate of Republican aspirants for these offices. The prospects of Republican victory in state elections has usually been dim, and thus the supply of candidates (especially for the lesser offices) limited. The state central committee has fulfilled the function of persuading persons to present themselves to the electorate as the party's candidates. Probably the main weakness of the state central committee has been its failure or inability to raise adequate finances to maintain a full-time staff, but in the past two years, serious efforts have been made to remedy this deficiency. The state party organization can be expected to strengthen its financial base and its staff resources now that it enjoys control of state government, and these gains should contribute to strengthening the Republican party in Kentucky.

4 | Democratic Factionalism

In his study of southern politics, V. O. Key, Jr., found three variations of factionalism prevailing in the state Democratic parties. In multifactional parties each candidate for major office constructed his own coalition of politicians and voters with little regard for previous factions. Bifactional parties were dominated by two factions that had some continuity and that selected candidates who divided most of the vote between them. A single faction dominated the Democratic party in several states, particularly ones in which the Republican party was challenging Democratic dominance during the 1940s—Virginia, Tennessee, and North Carolina.[1] The Kentucky Democratic party has had two clearly defined factions for most of the time since the 1930s, despite the strength of the Republican opposition. In twelve gubernatorial elections from 1923 through 1967 the median Republican vote was 45 percent; the party won three elections and never fell below 39 percent. The signs of growing Republican strength have not yet forced a truce in Democratic factional battles.

Two of the criteria of bifactionalism used by Key in *Southern Politics* are that most of the vote in the primary is usually divided between two persons and that the proportion of the winner is seldom much more than 50 percent. The Kentucky gubernatorial primaries meet these criteria, as shown in Table 4.1. In none of the eleven states analyzed in *Southern Politics* was the median percentage of the two top candidates so high and the winner's median percentage so close to 50 percent.[2] The runoff primary has only been used once in the Kentucky Democratic party—in 1935, when the top candidate (who lost the runoff) got only 45 percent of the vote and the two top candidates had only 87 percent. In the absence of a runoff, the leading politicians in each faction usually concen-

TABLE 4.1

Democratic Gubernatorial Primaries, 1939-1967

| Year | Number of Candidates | | Percent of Vote Received | |
	Total	*With 5 Percent or More of Vote*	*Winning Candidate*	*Top Two Candidates*
1939	4	2	52.5	98.3
1943	4	3	53.6	85.6
1947	3	2	54.9	98.3
1951	3	2	75.1	97.1
1955	3	2	51.4	99.2
1959	4	2	52.3	98.6
1963	4	2	53.8	97.0
1967	10	3	52.2	80.4
Median	4	2	53.1	97.7

trate their support behind a single candidate and discourage others from running; in the administration faction the governor plays a big part in selecting the candidate. In 1959, for example, Wilson Wyatt was persuaded to run for lieutenant governor rather than for governor in order to avoid splitting the vote of the Clements faction and to defeat the candidate selected by Governor Chandler.

The strongest, most persistent Democratic factions found in a southern state are those in Louisiana, where the Long and anti-Long factions have drawn most of their support from groups of voters having distinctly different geographic, socioeconomic, and ethnic characteristics.[3] This is not the case in Kentucky. The factional conflict is not between classes or regions or between urban and rural voters. When the same candidate represents his faction in several elections he may draw support repeatedly from some of the same counties, but these are likely to be the county in which he lives and those nearby. The difference between the factions often seems to be simply a difference between those in power and those who are seeking power.

[1] V. O. Key, Jr., *Southern Politics* (New York: Alfred A. Knopf, 1949), chap. 14.
[2] *Ibid.*, 17-18.
[3] Allan P. Sindler, *Huey Long's Louisiana* (Baltimore: Johns Hopkins Press, 1956), chaps. 2 and 9.

CONTINUITY OF FACTIONS

If these factions do not represent contrasting interests in the state, what gives them continuity? One important factor is that the incumbent governor tries to select his successor; this has been true of every governor since the early 1930s. Those state and local politicians, patronage employees, and other interests with a stake in the administration try to secure the election of the designated successor, and those groups that are out of power unite behind a challenger. This does not mean that all of the politicians and patronage seekers remain loyal to one faction. If the faction in power is defeated, some of its supporters are likely to shift sides in an effort to retain their positions, but most of them will work together as the opposition faction in an effort to win the next election.

Factional continuity implies not only some stability in the alliances among politicians but a consistent pattern of support for candidates of one faction over several elections by a substantial number of voters. We would expect not only that some voters would follow the advice of local politicians who remained allied with a faction but that other voters would develop a sense of identification with a faction, or at least with factional leaders, that might be comparable in its significance to party identification. In the absence of survey research data it is impossible to determine how many voters maintain such a sense of identification with a faction over a period of several elections. A study of factions in Louisiana led to the conclusion that the average voters were more consistently loyal to factional leaders than the politicians were, and this may be true in Kentucky.[4] At least there seem to be many Kentuckians who have retained the factional loyalties that they acquired in the 1930s and 1940s. The Combs-Breathitt faction has attracted a new generation of voters, but it is too early to tell how persistent these loyalties will be.

If the Kentucky factions are based only on personalities, they can be expected to have continuity only as long as a few strong personalities dominate the Democratic party. The history of modern factionalism in Kentucky has been largely a history of alternating

[4] *Ibid.*, chap. 9.

power—and direct clashes—between two men, A. B. "Happy" Chandler and Earle Clements, who have been the most successful in claiming the loyalties of both voters and politicians. Since the 1930s Chandler has commanded the loyalty of thousands of Kentuckians with his personal style of politics. During the period that Chandler was serving as baseball commissioner, Earle Clements became the dominant figure in the state Democratic party. His organizational skill in building a political base that reached from the county level to Washington made him the master of one faction.

When Chandler was elected lieutenant governor in 1931, he was only 33 years old, but he apparently already had his eye on the governorship. He fought the Laffoon administration to a deadlock on the question of imposing a sales tax, until the administration succeeded in stripping him of his powers as presiding officer of the Senate. Chandler forced the enactment of a compulsory primary law in 1935, by calling a special session during the governor's absence, and then launched his campaign against Tom Rhea, the administration's choice for governor. Chandler's campaign was one of the most colorful and energetic that the voters had seen. His speeches were brief and witty, interspersed with songs, his handshaking endurance was prodigious, and his rapport with the voters seemed instinctive. The sales tax, in the depths of the depression, provided him with a perfect issue. He challenged an administration that had all of the traditional advantages of an entrenched organization, and he defeated it. His greatest strength was in the prosperous counties of the Bluegrass—particularly those close to his home county of Woodford; his voting strength was less in western Kentucky and in the mountain Republican counties where the local politicians were most heavily dependent on the incumbent administration.[5]

In 1935 Chandler had run as a reformer, a candidate of the people challenging the entrenched machine. But in 1938 he ran against Senator Alben Barkley, who had the personal endorsement of President Roosevelt. This meant that he was running against the New Deal and challenging the policies of a president who had twice won resounding victories in Kentucky. Many of the reformers who had been attracted to Chandler deserted him in 1938; the increasingly powerful labor unions—particularly in the minefields—opposed

[5] J. B. Shannon, " 'Happy' Chandler: A Kentucky Epic," in J. T. Salter, ed., *The American Politician* (Chapel Hill: University of North Carolina Press, 1938), chap. 9.

him, and Chandler lost the primary by 70,000 votes. The struggle attracted national publicity, and notoriety, as a test of the relative weight of state and federal patronage. "Chandler marshaled the formidable patronage power of the state behind his candidacy. Every state employee was pressured to support the Governor, and every job was dispensed so as to serve his cause." Patronage was used for Barkley most extensively in the mountain counties: "In effect the gargantuan Relief program was transformed into a colossal and supremely effective political machine nourished by almost limitless patronage. . . . Barkley's campaign managers selected in each mountain county a trustworthy, loyal and astute local politician whose dependability was undoubted. . . . In the following weeks the politician carried a heavy responsibility. It had become his duty to build a political army within the framework of the swollen W.P.A."[6]

Despite Chandler's loss in 1938, his lieutenant governor and designated successor—Keen Johnson—defeated John Y. Brown in the 1939 gubernatorial primary. Johnson's greatest strength, like Chandler's, was in central Kentucky, and Brown carried the counties where the Rhea-Laffoon organization had been strong and did particularly well in the mountain counties, where he had labor's endorsement.

Although the Johnson administration had little difficulty in picking a successor, Lyter Donaldson, in the 1943 gubernatorial primary, he was defeated in the general election. This defeat and Chandler's resignation from the Senate in 1945 to become baseball commissioner left a vacuum in state politics that Earle Clements succeeded in filling when he won the governorship in 1947, after defeating Harry Lee Waterfield in the primary.

There was some continuity between the old Rhea-Laffoon organization and that which was built by Clements, particularly in the western part of the state. Clements had been elected to Congress in 1944 from the second district in western (but not far-western) Kentucky, and in 1947 much of his strongest support came from this region. He won backing from the state's congressmen in the gubernatorial race. During and after his term as governor, Clements helped to strengthen his factional control by developing strong

[6] Harry M. Caudill, *Night Comes to the Cumberlands* (Boston: Little, Brown, and Co., 1962), 209-10.

alliances with several of the state's congressmen. During the Clements and Wetherby administrations, Clements engineered the nomination of three congressmen, Carl Perkins, John Watts, and William Natcher, who remained loyal supporters of the Clements faction. Even as late as 1958, while Chandler was governor, Clements was able to bring about the election of one of his allies, Frank Stubblefield, who won a narrow primary victory in western Kentucky over a Chandler supporter, Representative Noble Gregory. One of the most important reasons for Clements' frequent victories in Democratic factional battles was his enduring alliance with the rejuvenated organization in Jefferson County. Another important factor was that Clements used the political powers of the governorship skillfully to enlarge the base of his organization. He maintained this organization after he was elected to the Senate in 1950 and was succeeded by Lawrence Wetherby as governor.

The Clements-Wetherby organization and its candidate for governor, Bert Combs, were defeated in 1955 by a coalition of the Chandler and Waterfield forces. Chandler, who had left his post as baseball commissioner in 1951, had failed to win an appointment from Governor Wetherby to fill a senatorial vacancy and had begun to rebuild his political fences. He still commanded a loyal following, concentrated particularly in the central part of the state, and in 1955 he waged an aggressive campaign against the Wetherby administration. Waterfield's strength complemented Chandler's. He had voting strength where Chandler did not, particularly in the far west and in a number of the southern Republican counties. Moreover, he was (like Clements) unusually skillful in building a grassroots political organization. The Chandler-Waterfield team, with its blend of personal campaigning and organizational skills and with a breadth of geographical support, narrowly defeated the entrenched organization and the relatively unknown candidate from eastern Kentucky whom it was running for the governorship.

The rematch in 1959 was almost as close, but the outcome was different. Lieutenant Governor Waterfield, running with Chandler's support, lost to Bert Combs by about 33,000 votes. Almost 30,000 of this margin was accounted for by Jefferson County, where the organization was able to take advantage of resentment over policies of the Chandler administration that appeared to be directed against Louisville. Combs made gains in most of the large cities and enlarged his base of support in the eastern part of the state.

In 1963 Edward T. Breathitt, selected by Governor Combs as the administration's candidate, defeated Chandler's bid for a third term as governor, but Waterfield, running on the Chandler ticket, was elected lieutenant governor. There were several reasons for Breathitt's decisive victory. Although Clements had left the administration and was supporting Chandler, most of the local politicians who had been associated with Clements saw no reason to sacrifice the advantages of alliance with the administration. After the departure of Clements, Combs showed great skill in maintaining the factional organization even though some of his resources—such as patronage —were declining. Combs, the first governor elected from eastern Kentucky since 1943, maintained the powerful support of that region for his administration by paying greater attention to its manifold needs than his predecessors had done. The Combs administration attracted widespread support for its programs, particularly in the areas of highways and education. By promising to reduce the sales tax that Combs had instituted, Chandler gained support among low-income urban voters but lost the votes of others who were afraid that a tax cut would jeopardize recent gains in the education program. In addition to benefiting from the political organization and the popularity of the Combs administration, Breathitt provided assets of his own. He had a strong following in the western part of the state, and he proved to be a skillful campaigner who used television effectively and whose youth contrasted with Chandler's age. The alliance between Chandler and Waterfield, which had survived victory in 1955 and defeat in 1959, was broken by the defeat of Chandler and the victory of Waterfield in 1963. Waterfield won in part because his opponent was running as an independent and there were frequent alliances at the county level between the supporters of Breathitt and Waterfield, alliances that caused deep resentment in the Chandler camp.

In 1967 the Breathitt administration selected as its gubernatorial candidate Henry Ward, a veteran administrator and legislator who had served as highway commissioner in both the Combs and Breathitt administrations. The antiadministration forces were badly divided. Chandler and Waterfield, now bitter rivals rather than allies, both sought the governorship. The unusually large field of ten gubernatorial candidates included two others who made serious races: J. D. Buckman, a veteran legislator who had supported the administration in recent years, and David Trapp, a Lexington businessman who relied heavily on professional public relations techniques. Despite the large number of candidates, the three major ones gathered 91 percent of the vote. Ward won a majority of over 52 percent, Chandler had 28 percent, and Waterfield had a little less than 11 percent. The administration won a lopsided victory in Jefferson County and held a substantial margin in both the eastern and western parts of the state; only in the Bluegrass did Chandler make a serious challenge, and there Ward held a narrow edge. Waterfield, who had never polled less than 43 percent of the vote in four previous statewide elections, ran a limited campaign with minimum financing and finished a poor third. Despite his active opposition to Governor Breathitt during most of his term as lieutenant governor, Waterfield failed to win the support of most anti-administration voters. Ward lost the general election to Louie Nunn, who had the open support of Chandler.

It is easier to trace the rise and fall of factions in recent political history than it is to provide solid evidence that there has been a continuity in individual voting patterns. It is easier to find politicians, from the state level to the precinct level, who have consistently been identified with one faction than it is to prove that these politicians have been able to win voters to the support of that faction with equal consistency. The only evidence of voting behavior that we have is what can be extracted from the county election returns, and the weaknesses of this source—compared to survey research data—should be made clear. A comparison of the county vote polled by the leaders of a faction in several elections does not tell us who cast these votes. A larger proportion of voters may vote for the same faction in successive elections in county A, even though the percentages polled by that faction are more consistent in county B. Moreover, gross election data do not tell us why people vote as they do. A person might vote consistently for one faction for several reasons. He might simply be following the advice of precinct leaders or other politicians without any awareness that he was supporting candidates in the same faction. He might be enthusiastic about a particular candidate, such as Chandler, and vote for him regularly without being aware of factions or necessarily voting for other candidates who had the endorsement of that one candidate. A voter might be aware of factional alignments and might identify with one of the factions,

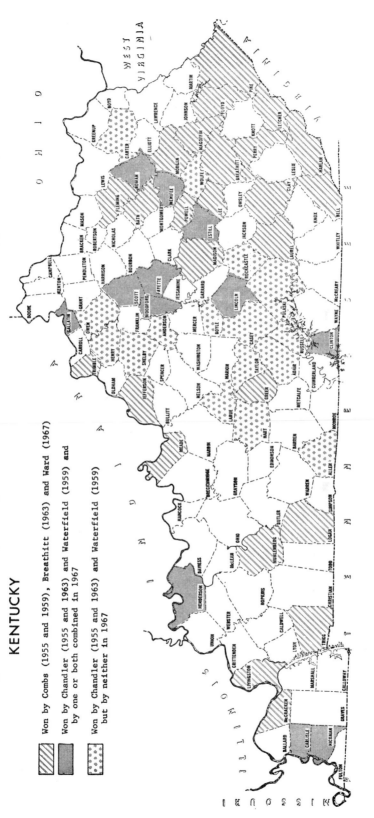

FIGURE 4.1

Kentucky Counties Consistently Won by Combs-Breathitt-Ward and Chandler-Waterfield Factions, 1955-1967

KENTUCKY

Won by Combs (1955 and 1959), Breathitt (1963) and Ward (1967)

Won by Chandler (1955 and 1963) and Waterfield (1959) and by one or both combined in 1967

Won by Chandler (1955 and 1963) and Waterfield (1959) but by neither in 1967 in the sense that voters often identify with a party and support it consistently in elections. This sense of identification might grow out of loyalty to a particular factional leader, such as Chandler, or strong approval or disapproval of the policies and programs adopted by a particular administration. In a different category would be the voter who is aware of factional alignments and who votes for or against a candidate to register approval or disapproval of the record of the administration with which that candidate is aligned.

The continuity of candidates in the 1955, 1959, 1963, and 1967 gubernatorial primaries gives us a chance to study the continuity of factional voting patterns to the extent that they can be measured by county voting records. There were 25 counties won by Combs in 1955 and 1959, by Breathitt in 1963, and also by Ward in 1967. There were 28 counties carried by Chandler in 1955 and 1963 and by Waterfield in 1959; but in only 12 of these counties did the combined vote of these two candidates constitute a plurality in 1967 (in most cases with Chandler alone winning the plurality). Almost one-third of the counties voted for the same faction in all four elections. As Figure 4.1 shows, more than half of the counties consistently won by Combs, Breathitt, and Ward were in eastern Kentucky, the area from which Combs came and which received greater attention during his administration. The counties most often in the Chandler or Waterfield column include a number in the Bluegrass, several southern Republican counties, and a few in the far-western part of the state.

Identification of the counties won consistently by a faction may be deceptive as a measurement of factional continuity because it tells nothing about the margin of victory. A better technique is to identify the top quartile of counties for each candidate (the 30 counties where his percentage of the vote is highest). What proportion of the counties appear in the top quartile for one faction in two or more elections? It should be kept in mind that we could expect two candidates chosen at random to have 7 or 8 of the same counties in their top quartile purely by chance, and three candidates would have 2 of the same counties among their top 30 by chance.

There are only 5 counties in the top quartile for Combs, Breathitt, or Ward in all four elections. (See Figure 4.2.) They include counties where strong political organizations have been allied with that

FIGURE 4.2

Kentucky Counties in Top Quartile for Combs, Breathitt, and Ward Three or Four Times, 1955-1967

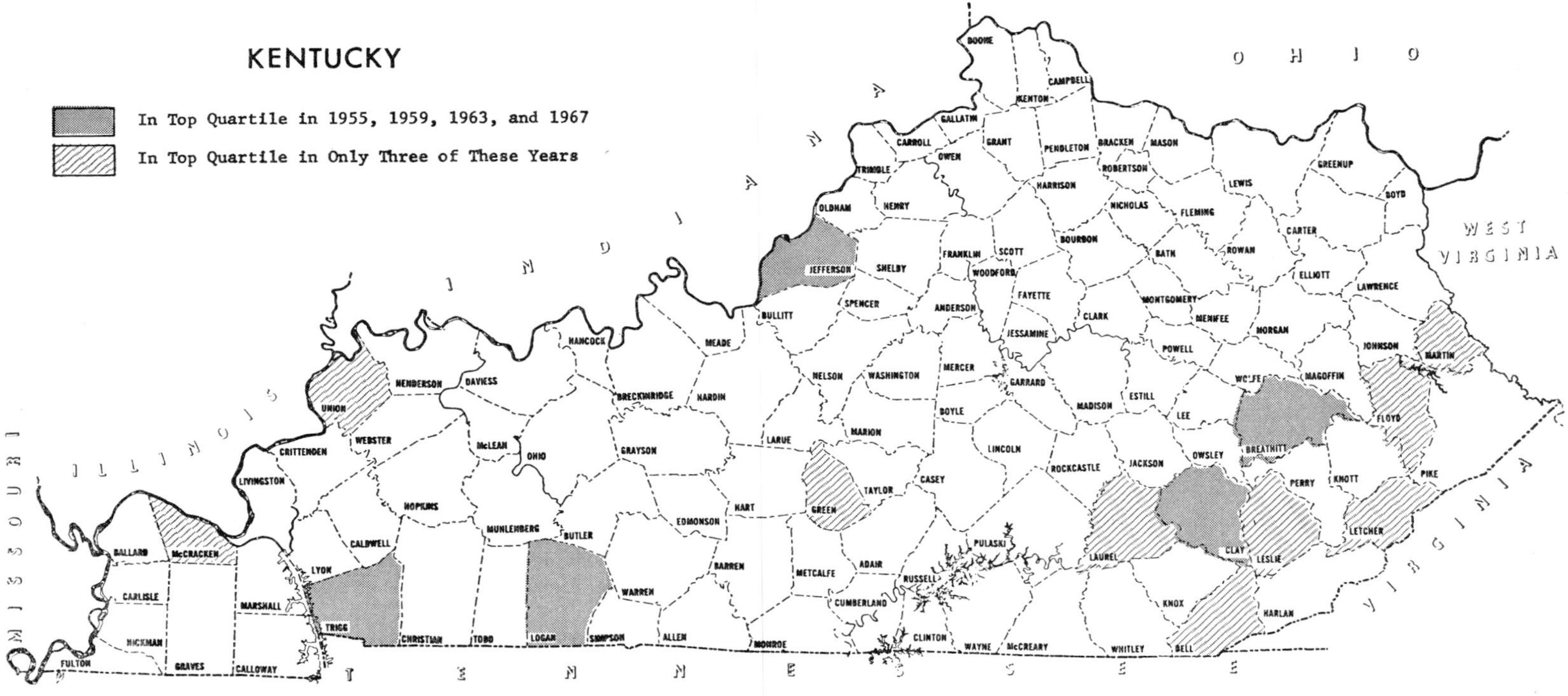

KENTUCKY

In Top Quartile in 1955, 1959, 1963, and 1967

In Top Quartile in Only Three of These Years

faction (Jefferson, Logan, and Breathitt). There were 9 additional counties that were in the top quartile in three of the four elections: 6 in all except 1959, 1 in all but 1963, and 2 in all but 1967. Although the counties that fell in the top quartile three or four times are not identical to those won consistently by this faction, they are concentrated in the same geographical areas, as a comparison of Figures 4.1 and 4.2 shows. We might expect the 1963 election to provide a sharp break in the pattern of factional continuity, both because a different man was running for governor and because the faction no longer had Clements' support. But this is not the case. There were 20 counties that ranked in the top quartile for Breathitt and for Combs in one or both of his elections, but only 2 counties that were in the top quartile in both Combs elections but not in 1963.

There is a surprising lack of continuity between the counties where Clements had the greatest voting strength and those ranking high for Combs, Breathitt, and Ward. In Clements' two crucial primaries, for governor in 1947 and for senator in 1956, there were 8 counties in the top quartile both times and 28 others in the top quartile once and carried by Clements in the other election. Of these 36 counties there were only 3 in the top quartile for Combs, Breathitt, and Ward in the four elections and only 1 other in the top quartile in three of the four elections. Most surprisingly, there were only 5 counties in the top quartile for Combs in 1955 and Clements in 1956. Clements was strong in a number of western and central counties which have not been consistently in the Combs-Breathitt-Ward column. Although the Clements organization was of continuing value to Combs and Breathitt in most counties, it is evident that Clements' vote-getting strength as a candidate differed substantially in geographic terms from that of Combs and Breathitt.

There are only 5 counties that were in the top quartile for Chandler in 1955 and 1963 and for Waterfield in 1959: Woodford and Hickman (their home counties), Clinton, Rowan, and Shelby. There were 14 others in the top quartile in two of the three elections. Because the Chandler-Waterfield faction was an alliance of two candidates who had run for office independently before they joined forces and who opposed each other in the 1967 race, it is necessary to identify the counties in which each was consistently strongest.

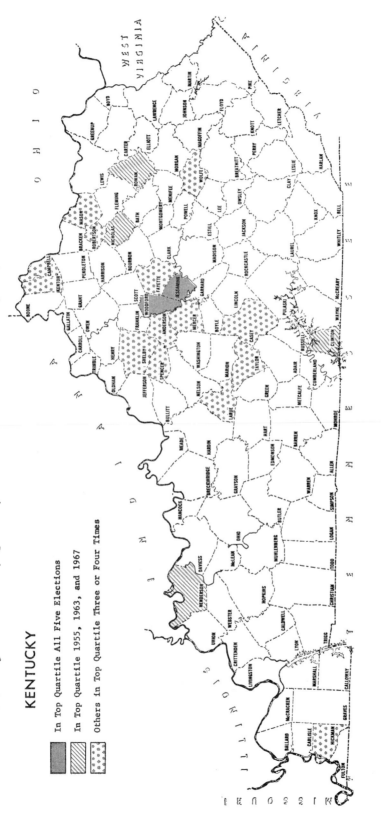

FIGURE 4.3

Kentucky Counties in Top Quartile for Chandler Three or More Times, 1935, 1938, 1955, 1963, and 1967

KENTUCKY

In Top Quartile All Five Elections

In Top Quartile 1955, 1963, and 1967

Others in Top Quartile Three or Four Times

Figure 4.3 shows the counties in the top quartile in at least three of five important primaries contested by Chandler: the 1935 gubernatorial runoff, the 1938 senatorial primary, and the gubernatorial primaries in 1955, 1963, and 1967. Figure 4.4 has comparable data for five primary races by Waterfield: gubernatorial in 1947, 1959, and 1967, lieutenant governor's race in 1955 and 1963. In Chandler's case, his home county of Woodford and adjoining Jessamine County were the only ones in the top quartile five times. Eighteen others were in the top quartile in three or four races out of five. The most consistently strong Chandler counties are concentrated in and around the Bluegrass. A larger number of counties—6—were in Waterfield's top quartile in all five elections, and all of these were clustered in the far west, in what is known as the Jackson Purchase, where Waterfield has consistently run a strong race. There were 16 other counties that were among the top 30 for Waterfield in three or four elections. In addition to his strength in the far west, Waterfield has run very well in a belt of traditional Republican counties in the southern (but not southeastern) mountains.

It is evident that, not only when they ran independently but also when they were allied, Chandler and Waterfield drew their greatest support from different groups of counties. There was relatively little overlap between these; there were only 6 counties that were in the top quartile for three or more of the races of each of the candidates (Figures 4.3 and 4.4). In 1955 and 1963 the two candidates ran on the same ticket, Chandler for governor and Waterfield for lieutenant governor. The number of counties in the top quartile of both candidates was 13 in 1955 and 14 in 1963, roughly double the number that might be expected by chance, but not an unusually high number for candidates slated together. There were only 4 counties in the top quartile of both Chandler and Waterfield in both 1955 and 1963; these were their two home counties and Clinton and Rowan. When the two men ran against each other in 1967, each won a negligible number of votes in the other's home county. Presumably during the years of their alliance both Chandler and Waterfield picked up some votes in every county from supporters of the other (and probably lost some votes from those who disliked the ally), but an analysis at the county level shows that during the period of the alliance each candidate maintained his own centers of

FIGURE 4.4

Kentucky Counties in Top Quartile for Waterfield Three or More Times, 1947, 1955, 1959, 1963, and 1967

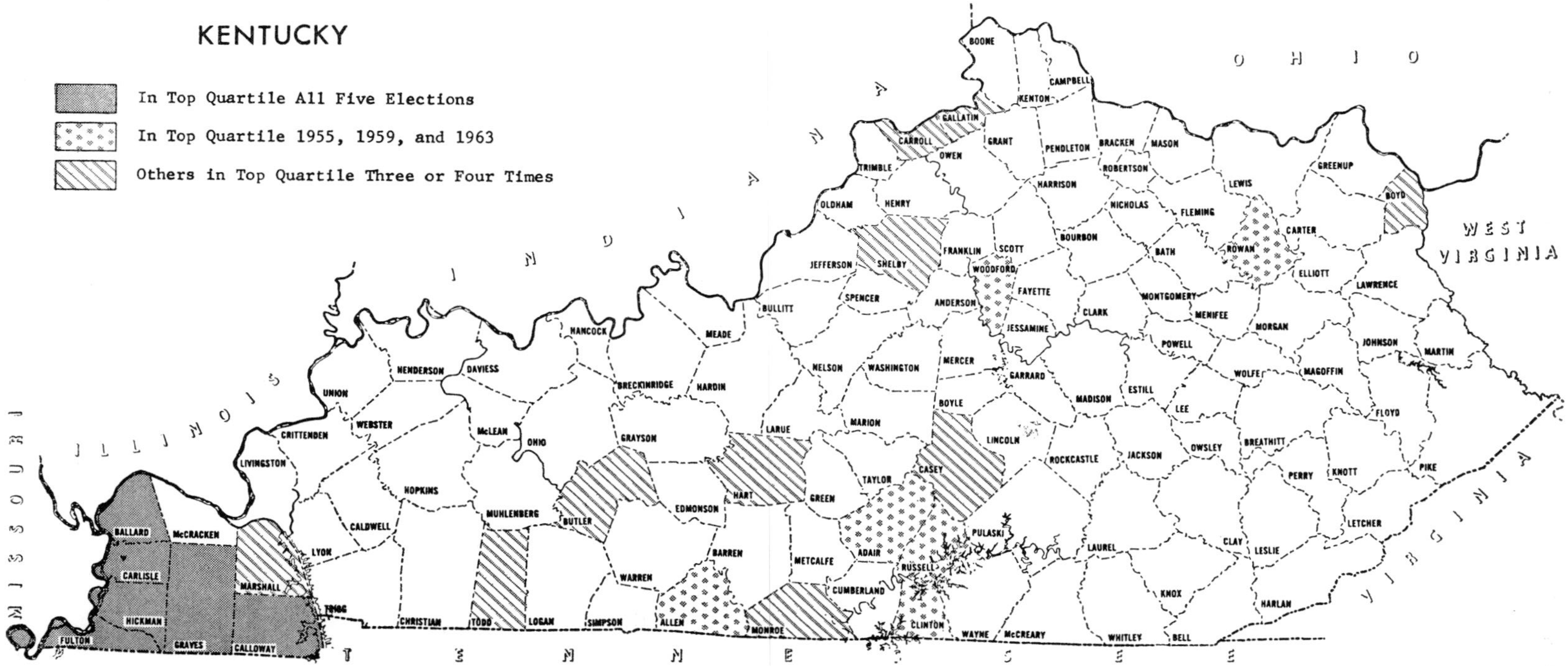

KENTUCKY

In Top Quartile All Five Elections

In Top Quartile 1955, 1959, and 1963

Others In Top Quartile Three or Four Times

strength and had difficulty in transferring much of this strength to the other. In the 1967 election both men continued to draw many of their votes from counties of traditional strength, but at greatly reduced levels. Waterfield's losses were particularly severe. Although the block of six counties in the far west continued to be in his top quartile, he only carried one of these—his home county of Hickman —and his percentage in the other five varied from 37 to 17. It is evident that the collapse of the alliance cost Waterfield more votes than it cost Chandler.

The analysis of counties by quartiles for both factions shows that the number of counties voting in all or most of the pertinent elections for the same faction is relatively small, though clearly larger than would occur by chance. (See Table 4.2.) These are

TABLE 4.2

Number of Counties Appearing in Top Quartile for Same Candidate or for Candidates of Same Faction in Two or More Democratic Primaries

| | | Counties in Top Quartile | |
Number of Primaries	Candidates and Elections*	Actually in Specified Primaries	Theoretically Would Occur by Chance
4	Combs (55 and 59), Breathitt (63), Ward (67)	5	½
3 or 4	Combs (55 and 59), Breathitt (63), Ward (67)	14	6
3	Combs (55 and 59), Breathitt (63)	7	2
2	Combs (55 and 59)	9	7½
2	Combs (55), Breathitt (63)	13	7½
2	Combs (59), Breathitt (63)	14	7½
2	Combs (55), Ward (67)	19	7½
2	Combs (59), Ward (67)	9	7½
2	Breathitt (63), Ward (67)	13	7½
3	Chandler (55 and 63), Waterfield (59)	5	2
2 or 3	Chandler (55 and 63), Waterfield (59)	19	19
5	Chandler (35, 38, 55, 63, 67)	2	⅛
3, 4 or 5	Chandler (35, 38, 55, 63, 67)	20	12½
3	Chandler (55, 63, 67)	6	2
5	Waterfield (47, 55, 59, 63, 67)	6	⅛
3, 4 or 5	Waterfield (47, 55, 59, 63, 67)	22	12½
3	Waterfield (55, 59, 63)	12	2

* All contests are gubernatorial primaries, except Chandler's 1938 senatorial race and Waterfield's race for lieutenant governor in 1955 and 1963. The 1935 Chandler race is the runoff primary.

mostly counties where the major candidates live or where there have been unusually strong local organizations allied with a state faction. The link between the strong Clements counties and those at the top of the Combs, Breathitt, and Ward lists is surprisingly weak, and there is relatively little overlap between the strong Chandler and Waterfield counties. On the other hand, an examination of the maps shows well-defined areas in which each of the candidates has usually been strongest. It is possible to identify counties usually voting heavily for Chandler or Waterfield or for Combs, Breathitt, or Ward. The voting link involving Combs, Breathitt, and Ward appears to be stronger than the other recent alliances. County voting data cannot prove anything about the motivations of individual voters, but the evidence from recent elections leads to one speculative conclusion. If there is more continuity in a candidate's strength than in a faction's strength at the polls, it seems likely that many voters are better informed about and more interested in candidates than factions and more likely to stick to a candidate than a faction in several elections. The factional voting record of counties in Democratic primaries is much less consistent than their partisan record in general elections, and this would suggest that over a period of time voters are much less likely to identify with a Democratic faction than they are to identify with one of the two parties.

SLATES FOR STATE OFFICE

The major candidates for governor in the Democratic primary often endorse candidates for other statewide offices and campaign with these candidates as a team. Factional lines are not usually crossed in the formation of a slate, but there is no certainty that candidates will run as a slate simply because they share factional loyalties. Candidates run together as a slate because it serves their mutual interests. The gubernatorial candidate looks for men running for lesser offices who have proven or potential vote-getting ability in various parts of the state or with various types of voters. He is trying to balance his ticket, just as party leaders in two-party states have traditionally done. He may persuade a political ally to run for office, but often he simply makes a choice among those who have already announced their candidacy. Unlike the leaders who are designing a partisan ticket, the gubernatorial candidate does not have to make an endorsement in every race. He may avoid doing so if there are two or more candidates allied with his faction running for an office, because an endorsement of one man would alienate supporters of the other. He may avoid an endorsement because a prominent candidate allied with the other faction has so much strength that he appears to be unbeatable and an endorsement of his opponent would be a liability.

The candidate who is running for a lesser statewide office for the first time faces enormous problems; he must raise funds, develop an organization in 120 counties, and attract the attention of the voters. If he can run on a slate with a gubernatorial candidate, he can rely heavily on the fund-raising and organizational efforts of that faction, and he hopes that voters who are supporting that candidate for governor will also vote for him because they realize that he is on the slate. He runs the risk that his gubernatorial ally will lose and that his identification with the slate will cost him votes. For the relatively unknown candidate who lacks a statewide following and organization the risks of being on a slate are easily outweighed by the potential advantages.

The candidate who has run in previous statewide races has a stronger bargaining position. He is less dependent on alliance with a gubernatorial candidate because he has been able to build up an organization and—particularly if he has won previous races—his name is more familiar to the voters. For these reasons he is most valuable to the gubernatorial candidate as a member of the slate. In recent primaries for lesser offices the most successful candidates have been the veterans of previous campaigns. In some states a man who has served several terms as treasurer or secretary of state, for example, is virtually unbeatable because his name is familiar and he has been able to establish political contacts and create an organizational base throughout the state. In Kentucky the constitutional bar on successive terms in one office prevents a man from becoming entrenched in one office, but the most successful candidates simply move from office to office. These candidates may join a slate in order to enhance their vote-getting ability, but they are not completely dependent on the factional organization, and some of them have been able to win despite the defeat of their gubernatorial running mates. Emerson "Doc" Beauchamp, who was elected lieutenant governor in 1951 on the Wetherby slate, ran successfully in 1959 and 1963 on the Combs and Breathitt slates for commissioner of agriculture and treasurer. Henry Carter, consistently slated with Combs or Breathitt, was elected treasurer in 1955 (despite Combs' defeat), secretary of state in 1959, and auditor in 1963. Thelma Stovall was elected secretary of state in 1955 on the Chandler slate and won terms as treasurer in 1959 and 1967 and secretary of state in 1963 despite the defeats of her running mates, Waterfield and Chandler. Wendell Butler, elected superintendent of public instruction in 1951, 1959, and 1967 and commissioner of agriculture in 1963, has been allied with different factions in the various races.

The contest for lieutenant governor is the most important of the races for lesser office, not because it is a powerful office but because it is regarded as a steppingstone to the governorship. From 1935 through 1967 there were eight primaries held during Democratic administrations. Twice the lieutenant governor who had recently succeeded to the governorship won a full term, once the lieutenant governor won, and three times the lieutenant governor ran but lost; none of the primaries was won by anyone holding any other elective state office. In choosing a running mate the gubernatorial candidate wants not only someone who can help him win votes but someone who will remain loyal and cooperate during the administration. Because of his political prominence, his authority as acting governor in the governor's absence, and his role as presiding officer of the Senate, the lieutenant governor can be a source of embarrassment to the governor and a political liability. Despite the apparent importance of the position gubernatorial candidates have endorsed candidates for lieutenant governor in recent years less often than those running for other state offices. In each of five Democratic primaries, from 1947 through 1963, only one of the major gubernatorial candidates endorsed a candidate for lieutenant governor, and in each case the endorsed candidate has won. In 1947 Clements endorsed Wetherby for lieutenant governor, but Waterfield endorsed no one. In 1951 Wetherby supported "Doc" Beauchamp, a leader of the Clements faction; the entire Wetherby slate won, in most cases by wide margins. But in 1955 the Clements faction and gubernatorial candidate Bert Combs did not make any choice for lieutenant governor, although the Jefferson County organization—allied with Clements—did so. Chandler and Waterfield ran successfully as a team in 1955, but four years later Waterfield ran alone, without making an endorsement for lieutenant governor. In 1959 the alliance of Combs and Wyatt as candidates for the two top offices occurred after Wyatt agreed to drop out of the governor's race. In 1963 Chandler and Waterfield again ran as a team, but only Waterfield won, while Breathitt did not endorse John Breckinridge, Waterfield's opponent. In 1967 the administration support was divided between Robert Matthews and Wendell Ford; Ford narrowly defeated Matthews in a four-man race. Chandler's ally ran a poor third. The record of recent elections suggests that an alliance between the candidates for governor and lieutenant governor usually benefits both men, but the candidates themselves have not consistently believed this to be true.

There is a more consistent record of endorsements for other statewide offices in recent elections. In 1951 Wetherby successfully endorsed a full slate of candidates for these six offices: secretary of state, attorney general, treasurer, auditor, superintendent of public instruction, and commissioner of agriculture, labor, and statistics. His relative weak opponent, Howell Vincent, made no endorsements. In the 1955, 1959, and 1963 elections both major gubernatorial candidates made endorsements—varying in firmness—for each of the six offices. Ten of the winners were endorsed by the winning gubernatorial candidate, and six were endorsed by the losing gubernatorial candidate; one winner had the support of both factions, and one had the support of neither. In no election did the winning gubernatorial candidate succeed in electing his entire slate. Chandler was particularly unsuccessful in 1955, when only two of his candidates, in addition to Waterfield, were elected. In 1967 the administration endorsed candidates for all six offices, and all but one were nominated. Chandler did not have a comparable slate.[7]

Participation on a slate helps a candidate if it wins votes for him, and this may occur either directly or indirectly. Slating may have a direct impact when the voter knows that two or more candidates are on the same ticket; it has an indirect impact when local political organizations work for several candidates. An alliance of candidates for the two top positions, such as the Chandler-Waterfield or Combs-Wyatt teams, is usually well known to the public. The candidates appear together in person and on radio and television;

[7] A candidate for clerk of the Court of Appeals is also often slated.

advertisements—in newspapers, on billboards, on bumper stickers—link their names together; and news stories in the press and other media frequently refer to the alliance. There is much less publicity about the slating of candidates for lower office, partly because no one pays so much attention to them. The reader of newspapers and the radio-television listener would rarely find any reference to such slates, either in political advertising or in news stories. The careful newspaper reader might not find out which candidates were running on which slate until the election was over and the results were being analyzed. In the closing days of the campaign the candidates for state office slated with a gubernatorial candidate frequently travel with him from courthouse to courthouse, where they are briefly introduced to the crowd.

The impact of slating would be minimal if only its public effects were measured. The major advantage a candidate gains from being slated with a gubernatorial candidate is organizational. Throughout the state, county factional leaders pass the word to precinct workers that his name is on the slate. At the precinct level there is frequent reliance on sample ballots handed out on election eve or at the polls. Because the ballot is long and most voters are unfamiliar with many of the candidates for state offices, it is probable that the advice given and the sample ballots distributed by precinct leaders influence many of the voters who know and trust the precinct leaders. The candidate who is on the administration slate can also count on the votes of most state workers, particularly those holding patronage jobs. The votes cast by those persons who follow the advice of county and precinct leaders assume greater importance because many other voters, out of ignorance or disinterest, go to the polls without casting any vote for the lesser state offices. In the 1955, 1959, and 1963 gubernatorial primaries the total vote cast for lieutenant governor ranged from 75 to 84 percent of the vote for governor, but the vote for the other six state offices ranged from 37 to 55 percent of the gubernatorial vote, with a median of only 49 percent. (The median was 53 percent for secretary of state, 52 percent for attorney general, 49 percent for both auditor and superintendent of public instruction, and 47 percent for both treasurer and commissioner of agriculture.)

Because the effectiveness of slating depends on the work of local factional leaders, there are occasionally differences between the slate announced by a gubernatorial candidate and the slates that appear on local sample ballots. The gubernatorial candidate cannot guarantee to those he endorses that the endorsement will be effective in 120 counties. Local factional leaders may decide to support some other candidate for one of the lesser state offices because he comes from that area or is particularly popular in the county and they fear that the failure to put him on the slate would hurt their gubernatorial candidate. They may avoid slating anyone for a particular office. In some cases local leaders of two factions will make a trade involving two of the lesser offices. Sometimes the decisions of local leaders do not become known until sample ballots are distributed on election day. But if a gubernatorial candidate becomes aware that there is resistance in one part of the state to a candidate whom he has endorsed, he may let the county leaders in that area know he is not insisting that the candidate appear on the slate.

Slating arrangements are carried out in an atmosphere of mystery and even intrigue, as state and local politicians maneuver at the last moment to make the deals that they believe will enhance the prospects of the particular candidate to whom they have the greatest loyalty. A comprehensive statewide study of slating in a primary would require the collection of sample ballots distributed by two or more factional organizations in every county and even modifications in the ballot made by precinct leaders in some counties. Just a cursory examination of the slating arrangements in the 1963 Democratic primary gives some idea of their complexity. In the lieutenant governor's race Harry Lee Waterfield was consistently identified as Chandler's running mate in personal appearances, advertising, and news stories. Waterfield's opponent, John Breckinridge, had been elected attorney general on the Combs ticket in 1959, but he ran as an independent in 1963. Negotiations between Breathitt and Breckinridge never led to an alliance between them, but in some counties Breckinridge was invited to appear at rallies with the Breathitt slate of candidates, and some leaders in the Combs administration apparently put pressure on factional leaders in some counties to support Breckinridge. In about one-fourth of the counties the local organizations supporting Breathitt put Breckinridge on their slate. In roughly half as many counties, predominantly in western Kentucky, the Breathitt organization endorsed Waterfield for lieutenant governor, and in some cases where this occurred, at least some of the politicians working for Waterfield threw their support to Breathitt. In more than half of the counties there was no consistent pattern of slating for lieutenant governor by the Breathitt organization; it remained neutral, leaving its precinct leaders free to work for either candidate or none. The Breathitt organization endorsed an entire slate of candidates for the other statewide races, although some of the local organizations may occasionally have failed to go along, particularly in the case of Thelma Stovall, running for secretary of state. Chandler also endorsed a full slate of candidates, but there were rumors that the Chandler organization concentrated its efforts on the races for lieutenant governor and secretary of state, and in most counties gave no effective support to the other candidates, who were running against better known and often veteran candidates.

The difficulties of using gross county election data to estimate the extent of factional voting have already been described. But when the objective is to determine how much voters were influenced by slating for state offices, the difficulty is compounded by the smaller number of votes cast in races for the lesser offices and also in some races by the presence of several candidates unendorsed by either faction. Another complication is the occasional failure of local leaders to slate the candidate for a particular office. Because candidates are dropped from the slate in those counties where their opponent is particularly strong, a poor showing by the candidate in that county could not be considered good evidence of the effects of slating and nonslating. A comparison of the top quartile of counties (based on percentage of the vote) for two candidates can tell us how much overlap there is in the centers of their voting strength, and from that we can only speculate about how much this result was affected by slating. (By chance we would expect to find 7½ counties in the top quartile of two candidates.)

In 1963 there were 14 counties, mostly Republican ones, in the top quartile for both Chandler and Waterfield, who were running as a team for governor and lieutenant governor. Although Breathitt and Breckinridge were not slated together in most counties, there were 20 counties in the top quartile for both men, including 16 of the 20 counties that Breckinridge was able to carry. Breckinridge apparently benefited both from being slated with Breathitt in some counties and from being identified in the voters' minds with the

Combs-Breathitt faction. All 11 of the counties where Breckinridge was slated and which were in Breathitt's top quartile were also in Breckinridge's top quartile; 9 of the 19 other counties in the top quartile for Breathitt were also among Breckinridge's top 30. Among the remaining counties, 5 out of 16 where Breckinridge was slated and only 5 out of 74 where he was not were in his top quartile. In Jefferson County, where the regular organization slated no one for governor and Waterfield for lieutenant governor, Breckinridge won, running close to Breathitt in the upper-income precincts but far behind in the lower-income precincts, where slating probably has a greater effect.

The race for secretary of state in 1963 involved two principal candidates. Thelma Stovall, who had long been identified with Chandler and was consistently slated by the Chandler organization, had 18 counties of her top 30 that were identical to those in the top quartile for Chandler. John Moloney, who was a less prominent member of the Breathitt slate, shared 16 counties in the top quartile with Breathitt. The race for attorney general was confused by a third candidate, who ran slightly ahead of the third-place candidate endorsed by Chandler. The Breathitt candidate, Robert Matthews, shared 11 counties in the top quartile with Breathitt; the Chandler candidate, R. K. Grantz, who was less consistently slated by county organizations, had 12 counties in the top quartile with Chandler. One additional race, in which slating does not always occur, involved the clerk of the Court of Appeals. In 1963 there were two candidates, each slated with one faction; one had 15 and one had 12 counties in the top quartile with his gubernatorial candidate. The election returns in 1963 also demonstrated the importance of geography in some of the races for lesser offices. The home city of each candidate is listed on the ballot and probably affects the choice of many voters, particularly those who have no other information about the candidates. In 1963 several of the candidates who were not well known across the state had their highest percentages mainly in counties that either were strongly carried by their gubernatorial candidate or were close to their home county.

In the 1959 primary the partnership between Combs and Wyatt was well publicized throughout the campaign. In the race for lieutenant governor, Wyatt faced six opponents, three of whom might be considered serious contenders and all of whom had at least pockets of local strength. There were 17 counties that were in the top 30 for both Combs and Wyatt, a figure that suggests the alliance was recognized by the voters and implemented by county organizations. Breckinridge, running for attorney general against three opponents, had 12 counties out of his top 30 that were in the top quartile of Combs counties.

The record of recent elections for state offices shows that the winning candidates have almost always been those who were slated with one of the gubernatorial candidates, though not necessarily with the winner. Analysis of county voting in several of these races shows that the top-ranking counties of these candidates coincided with the top-ranking counties of the gubernatorial candidate more often than would be dictated by chance and sometimes to a high degree. Slating has an impact both because some voters identify the candidate with a faction and because factional leaders in most counties work for the entire slate. It is probable, but difficult to prove, that voters are more likely to be familiar with the factional affiliation of the more prominent candidates, particularly those running for lieutenant governor, and that it is the least prominent candidates who are most dependent on the work of county organizations in behalf of the slate.

LEGISLATIVE SLATING

One of the least publicized and understood aspects of Democratic primaries is the endorsement of legislative candidates by the governor or other factional leaders. This is not a common practice in states dominated by one party; Louisiana is the only state where there is evidence of legislative slating on a scale comparable to that in Kentucky.[8] The governor of Kentucky, when he is a Democrat, endorses candidates in many of the contested legislative primaries that occur in the middle of his term. His major reason for doing so is to insure the nomination and election of men who will support his program in the legislature. At the halfway point in his administration, the governor has usually exhausted many of his political resources and distributed most of the available patronage; the legislative honeymoon of the first session is over; and his inability to run for reelection has begun to erode his power. The prospects for his

[8] Sindler, *Huey Long's Louisiana*, 273-82.

legislative program in the second session will be improved if he can elect men who are identified with his faction or have a legislative record of support for his program, and if he can defeat any who have regularly voted against his program. Moreover, legislative candidates will be indebted to him if the support of his organization is—or appears to be—decisive in their renomination. The governor may also support a candidate in deference to the wishes of local politicians who belong to his faction. Most legislative candidates, in turn, are eager to have the support of the county organizations allied with the administration, unless they believe that the governor and his programs are unpopular in their district.

Gubernatorial endorsements of legislative candidates during a gubernatorial campaign occur much less often, however. The governor and the candidate he is supporting to succeed him concentrate their attention and resources on the gubernatorial campaign. They are wary of alienating either voters or local politicians by choosing sides in legislative primaries. The legislative candidate has equally good reasons for avoiding public identification with a gubernatorial candidate. If the candidate for governor fails to carry his district, it may cost the legislative candidate votes; and if the other candidate is elected governor, he may treat the legislator as an opponent and deprive him of the benefits that a governor has at his disposal. Legislative candidates who are well known for their factional loyalties may take a public stand in gubernatorial primaries and may receive organizational help from the same politicians who are active in the gubernatorial race, but they are not likely to emphasize their factional alignment in their campaigns. Only in Jefferson County are legislative endorsements regularly made in every primary election; in this case the county organization makes the endorsement after consultation with state leaders of the allied faction.

During the gubernatorial campaign the candidate of the opposition faction has the same reasons as his opponent for avoiding entanglement in legislative primaries, but during a midterm election both the state and local leaders of the opposition faction may give their support to legislative candidates who are running against the governor's supporters. The motive may be to embarrass the governor politically and to demonstrate that their faction is growing in strength, or it may be simply to help individual legislators whom the governor is trying to purge. The opposition faction lacks many of the resources of the administration, however. It has no claim on the loyalties of most state workers, its county organizations are likely to be undernourished, and it faces recruiting problems because the off-year election stirs up much less interest than the gubernatorial race. A legislative candidate who is opposed by the administration may be able to get help from county politicians and factional organizations with which he has been allied, but he is not likely to get more than an encouraging word from state leaders of the opposition faction.

When a legislative candidate wins the endorsement of the governor or some other factional leader, it means that he can expect to receive organizational assistance: funds, workers in the campaign and at the polls, and the votes of state workers or others who are responsive to organizational leadership. These resources are usually greater if he is endorsed by the governor rather than by the governor's opponents. The factional endorsement of a legislative candidate is not likely to have much direct impact on the voters because it is not publicized. The average voter is not likely to hear about it. The candidates rarely talk about their endorsement or stress it in their advertising. The press is likely to describe as factional conflicts some of the primary contests between men who are prominently associated with different factions, but it does not provide a comprehensive guide to the legislative races in which one or both candidates enjoy factional endorsement. The careful reader of a rural county newspaper often finds no clue to legislative slating in either the news stories or the advertisements. The governor does not announce the list of candidates who have his support, nor does he go from county to county giving his blessing to candidates and urging the voters to support them. Public speeches or statements by the governor in behalf of a particular candidate are rare, and when given they usually take the form of a cautious statement that legislator X is an old friend or has been a valued member of the legislature.

During the 1965 primary election Governor Breathitt visited a number of counties to speak in behalf of the candidates he had endorsed. He also broke precedent by making statements to the press and in a television broadcast asking the voters to elect senators who would support the administration. The battle was concentrated in the Senate because during the 1964 session Lieutenant Governor Waterfield had dominated that body and had been given authority under the Senate rules to appoint members of committees and assign bills to committees. As the factional contest between Breathitt and Waterfield grew more intense, the governor decided that the lieutenant governor must be stripped of these powers in the 1966 session. The administration insisted that those candidates whom it supported commit themselves to vote for such a change in the Senate rules. In a number of senatorial contests Waterfield supported men who were running against the administration candidates, and as the campaign progressed, the press identified ten senatorial races as contests between Breathitt and Waterfield candidates. Both men charged the other with endorsing a slate of candidates who were pledged to support one-man rule and domination of the Senate by the other. Breathitt said that committee assignments should "reflect the wishes of our *legislature as a whole* rather than the personal preference of any single individual with dictatorial powers," and expressed the hope that the voters would "nominate and elect courageous men and women who will stand by the Senate's traditional freedom to choose its own committee organization." The governor did not directly announce which candidates he was supporting, although the information was available in the press. Instead, he told the voters: "It is very important that you find out how the candidates for the Senate in your district stand on this question: Shall the Senate select its own committee organization, or shall one man assume the dictatorial power to control the Senate?"[9]

The method for selecting committees is a complex, technical issue that does not seem either simple enough or interesting enough to arouse support from the voters. As we shall see from polling data, few voters seem to have understood exactly what the controversy was about, but many of them realized that the fundamental issue was a struggle between the governor and the lieutenant governor for control of the Senate. By his open intervention in the senatorial primaries, Breathitt risked a serious blow to his prestige and the alienation of the men he opposed unsuccessfully, should the voters reject his advice. But the administration candidates won seven of the ten races that had been billed as a test of strength, Breathitt's

[9] Text of telecast by Governor Edward T. Breathitt.

influence in the legislature was enhanced, and the rules were changed to reduce the lieutenant governor's power.

Frequency of Slating. It is difficult to draw a comprehensive picture showing how extensively legislative candidates are slated because the support from both the administration and opposition factions is usually provided quietly and takes the form of organizational support rather than public appeals to the voters. Press accounts of factionalism in legislative primaries focus attention only on those races in which the candidates are prominently identified with opposing factions. Moreover, endorsements vary in their intensity and effectiveness. Local leaders of the administration faction may be working for a candidate at the request of the governor. In some districts the local leaders of a faction may be divided with regard to a legislative primary and may work for different candidates whether or not the governor has indicated his preference. The resources available to the opposition faction are limited, and a candidate identified with that faction may receive little tangible help from it.

Only in Jefferson County has the slating of legislative candidates consistently occurred. It has been the standard practice of the regular Democratic organization to endorse a full slate of candidates for legislative as well as local office. This practice has discouraged candidates from running on their own initiative without the organization's support, and frequently the legislative primaries have been uncontested. In some years, particularly when factional conflicts have been strong at the state level, there has been an opposition slate of candidates for some of the legislative seats. In gubernatorial election years one reason for an opposition slate may be to meet the legal requirements necessary to give a gubernatorial candidate a share of election officials at the polls. Almost all of the legislative candidates supported by the regular organization have won in Jefferson County, with or without opposition. In the postwar period the largest proportion of legislative races contested by opposing slates in Jefferson County have occurred in 1947, 1949, 1955, and 1959. In 1961 Chandler supporters ran only a few legislative candidates, and in 1965 there were just a few independent candidates challenging the organization. In 1963, the year when it made no gubernatorial endorsement, the organization endorsed a coalition slate of legislative candidates, which ran successfully against a scattering of independent candidates.

In the state as a whole, the extent of gubernatorial endorsements in midterm legislative primaries has varied with the circumstance of factional strife but seems to be increasing. Press accounts suggest that factional conflicts were frequent in the 1949 primaries, during Clements' administration, occurring in perhaps half of the contested primaries. Four years later Governor Wetherby was reported to be working to assure the election of friendly legislators, but there were few accounts in the press of primary contests between friends and foes of the administration. In 1957 the proportion of publicized factional conflicts increased, and the losses suffered by supporters of Governor Chandler in several of these races strengthened the "rebel" movement in the legislature during the remainder of his term.

In 1961 and 1965 questionnaires were sent to all the Democratic candidates running in contested Democratic primaries. The information from the questionnaires pertaining to factional endorsement of candidates is summarized in Table 4.3. The senatorial primaries attract greater attention from the factions because the stakes are higher in these races; the senators have greater prestige and longer terms, and the outcome of a few elections will have a greater effect on controlling that branch of the legislature. In both years the administration endorsed a candidate in each of the senate races covered by the questionnaires (all but two of the contested primaries). In only a few of the 1961 Senate races did the opposing candidates report that they had factional support. In 1965 there were ten highly publicized races in which the Breathitt administration and Lieutenant Governor Waterfield supported opposing candidates, and in the other two contested races Breathitt supported a candidate but Waterfield remained neutral. Questionnaires from 52 of the 67 contested House primaries in 1961 showed that there were 38 races in which the administration endorsed a candidate, 6 others in which only the opposition faction is reported to have endorsed anyone, and 8 races in which no endorsements were reported. Although the data are incomplete, it is clear that the administration expressed a preference in about three-fourths of the contested House primaries, and that the opposition faction was much less active. In 1965 the administration was reported by the candi-

TABLE 4.3

Factionalism in 1961 and 1965 Democratic
Legislative Primaries as Described by Candidates

	1961 No. of Candidates			1961 No. of Districts			1965 No. of Candidates			1965 No. of Districts		
	S	H	Tot	S	H	Tot	S	H	Tot	S	H	Tot
Total contested primaries				13	67	80				12	55	67
Primaries reported in poll				12	52	64				11	45	56
Candidates who responded	22	90	112				16	67	83			
Some factional endorsements				12	44	56				11	43	54
No factional endorsements				0	8	8				0	2	2
Respondents endorsed by administration faction	13	38	51				10	20	30			
Respondents endorsed only by opposition faction	4	13	17				4	a	4			
Respondents not endorsed	5	39	44				2	25	27			
Respondents reporting opponent had administration endorsement	a	a	a				6	23	29			
Winners endorsed by administration faction				10	30	40				8	29	37
Winners endorsed only by opposition faction				2	6	8				3	a	3
Winners not endorsed				0	7	7				0	16	16

a Question not asked in this poll. The House respondents in 1965 who are in the category of "not endorsed" probably include a few who had support from the Waterfield faction.

dates to have endorsed someone in 43 of the 45 contested primaries from which answers were received. Although the 1965 questionnaire did not cover endorsement by the opposition faction, it appears that Waterfield and his factional allies concentrated most of their efforts on Senate rather than House races.[10]

The data on contested primaries probably underestimate the interest of the administration in legislative elections because in some

[10] Questionnaires were sent to all Democrats in contested races. In 1961 questionnaires were received from 22 of 31 Senate candidates, including 12 of the 13 winners, and from 90 of 180 House candidates, including 43 of the 67 winners and a good proportion of the candidates who ran second; the relatively minor candidates were least likely to respond. In 1965 questionnaires were received from 16 of 31 Senate candidates, including 8 of the 12 winners, and from 67 of 137 House candidates, including 26 of 55 winners in contested primaries. The questions included in the two years were not identical.

districts the administration's support for a candidate is enough of a deterrent to prevent other candidates from entering the primary. In 1965, questionnaires were sent to House candidates in uncontested primaries. Nine of the 20 responding said they had the governor's support in getting the nomination, and several of these specifically said that he discouraged others from running or did not encourage others; one said the governor tried but failed to find an opponent.

In 1961 some of the candidates who were supported by the administration, particularly in House races, received some support from other factions. This was usually a case in which some of the local leaders of both factions were supporting a candidate, whether or not the governor had indicated his choice. Some administration candidates claimed that they had some support from politicians aligned with Chandler. The allegiance of Clements supporters was unpredictable in 1961, less than a year after he had left the administration; candidates with administration backing encountered support from the Clements groups in some counties and opposition from them in others. In some races factional lines were tangled. In one Senate race, for example, the reports from both candidates confirm that one of them had the support of Combs, Clements, Chandler, and Waterfield; the other, who lost, had some help from Wyatt supporters. In another legislative primary both candidates insisted that the administration had worked against them. (The 1965 House poll did not ask about other factional support.)

Advantages of Factional Support. It is clear from Table 4.3 that factional support, preferably from the administration, is an asset to a candidate. Of the 55 winners responding in 1961, 48 had some factional endorsement. Forty of the 51 respondents who had the administration's backing won, compared to 8 out of 17 with backing from an opposition faction, and only 7 winners out of 44 candidates who had no factional endorsement. The 1965 data cover all districts in which any candidate responded, because candidates were asked about administration backing of their opponent as well as themselves. In 1965 there were 54 races reported in which the administration made an endorsement; the endorsee won 37 and lost 17 of these to candidates who were either independent or had some support from the opposition faction.

Most candidates also agree on the importance of factional support, particularly if it comes from the administration. Candidates who had administration support and those who faced an opponent with administration endorsement were asked whether these endorsements affected the campaign. It is obvious from Table 4.4 that most

TABLE 4.4

Advantages of Administration Endorsement in 1961 and 1965 Democratic Legislative Primaries as Described by Candidates

	Winner or Loser	Candidates Endorsed by Administration		Candidates Not Endorsed by Administration	
		1961	1965	1961	1965
Candidates who thought administration endorsement was asset to its recipient	Winners	21	17	0	8
	Losers	0	6	30	33
Candidates who thought administration endorsement was liability to its recipient	Winners	1	1	5	1
	Losers	5	0	2	0
Candidates who thought administration endorsement made no difference	Winners	11	4	3	2
	Losers	3	2	6	5
Kinds of Tangible Help Reported Received by Administration-Endorsed Candidate					
State workers (votes, funds, work at polls)		0	15	7	22
Organizational help, workers		1	8	0	8
Personal appearance in county by governor		0	2	0	2
Governor's endorsement		0	3	0	3
Financial aid		0	3	12	16
State projects in county		0	0	1	2
Local slates organized		0	0	1	2
Did Administration-Endorsed Candidate Get Financial Aid as Result of Endorsement and Was It Important to Campaign? (House Candidates—1965)					
Yes—Very important			0		23
Yes—Somewhat helpful			3		8
Yes—Not important			4		0
No aid received			13		3
Don't know			0		9

winning candidates who had administration support considered it an asset, very few considered it a liability, and the remainder believed that it made little difference. Those who lost despite administration support were about evenly divided on its value. Several of the candidates said that they benefited from organizational assistance but were hurt by the administration's unpopularity. In answer to a question in the 1965 poll most administration candidates described this support as "somewhat helpful" rather than "very important." The overwhelming majority of candidates who were defeated by an administration-endorsed opponent believed that this endorsement was a factor in their defeat; most of these in 1965 believed that such support was "very important" to their opponent and not merely "somewhat helpful." Those who defeated administration candidates were divided on the effects of administration endorsement. It is worth noting that both the administration losers and opposition winners who thought the endorsements had some effect almost unanimously agreed that administration support was a liability in 1961 and an asset in 1965. In general it is true that losing candidates who did not have administration support attributed greater importance to it than the winners who had such support and who may have been better able to evaluate its importance.

It is significant that most candidates judged administration endorsement to be of some importance. The significance of these beliefs lies in their effect on the candidates' behavior. Candidates are more likely to make commitments to the administration if they believe that its endorsement has some value. But these views of the candidates do not necessarily measure accurately the importance of administration endorsements. In 1961 a number of candidates cited the sales tax, enacted by the Combs administration, as an important factor either helping or hurting the administration's candidate, but there is no evidence to show that this issue had a great impact on the voters. It is very likely that some of the defeated candidates, searching for a scapegoat to explain their loss, exaggerated the effect of the administration's opposition, just as some of them appear to have exaggerated the resources devoted by the opposition to defeating them.

What are the specific advantages of being the administration's candidate? Those candidates who enjoyed that position tended to emphasize the popularity of the administration and its policies, while those who had been beaten by administration candidates put greater stress on the more tangible assets. There is no evidence concerning popular attitudes toward the administration, nor is it clear what proportion of the voters were aware of the administration's endorsement in a particular race. Legislators in 1961 were asked how often the voters asked them about their support of or opposition to the administration, and their answers varied widely. One-third said either that the voters generally knew this or that they often asked; another 40 percent encountered such questions only occasionally or rarely; and one-fourth said they were never asked. Relatively few administration candidates in either election said that they emphasized their endorsement during the campaign.

Table 4.4 summarizes the most frequently mentioned kinds of tangible help that administration candidates received, or their opponents thought they received, from the administration. (The question about tangible assistance was asked more precisely in the 1965 questionnaire; this probably accounts for the larger number of pertinent responses in that year.) The form of assistance most often mentioned, both by supporters of the administration and by their opponents, is the assistance given by state workers. They are useful in several ways, which were summarized by one losing candidate: "All state workers were assessed and instructed to work and vote against me." Administration supporters confirm that state workers were valuable not only for their votes but also for their assistance in the campaign. These are principally those holding patronage jobs, such as in the highway department. One senatorial candidate said, "State workers in every county were valuable as campaign workers. It was a big factor in my victory." But administration candidates did not cite state workers as a source of financing, and several of them emphasized that state workers were not assessed for funds. In Franklin County (Frankfort) the press reported in 1961 that the governor had told a group of high-ranking state employees that they should take an active part in the legislative primary in that county. In a southeastern mountain district one candidate said that the administration enlisted the support not only of state employees but also of schoolteachers and schoolbus drivers.

Administration candidates in many counties can recruit to work at the polls not only persons employed by the state but also the precinct workers who are loyal to the administration faction.

Although the administration could assist a candidate greatly by announcing state projects for his county, this form of assistance was mentioned by only a few candidates and appears to be seldom employed in legislative primaries. One losing candidate did assert that the governor had made a flying trip to promise both highway and dam projects in the district. The administration must exercise care in dispensing such favors because they are limited in number, and most of them seem to be employed for purposes that have a higher priority, such as winning gubernatorial primaries or bargaining with the elected legislators when important legislation is at stake.

How important are the financial contributions that the administration makes on behalf of its candidate? The evidence is contradictory. (See Table 4.4.) Opponents cited financial aid to administration candidates almost as frequently as they mentioned the assistance of state workers, but only 3 administration candidates out of the 81 polled in two years made any reference to financial aid when they were asked in what way their endorsement helped them or what tangible aid they received. The contrast was sharpest in answers to a specific question directed to House candidates in 1965. Administration candidates were asked whether they received any financial help, directly or indirectly, as a result of their support from Governor Breathitt and were asked to evaluate the importance of any such financial help to their campaign. Candidates were also asked whether their opponent got financial help from the administration and how important it was. Only 7 of 20 administration candidates said they received such help, and only 3 of these considered it helpful. But most of the opponents believed that administration candidates got financial aid and they generally considered it very important.

Some of the opponents were eloquent in describing the role played by money from the administration in their defeat. Their sentiments can be summarized by two comments: "Free elections—bah—bought and paid for!" "The administration had a lot of money and they knew *how* to spend it." Those who claimed that large sums of money were spent by the administration usually asserted that most of the funds went to buy votes. One losing candidate said that the "floater" (bought) vote in his senatorial district was over 3,000, and he claimed that his opponent, with administration help, spent $12,000 in the campaign. One candidate in a county notorious for the size of its floater vote said that the administration was "reported" to have spent $30,000 to support its candidate in a legislative race in which the total vote cast was about 6,200.

These assertions that legislative candidates have received many thousands of dollars directly from the state administration faction must be considered exaggerations. Several persons active in the administration faction at the state level emphasized that financial aid was much less important than organizational help in the legislative primaries. They said that the administration faction did not have large sums of money to disburse and did not consider individual primary contests important enough to justify a major financial commitment. One person who was thoroughly familiar with the 1961 campaign estimates that no more than $15,000 was disbursed by the state factional leadership, with the amounts allocated to specific candidates ranging from $100 to $500. It is noteworthy that none of the administration candidates mentioned financial aid in the 1961 questionnaire, and that only a few did so in 1965 in response to a more specific question. Probably the administration's endorsement gives a candidate more indirect than direct financial assistance. In some districts the state workers holding patronage jobs are expected to contribute funds to the campaign, and in large districts this could account for several thousand dollars. It is also probable that contractors and other business interests, which would normally contribute to gubernatorial campaigns, are more likely to support those candidates in legislative primaries who have the administration's support. In short, the administration's endorsement gives the candidate access to sources of funds, just as it gives him access to state patronage employees and other political workers who are loyal to the administration faction. It is impossible to put a price tag on the value of this accessibility.

The tangible advantages of association with an opposition faction are less obvious and in most counties smaller. Although several opposition candidates expressed the belief that they profited from the administration's unpopularity, relatively few described specific benefits that were gained from the opposition faction. The only advantage to be expected is that those politicians in the opposition faction will help the candidate to set up an organization, raise some funds, get out the vote on election day; this is valuable in those counties where the opposition faction has a strong organization. Several senatorial candidates in 1965 commented that they received little tangible help from Waterfield. Two mentioned financial contributions from supporters of Waterfield, and one of these said that he raised $750 from this source. Waterfield concentrated his efforts on five senatorial primaries where he believed his candidates were in the strongest position; the candidates he supported won three of these races and lost the other two by narrow margins. Waterfield's most direct contribution was to send some 10,000 letters to voters, principally in these five senatorial districts, urging them to support the candidates whom he had endorsed.

Legislative Slating and the Voter. The primary election returns and the testimony of candidates support the belief that endorsement by the administration is usually an asset and support from an opposition faction is sometimes an asset to a legislative candidate. To estimate the impact of slating more precisely would require a study of why voters vote as they do in legislative primaries, and such a study necessitates interviewing voters. It is doubtful that interviews alone would be effective, however, because many persons would not recognize that their vote had been affected by slating. The legislative slate, as we have described it, is like an iceberg. The endorsements that are well enough publicized to be visible to the average voter are less important than the organizational work that goes on below the surface. The voter may cast his vote for the administration's candidate because he has seen him on a television program paid for by the administration faction, because he has been asked to do so by a friend who is a state worker or a politician working for the administration faction, or because the candidate's name was on a sample ballot handed to him at the polls by someone working for the administration faction. The average voter might only remember that he had seen the candidate on television, been told that he was a "good man," or heard the name somewhere; he might neither know nor care that the candidate had been endorsed by the governor.

Survey research techniques cannot adequately measure the indirect effects of slating (i.e., the organizational effects); they can only measure the direct effect on voters by showing how many knew and cared about factional endorsements. If this is our objective, to determine how much Kentucky Democratic voters know about and are influenced by factional slating of legislative candidates, there are still serious limitations on what we can expect from a survey. To reach conclusions about Kentucky Democratic voters, it would be necessary to survey a sample of voters drawn from a population that included all districts that had legislative primary contests, or at least all races where slating occurred. But we have seen how much slating varies from district to district in the amount of publicity that accompanies it and the extent to which a faction commits its prestige and its resources. Relatively few factional contests at the legislative level are publicized as such, and only the better informed voters are likely to be aware of legislative slates when they do become publicized. To conduct a comprehensive study of slating would require a large sample in each of a great many legislative districts as well as polling an unusually large number of voters in order to find enough respondents who were directly influenced by slating.

Lacking the resources for such an extensive survey, we have conducted surveys of voters in five legislative districts in an effort to get some fragmentary evidence that would at least permit speculation about the direct effects of legislative slating on the voters. The five Democratic primaries include two House races in Lexington, one in 1961 and another in 1963, and senatorial contests in 1965 in Owensboro, Richmond, and Georgetown. The polling was done in urban rather than rural areas for reasons of convenience. In each city several precincts were selected, ranging in number from three to five. All of the precincts were in middle or upper income areas; these were chosen because it was assumed that the voters were more likely to be informed about slating and less likely to be simply responding to the advice of precinct workers than would be true of voters in the lowest income precincts. Other criteria used in selecting precincts included achieving some socioeconomic and geographical balance (within the limits just mentioned), avoiding the home precinct of candidates, and picking a group of precincts where the proportion of vote for the two candidates approximated that in the whole county. Within each of the precincts, names were selected entirely at random from lists of all those who had voted in the Democratic primary according to records of the county clerk.[11]

The 1961 primary race involved two prominent men: John Y. Brown had repeatedly run for state and legislative office, and Ted Osborn was the incumbent legislator. Neither man was closely associated with a single faction, and the Combs administration maintained a strict neutrality in the race. The 1963 primary involved two men of much less prominence, neither of whom were incumbent legislators. Charles Tackett had the support of the Breathitt organization, and Darrell Hancock was backed by the Chandler organization, but neither candidate mentioned this factional support in his campaign, nor was it publicized in the Lexington press. A voter who knew the candidates well might guess at their factional support because of their previous identification with the two factions. The only solid evidence of factional alignment available to the voters was in sample ballots, which appear to have been handed out quite regularly in most of the precincts. The Breathitt ticket included Tackett on a long list; the Chandler ticket listed only Chandler, Waterfield, and Hancock.

The results of the two polls are summarized in Table 4.5. It is surprising to discover that in 1961 one-sixth of the voters, when asked, thought that one or both of the candidates had factional support, even though neither one did in reality. Whatever the reason for this belief, it had a negligible effect on the way respondents voted. In 1963, when factional alignments were real but poorly publicized, almost one-fourth of the voters were informed about the alignments; about one out of seven said that this influenced their vote. It is possible that some voters were influenced by sample ballots but did not recognize or had forgotten that these constituted a factional slate. The coincidence with the gubernatorial race permits us to explore this possibility. A large majority of the Tackett voters also voted for Breathitt, but the Hancock voters were almost evenly divided in their gubernatorial vote. All of the Tackett voters

---

[11] The 1961 Lexington interviews were conducted by students in a political science class and those in 1963 were done by a graduate assistant. The 1965 interviews were conducted principally by the authors and two graduate assistants. The use of student assistants and the pressure of time limited the number of callbacks that were feasible and resulted in a relatively low rate of response. In the 1963 study, if the person chosen at random were not home but another person in the household had voted, the latter was interviewed.

TABLE 4.5

Factors Affecting Voter Decisions in Two Fayette County Legislative Primaries, 1961 and 1963

	1961 No. Voters for		1963 No. Voters for	
	Osborn (71)	Brown (110)	Tackett[a] (45)	Hancock[b] (38)
Voters' Viewpoints on Factions				
Thought one or both candidates had factional support	10	25	11	8
Did not think either had factional support	61	85	34	30
Gave factional support as reason for vote, on own initiative	1	0	6	2
Said factionalism affected vote, when asked	3	2	8	4
Said factionalism did not affect vote, when asked	7	23	3	4
Voted for gubernatorial and legislative candidates on same ticket	....	....	30	19
Voted for gubernatorial and legislative candidates not on same ticket	....	....	13	18
Other Reasons Given for Vote				
Knew candidate or his family personally	22	41	10	14
Personal qualities of candidate or his opponent	32	53	6	6
Program or record of candidate or his opponent	11	32	0	0
Candidate called on him in person	0	0	14	1
Supporters of the candidate persuaded him	4	1	4	6

[a] Endorsed by Breathitt organization.
[b] Endorsed by Chandler organization.

who knew about the slating voted for Breathitt; five of eight similarly informed Hancock voters cast a ballot for Chandler. A summary of the other reasons offered by the voters emphasizes, above all, the advantage enjoyed by a candidate who has a large number of friends and acquaintances. Even in an urban district, those who know the candidate can constitute an important block of voters. The candidate who is not well known may, as Tackett did, win a lot of votes from door-to-door campaigning. None of the voters polled in 1963 made any reference to issues, and most of those in 1961 who explained their vote by reference to issues were speaking in very general terms. The only exception to this was in the case of John Y. Brown, whose preference for a sales tax over an income tax had been well publicized for many years and was referred to by fifteen voters. The conclusion from the Lexington polls is that the voters were often confused and ill informed about factional endorsements, but that a substantial number of the supporters of the administration candidate in 1963 appear to have been influenced, consciously or unconsciously, by the administration's endorsement. (This was particularly true in one of the three precincts, the one in which that legislative candidate worked at the polls.)

The senatorial primaries of 1965 offered an excellent opportunity to test the direct effects of legislative slating through interviews because the governor took a public stand on these races and the conflict between candidates endorsed by Breathitt and those endorsed by Waterfield was well publicized in the press. Three surveys were conducted, in Owensboro (Daviess County), Richmond (Madison County), and Georgetown (Scott County). (Each senatorial district included other counties also.) In Owensboro the administration endorsed Wendell Ford, who had been an administrative assistant to Governor Combs and was the Breathitt administration's contact man in Daviess County. Waterfield supported the incumbent, H. C. "Cap" Gardner, who had been identified with the Chandler faction and who had been picked by Lieutenant Governor Waterfield to serve as majority leader of the Senate in the 1964 session. The race was highly publicized in the state newspapers. In Richmond the administration was supporting Guy Duerson, and Waterfield endorsed Edward Murphy; neither was an incumbent, and there was a minor third candidate. The race received little attention in the state. In Georgetown the administration was supporting Lawrence Wetherby, a former governor and a charter member of the Clements-Combs-Breathitt faction, who was scheduled to become president pro tem of the Senate in 1966. His major opponent was the incumbent, Marvin Edwards. There were three other minor candidates. Although the Wetherby-Edwards race was described in the press as a major factional contest (and although Wetherby's loss would have been a major blow to the administration's prestige), Waterfield said that he did not devote much attention

TABLE 4.6
Effect of Factions on Voter Decisions in Three Senatorial Primaries, 1965

Voters' Viewpoints on Factions	OWENSBORO Number of Voters for		RICHMOND Number of Voters for		GEORGETOWN Number of Voters for		No. of Votes Cast in All Three Races		Percent Votes Cast in All Three Races	
	Ford	Gardner	Duerson	Murphy	Wetherby	Edwards	Pro-admin. Cand.	Anti-admin. Cand.	Pro-admin. Cand.	Anti-admin. Cand.
Knew factional support of both candidates	16	21	10	7	2	2	28	30	35	33
Knew only of Breathitt support	8	13	3	3	4	6	15	22	19	24
Knew only of Waterfield support	0	0	0	1	0	0	0	1	0	1
Knew nothing of factional support	15	7	7	18	15	12	37	37	46	41
Gave factional support as reason for vote, on own initiative	4	12	7	1	2	1	13	14	16	16
Said factionalism affected vote, when asked	7	17	10	1	3	3	20	21	25	23
Said factionalism did not affect vote, when asked	17	17	3	10	3	5	23	32	29	36
Totals	39	41	20	29	21	20	80	90	100	100

Ford, Duerson, and Wetherby were supported by the Breathitt administration. Gardner, Murphy, and Edwards had varying degrees of support from Waterfield.

to this race, and Edwards said that he did not receive any help from Waterfield. In his advertising, Edwards criticized the governor for attempting to dictate the choice of senators. By seeking renomination, Edwards was violating the Democratic party rotation agreement that applied to this district, but not a single voter who was interviewed made any reference to the rotation principle. All three races were relatively close. Two administration candidates, Ford and Wetherby, and one opposition candidate, Murphy, were nominated in the primary.

Because the number of voters interviewed was so small, the data must be considered as suggestive rather than conclusive. We must be particularly cautious about the findings in individual races where the samples are very small. For this reason, percentages are given in Table 4.6 only for the total and not for each race. Slightly more than half of the voters knew that Governor Breathitt was supporting a candidate and knew which one it was; about one-third of the voters knew that Waterfield was supporting the other. The voters were best informed in Owensboro, where the bitterly contested race had attracted the most attention. Almost three-fourths of the voters there knew that Breathitt had endorsed Ford and almost half knew that Waterfield had endorsed Gardner. Voters were least informed about factionalism in Georgetown. It is perhaps surprising that only one-third of them knew about Breathitt's endorsement of Wetherby; it is understandable that only 4 out of 41 identified Edwards with Waterfield, because the alliance was a hazy one.

The voters were asked early in the interview why they had voted as they did, and later those who had accurate information about the endorsement of at least one candidate were asked if this support affected their vote in any way. One voter in four said that factionalism affected their vote, and a majority of these independently mentioned this earlier in the interview. The differences among the legislative races are substantial enough to make us cautious about any broad conclusions regarding the impact of factionalism on legislative primaries. Probably the effects are different in every legislative district. The samples of voters are too small to permit any accurate judgment about the effect of the administration's intervention on each race. In Owensboro, the opposition candidate appears to have profited most from factionalism, and in Richmond it was the administration candidate who gained; but both of these men were defeated. In Georgetown, factionalism seems to have had little effect insofar as the respondents were concerned.

In Owensboro, many of the voters were critical of the Breathitt administration. Twenty-one percent said that Breathitt was doing a poor job (compared to only 1 percent in the other two cities), and 39 percent described his performance as excellent or good (compared to 68 percent in the other cities). The voters felt that Owensboro had been neglected by the administration, particularly with regard to improved highway construction linking the city with other parts of the state. Ford believed that the unpopularity of the administration hurt his chances with many of the voters. These criticisms of the Breathitt administration were expressed by a number of voters in explaining the factional implications of their vote for Gardner; others simply said that they were against "machine control" or "hand-picked candidates." Ford gained some votes from discontented voters, however, either because they blamed Senator Gardner for failure to get action or because they thought Owensboro would benefit from having a senator in office who was friendly to the administration.

In Richmond, on the other hand, half of Duerson's support (among the respondents) came from persons who were either vocally enthusiastic about the Breathitt administration or critical of Waterfield. Several, including respondents connected with the state college, specifically mentioned the administration's education policies. Although Murphy's factional alignment was almost as well known as his opponent's, it was mentioned by only one of his supporters as a reason for his vote.

Voters in the three cities were asked whether or not they had heard about the disagreement between Breathitt and Waterfield on how the Senate should be organized, and if so, they were asked what the disagreement was about. Breathitt in his public statements had urged the voters to determine the views of senatorial candidates on this issue. Although 56 percent said they had heard of the disagreement, only 18 percent were able to describe it with some accuracy, either as a struggle for control of the Senate or as a conflict over the organization of committees; very few of these had any more explicit information. Almost all of these who had some accurate knowledge of the dispute also knew the factional endorsement of one or both candidates.

Among those voters who described Governor Breathitt's performances as excellent or good, 52 percent supported administration candidates; of those who evaluated it as fair or poor, 42 percent supported administration candidates. The differences between these two groups were greater in the case of voters who were aware of the factional alignment of candidates. A comparison of voting records of those persons who had voted for Breathitt with those who had voted for Chandler in 1963 showed no meaningful differences, partly because some voters had changed their attitude toward Breathitt since the 1963 primary and probably in part because some voters did not remember accurately how they had voted in 1963.

The reasons, other than factionalism, that voters most frequently gave to explain their votes were similar to those revealed by the Lexington polls. (Some voters in each instance gave more than one reason.) Thirty-one percent said that they or others in their family were personally acquainted with the candidate, and this figure was 42 percent in the case of those supporting the three candidates who were running in their home county. ("I've known him all his life, and I don't know anything bad about him.") Thirty-six percent mentioned the personal attributes or the qualifications of the candidates or their opponents. This included those who preferred to vote for an incumbent. It also included voters who had done business with a candidate and who were satisfied—or in a few cases dissatisfied. ("He makes good sausages." "I've done business with him for years." "He sold me something defective in his store, and I wouldn't want the county run that way.") Eleven percent made some reference to issues, in most cases simply expressing the view that one candidate or the other could do more for the county, or had not done much for it. Eleven percent explained their vote by reference to the campaigning of one or both candidates, although only a few emphasized personal visits from a candidate. Several said they voted for one man because they did not like the other's campaign tactics. Another 11 percent said that some other person, often a member of the family, had urged him to vote as they did.

These fragmentary insights into the motivations of those who vote in legislative primaries suggest several conclusions. There is no evidence that factional loyalty in Kentucky is as strong as party loyalty and is a sufficient reason, in the minds of many voters, for voting for a particular candidate. Factionalism usually appears less important than personal qualities if the voter knows something about the candidate, and it is of little importance to those voters who know (and like) one of the candidates. The factional implications of legislative primaries are seldom publicized, and even in 1965, when the senatorial primaries were repeatedly described in the press as a test of the administration's prestige, voters were much more likely to be conscious of factionalism in some districts than in others. Voting decisions in legislative primaries may be influenced by factionalism for several reasons: the prominent identification of a candidate with a faction, the existence of a highly salient issue that arouses strong pro- or anti-administration sentiments, or the belief that the administration has treated a county well or poorly.

Those voters who were best informed tended to come from the higher income (and presumably higher education) sections, although no precise correlations with income or education were attempted. It is probable that in lower income precincts voters are less informed about factional alignments and are more dependent on sample ballots and the advice of precinct workers; in these areas the indirect, organizational effects of factionalism would be more important than the direct effects. The value of a strong organization is not limited to a few precincts, however, as the use of sample ballots (with no other publicity) in the 1963 Lexington primary illustrates.

Although the practice is not new, there appears to be a greater willingness of governors to intervene in midterm legislative primaries. The senatorial primaries in 1965 were characterized by an unprecedented commitment of the governor's prestige, while in the House races the administration expressed a clear, but usually unpublicized, choice in an extraordinarily high proportion of the contested races and helped candidates to avoid competition in other districts. It seems clear from the candidate questionnaires that administration support in most districts is valuable, principally because it makes available manpower and other organizational assistance. It also seems clear that those candidates who are defeated by administration endorsees often exaggerate the importance of the administration's help, particularly in the area of financing. The value of open, publicized endorsement by the administration is far less sure, both because voters are often unaware of it and because an administration is likely to be unpopular in some districts. Many candidates were reluctant to advertise their alignment with the administration. Some candidates attributed their victory or their defeat to the level of the administration's popularity, but it is doubtful how much evidence they had to support these judgments. The evidence from interviews with voters suggests that those voters who are directly affected by factional alignments are likely to include both the most enthusiastic supporters and the strongest critics of the administration.

5 | The Kentucky Voter

The partisan political configuration in Kentucky, as elsewhere, is influenced by inherited partisan affiliation. "The party system of a state . . . is not the creation of a day. Its form bears the imprint of events long past and its practices are often dictated by customs of long forgotten origin."[1] As we noted in chapter 1, the Civil War and the Reconstruction period had a significant impact upon the state. A century later, this impact is still evident.

Figure 5.1 reveals the force of tradition in voting—showing those counties with a persistent attachment to one party in presidential elections since 1872.[2] Twenty-three counties have always returned majorities for Democratic presidential candidates; fourteen counties have strayed from the Democratic fold only once, and eight only twice. Of the eight counties which have twice deviated, seven of them did so in 1928 and 1960, leading to a strong presumption that the Catholicism of the Democratic candidates was the decisive factor. Of the fourteen which have voted Republican only once, ten did so for Hoover in 1928, leading to the same presumption.

Eleven counties have always gone Republican in presidential elections since 1872. Mainly in the southeastern part of the state, these counties are part of the post-Civil War phenomenon known as "mountain Republicanism," which includes areas in western Virginia, western North Carolina, eastern Tennessee, and a few counties in Georgia and Alabama. Of the six usually Republican counties, three have broken away only once, in 1964.

Figure 5.1 also shows traditional partisan allegiances dating from

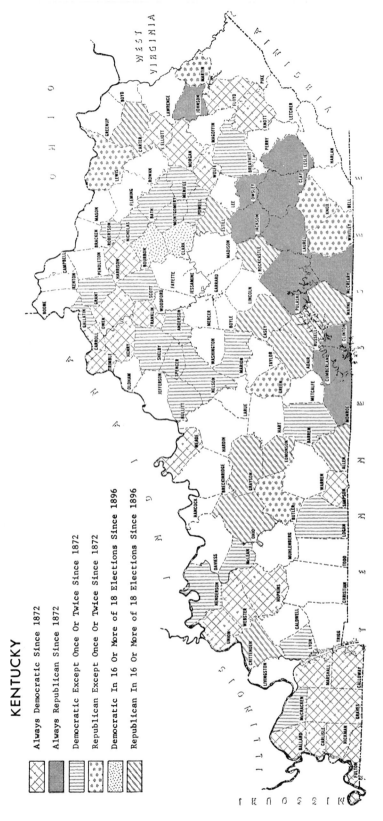

FIGURE 5.1

Kentucky Counties with Long-Established Traditional Voting Behavior in Presidential Elections

KENTUCKY

Always Democratic Since 1872

Always Republican Since 1872

Democratic Except Once Or Twice Since 1872

Republican Except Once Or Twice Since 1872

Democratic In 16 Or More of 18 Elections Since 1896

Republican In 16 Or More of 18 Elections Since 1896

1896. Voting patterns in these counties had fluctuated during the period following the Civil War; however, in the 1896 McKinley-Bryan election the struggle over monetary policy provoked such fervent emotions that voting patterns were established in many counties that have endured to the present.[3]

Tradition can influence voting behavior in localities where the two-party vote is persistently close. In a particular county the result can be a nearly even partisan division. Eight counties in Kentucky that can be classified as marginal appear to have had this pattern set as a result of the Civil War and its aftermath. They have shown a fairly consistently close division of their vote in presidential elections since 1872, and have fluctuated, with varying degrees of impartiality, from the Democrats to the Republicans. The average percentage of the two-party vote in these counties for the 24 presidential elections has varied from about 50-50 to a 54-46 percent Democratic advantage. Of 192 possible majorities, Democratic candidates have won 101, Republicans 91. When the vote is persistently close for nearly a century, traditional allegiances handed down through generations appear to dominate the voting pattern.[4]

We find that a total of 82 counties, which are predominantly rural, have followed a traditional allegiance for one of the two parties, or a closely balanced fluctuation between them, since 1896

[1] V. O. Key, Jr., *American State Politics: An Introduction* (New York: Alfred A. Knopf, 1956), 217.

[2] The year 1872 is chosen as a point of departure because not until then were the full effects of the changes wrought by the Civil War and Reconstruction felt (specifically, Negro voting). Presidential elections are used because deviations are more likely to occur in such elections, and thus a survey of them will reveal the bedrock of traditional attachment to one party. See the observation by Key that "presidential voting preferences are more volatile than those in state and local elections." V. O. Key, Jr., *Politics, Parties, and Pressure Groups* (New York: Thomas Y. Crowell, 1958), 337. In some instances, a county was considered as carried by one party when that party's candidate obtained only a plurality of the vote. For those counties formed since 1872, the results in the original county were used in determining classification. For 1912, the Progressive (Bull Moose) vote was also counted as Republican.

[3] John H. Fenton, *Politics in the Border States* (New Orleans: Hauser Press, 1956), 63, says that many of the counties which were Republican after the 1896 election were put on the Republican path because of judicious use of money furnished Republican organizations therein by anti-Populist business elements. This money was important, says Fenton, in enabling the Republicans to gain control of local offices, thereby helping to maintain a Republican majority in the county.

[4] The counties, number of victories of Republican candidates, and average Republican percentage of the vote are as follows: Caldwell, 12, 49 percent; Hancock, 12, 46 percent; Hart, 10, 47 percent; Lawrence, 14, 49 percent; Lincoln, 6, 47 percent; Madison, 10, 48 percent; Muhlenberg, 15, 49 percent; and Washington, 12, 48 percent.

or earlier. In 50 of these counties all of the population resided in rural areas in 1960. In only three (Franklin, Henderson, and McCracken) did more than half of the populace live in urban areas. In the remaining counties, over half of the population lived in rural areas. It is generally acknowledged that in rural areas there are fewer forces to upset tradition than is the case in cities, though this contrast may be declining today with improvements in facilities for transportation and communication (especially television). Even so, the durability of devotion to one party in most rural areas is impressive. V. O. Key's surmise that "rural communities retain a greater capacity to transmit and maintain party loyalties than do metropolitan communities"[5] seems borne out in Kentucky.

PATTERNS OF STATE VOTING SINCE 1920

What type of party system does Kentucky have at present? There is no commonly accepted typology of party systems, and thus we must be arbitrary in our definitions. First of all, the state's "norm" in voting behavior must be determined. How many years must elapse before the norm is manifested? The 46 years of the period from 1920 to 1966 is an arbitrary period, but it is tenable because "it seems long enough to overcome the effects of any aberration from the state's 'norm.' "[6] Next, an arbitrary choice of election statistics must be made. Those used here are for presidential, United States senatorial, and gubernatorial elections "because they are generally regarded as the most important and because they are the only [sic] offices voted upon by state-wide constituencies."[7] From analysis of this statistical data, Kentucky can be classified as a two-party (or competitive) state, since the minority (Republican) party has won 16 of 44 statewide elections (36.4 percent). Table 5.1 contains the Republican statistics for each election during the period.

Table 5.1 shows a fairly competitive situation in Kentucky during the 1920 decade. The state's governor was a Republican until 1923 (elected in 1919), and another Republican was elected governor in

[5] *Politics, Parties, and Pressure Groups*, 267.

[6] Austin Ranney and Willmoore Kendall, *Democracy and the American Party System* (New York: Harcourt, Brace & Co., 1956), 161. Ranney and Kendall use only a 40-year period.

[7] *Ibid.* Of course, there are other state offices (lieutenant governor, treasurer, etc.) voted upon by statewide constituencies in many states, including Kentucky.

TABLE 5.1

Republican Percentage of Two-Party Vote in
Statewide Elections, 1920-1967

Year	President	U. S. Senator	Governor
1920	49.6	50.3	
1923			46.2
1924	51.4	51.6	
1926		48.2	
1927			52.1
1928	59.4		
1930		47.9	
1931			45.6
1932	40.5	40.6	
1935			45.3
1936	40.5	40.4	
1938		38.0	
1939			43.5
1940	42.4	41.7	
1942		44.7	
1943			50.8
1944	45.4	45.0	
1946		53.4	
1947			42.6
1948	42.2	48.5	
1950		45.4	
1951			45.4
1952	49.96	51.5	
1954		45.5	
1955			41.7
1956	54.6	50.3 (Morton)	
		53.2 (Cooper)	
1959			39.4
1960	53.6	59.1	
1962		52.1	
1963			49.3
1964	35.7		
1966		64.3	
1967			51.6

1927.[8] There were two Republican United States senators during this decade, and the Republicans carried Kentucky in the 1924 and 1928 presidential elections. Religion was undoubtedly a significant factor in Hoover's win in 1928, although the Republican victory in

[8] There were many irregularities in this election, and assertions that it was a stolen election. Jasper B. Shannon, "The Political Process In Kentucky," *Kentucky Law Journal,* XLV (1957), 427.

1924 suggests that it was not necessarily decisive. The economic depression beginning in 1929 helped the Democrats in Kentucky, as elsewhere in the nation. The state was solidly Democratic during the 1930 decade and on until the end of World War II, with one exception. This was in the gubernatorial election in the war year of 1943, when Judge Simeon S. Willis narrowly defeated the Democratic candidate. A factor undoubtedly contributing to the Democratic defeat that year was a bitterly fought Democratic primary for the gubernatorial nomination. The party split was not healed before the general election, and the Republican nominee benefited.

The two decades since the end of World War II have shown closer competition in statewide politics. Republicans have won seven of the ten United States senatorial elections during this period. Senator John Sherman Cooper has proved an extremely popular votegetter, and has won five of the seven times he has been a candidate. Senator Thruston B. Morton has been victorious both times he has run. His initial victory (in 1956) almost certainly was because of bitter factional wrangling in the Democratic party between the then governor, A. B. Chandler, and the then incumbent senator, Earle Clements. Chandler's lack of support for Clements was an open secret and was of crucial importance in Morton's narrow (50.3 percent) margin of victory.

In presidential elections during the past twenty years, the Democrats have won a bare majority of the times. Harry Truman won easily in 1948, but Adlai Stevenson had a microscopic majority of 700 votes in 1952. Dwight Eisenhower's large margin in 1956 was not equaled by Richard Nixon in 1960, who benefited substantially from the religious issue. Johnson's 1964 percentage in Kentucky was greater than his percentage in the nation, as many traditional Republican areas deserted the Goldwater candidacy in huge numbers. The "racial backlash," which led many persons to expect a very close outcome in the state, was apparently almost completely overridden by voter concerns over such issues as social security, the farm support program, and the Tennessee Valley Authority.

In the postwar period the Democrats have had the greatest success in gubernatorial elections, winning five of six times. The 1963 election was the closest one since the last Republican victory twenty years earlier. The racial issue apparently gained many votes for the Republican candidate, who was also aided by a Democratic split, again growing out of a bitter primary for the gubernatorial nomination. In 1967 the same Republican candidate, Louie B. Nunn, ran again and won 51.6 percent of the vote. Once again he was aided by splits within the Democratic party.

PATTERNS OF COUNTY VOTING SINCE 1920

It is now pertinent to attempt a closer analysis of the period. It is assumed that a 46-year period will show a norm; that is, a county can be classified as either "normally" Democratic or Republican by its voting record in statewide races during this period. Such a technique does not, however, show developments or trends because it necessitates wrenching the county out of a context in which time is an important element. The year from which one starts may have been a year in which a previously existing development had reached its climax, or in which a previously determined pattern was still exerting influence but which would subsequently be altered by events. It may have been a year of the unusual or abnormal resulting from a set of circumstances unique to that year. The 1920 election, for example, was "abnormal" in the sense that it was the first national election in which the reaction to the World War I and its aftermath was reflected. For the purposes of discussion, however, we will assume that the 46-year period will reflect "normal" voting behavior.

The next problem is to establish categories of classification. We will obviously use percentages of the two-party vote, and also the percentages of victory of one party for each county. A county with a very high average percentage of the vote for one party almost always is one that consistently is carried by that party's candidate, and thus is a one-party county. Occasionally, one party will win all or nearly all of the elections in one county by a relatively narrow margin (say, 52 or 53 percent of the vote), and thus on the basis of partisan victories the county could be called a Republican or Democratic county, as much so as if the vote had been consistently 70 or 75 percent Republican or Democratic. To ignore the percentage of the vote, therefore, can give rise to an unclear picture of the partisan situation in the county. Hence, in our classifications, we consider both percentage of victories and percentage of the vote.

A county is classified as "Strongly" one-party when the one party

FIGURE 5.2
Seven-Way Classification of Kentucky Counties Based on Statewide Elections, 1920-1966

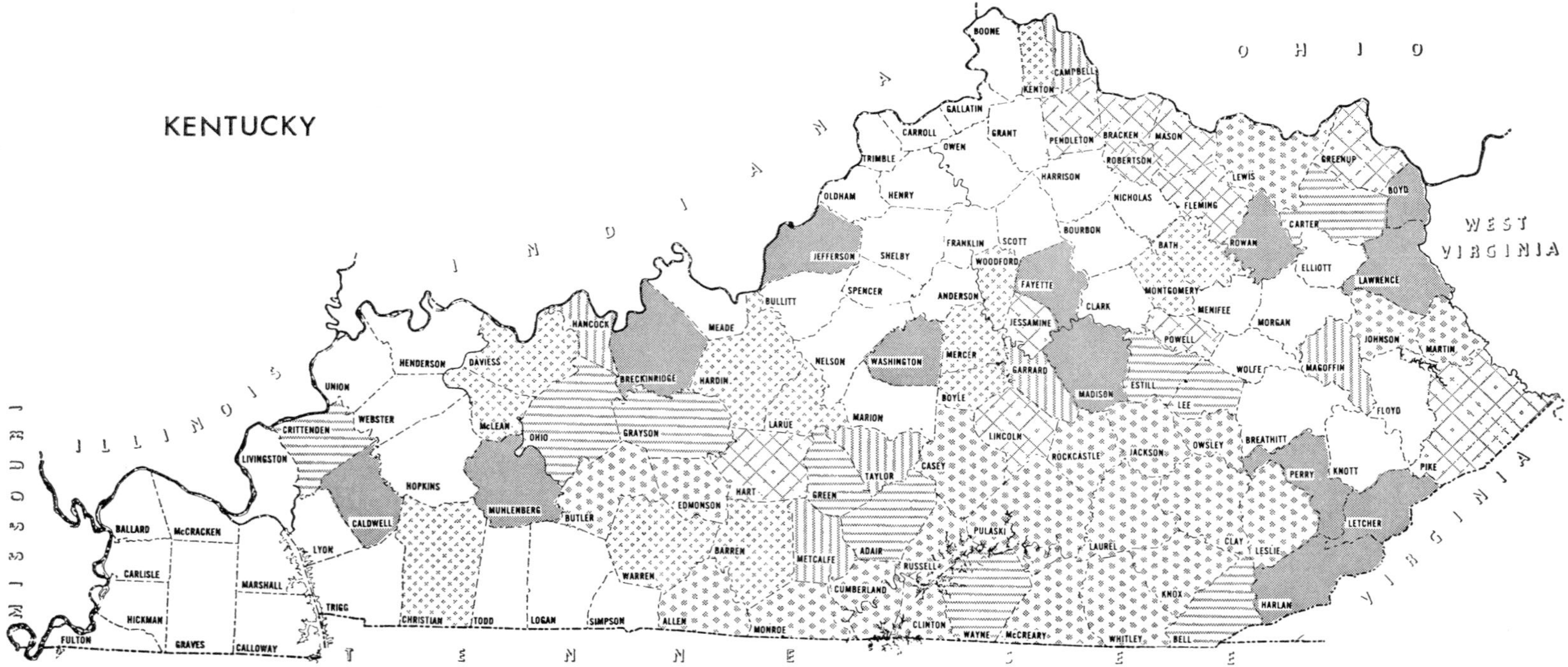

KENTUCKY

Strongly Democratic: Democratic majority in 2/3 or more races with median of average percentage of vote 60 or more

Democratic: Same with median of average percentage of vote 55 to 59.9

Democratically Inclined: Democratic majority in 60 percent or more of races with a median of average percentage of vote less than 55

Strongly Republican: Same criterion as for Strongly Democratic

Republican: Same criterion as for Democratic

Republican Inclined: Same criterion as for Democratically Inclined

Marginal: Won by neither party 60 percent of the elections has won the county in at least two-thirds (29) of the elections (a total of 43), with the median of the average percentage of the vote at least 60. This figure (the median of the average percentage of the vote) is derived as follows: the average Republican percentage of the vote in gubernatorial races for the period 1923-1963 is computed; the same figure in United States Senate races for 1920-1966 is computed; and the same is done for presidential races, 1920-1964. The middle (median) of these percentages is then ascertained. For example, Fayette County shows an average Republican percentage of the two-party vote of 51.9 in United States Senate races, 50.4 in presidential races, and 49.0 in gubernatorial races. Its median of the average Republican percentage of the vote is, therefore, 50.4. There is, as would be expected, some variation of the vote of many counties in national elections and in gubernatorial elections. In fact, some counties which return Republican majorities in national races show a decidedly Democratic performance in gubernatorial races; in a sense, they could be categorized Republican nationally, but Democratic in state races. However, the "normal" partisan preference of the county is assumed to be more correctly shown by using the median of the average percentage of the vote in the three races.

A county is classified as "Republican" or "Democratic" when the particular party has won two-thirds of the races with a median of the average percentage of the vote from 55 to 59.9. A county is classified as "Inclined" to one party when that party has won 60 percent or more of the elections, with the median of the average percentage of the vote of less than 55. The essential criterion used for this classification is the median of the average percentage of the vote. Some of the Inclined counties have been won by one party in over 80 percent of the elections. A county is classified as "Marginal" when neither party has won 60 percent of the elections therein. The median of the average percentage of the vote was not included in this classification, because it varied so many times from the rather close limits within which it would have had to be established. Figure 5.2 is a map showing the classifications of the 120 counties of Kentucky when the foregoing seven-way system of classification is used.

One can also classify the counties on the basis of the median of average percentage of the vote, disregarding the number of elections

KENTUCKY

Figure 5.3

Three-Way Classification of Kentucky Counties Based on Statewide Elections, 1920-1966

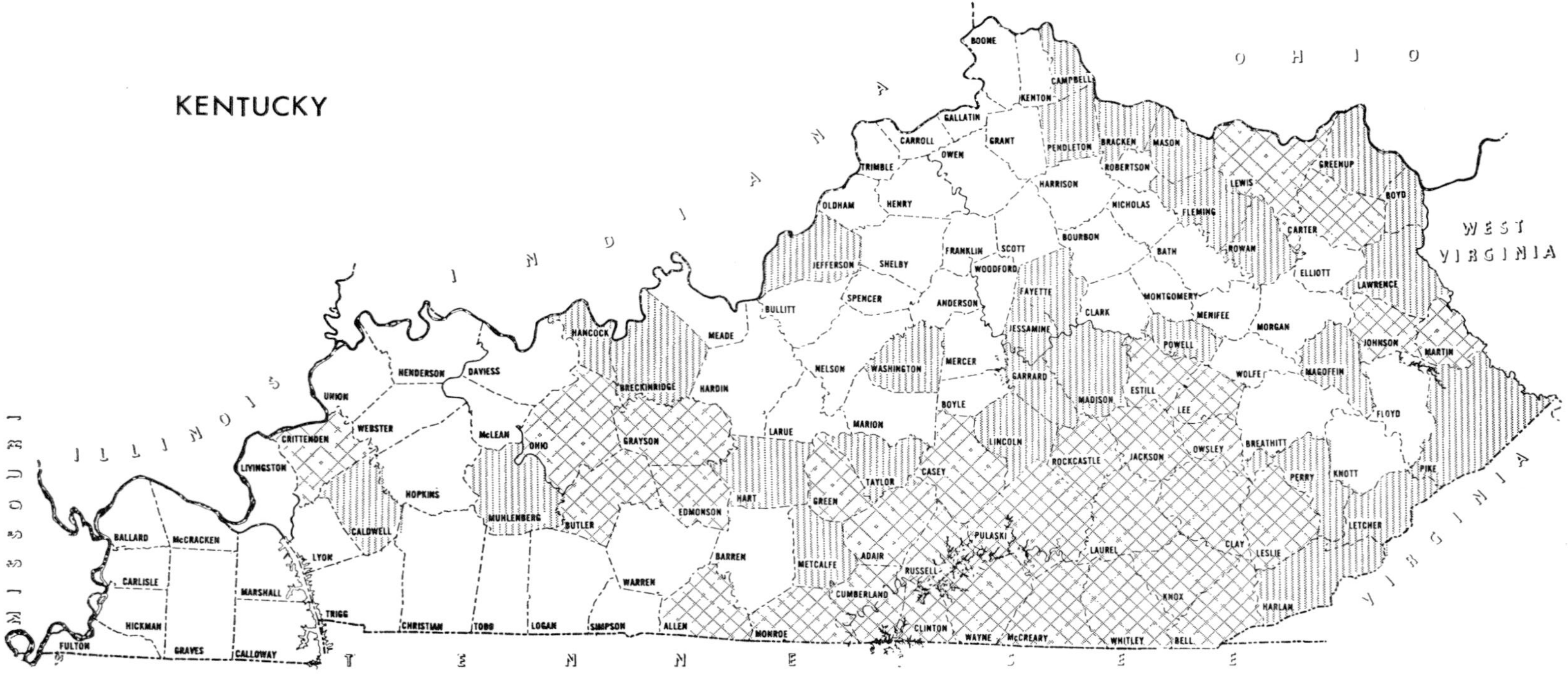

Democratic: Median of average percentage of vote 55 or more (frequency of victories disregarded)

Republican: Median of average percentage of vote 55 or more (frequency of victories disregarded)

Marginal: Median of average percentage of vote less than 55 for either party (frequency of victories disregarded) won by either party. Using as a criterion for such classification a median of the average percentage of the vote of less than 55 for the Marginal classification, one finds that all 16 of the counties classified as Inclined to one party by the previous method are now classified as Marginal. Figure 5.3 illustrates the difference. This criterion of Marginal (median of average percentage of vote less than 55, with frequency of victories disregarded) will be used in what follows, unless otherwise indicated.

TABLE 5.2

Increasing Importance of Marginal Counties

	PER THREE-WAY CLASSIFICATION					
	Total Population			Percentage of Population		
Year	*Marginal*	*Democratic*	*Republican*	*Marginal*	*Democratic*	*Republican*
1960	1,369,221	1,200,205	468,730	45.0	39.6	15.4
1950	1,264,568	1,127,978	552,260	42.9	38.4	18.7
1940	1,152,330	1,101,941	591,356	40.5	38.7	20.8

	PERCENTAGE OF POPULATION CHANGE			
	Marginal	*Democratic*	*Republican*	*Kentucky*
1950-1960	8.3	6.4	−15.1	3.2
1940-1960	18.9	8.9	−20.7	6.7

	PER SEVEN-WAY CLASSIFICATION					
	Total Population			Percentage of Population		
Year	*Marginal*	*Democratic*[a]	*Republican*[a]	*Marginal*	*Democratic*[a]	*Republican*[a]
1960	1,036,376	1,395,362	606,418	34.1	46.0	19.9
1950	925,729	1,335,490	683,587	31.8	45.0	23.2
1940	815,236	1,306,501	723,890	28.6	45.9	25.5

	PERCENTAGE OF POPULATION CHANGE		
	Marginal	*Democratic*	*Republican*
1950-1960	11.9	4.5	−11.3
1940-1960	27.1	6.8	−16.2

[a] Democratic includes Democratic Inclined and Strongly Democratic; Republican includes Republican Inclined and Strongly Republican.

Analysis of the counties using the three-way classification reveals that the Marginal counties are of greatest importance in determining the victors in statewide races. The indications, too, are that these counties will become increasingly important in this respect. Table 5.2 illustrates these facts statistically.

Nearly all of the important urbanized-industrialized counties of the state are included within the Marginal classification.[9] Jefferson County alone constitutes over one-fifth of the population of Kentucky. Adding the five next most important urban-industrial counties (Fayette, Kenton, Campbell, Daviess, and Boyd) produces a population (1,073,107) that in 1960 was over one-third of the entire state. In the process of increasing industrialization and urbanization of Kentucky,[10] these counties become of greater and greater importance in influencing the outcome of statewide races. More and more persons leave the rural-agricultural areas of the state in search of better living and end up in these urban and industrial counties. The table shows that losses in the Republican counties have been greatest in the 1940-1960 period. Democratic counties, while gaining population absolutely, have gained less than the Marginal counties. Because Democratic counties are generally wealthier than the traditional Republican counties, there is less pressure on their residents to migrate in search of better economic opportunities.

Another significant fact resulting from an analysis of the counties is that most of the really poverty-stricken counties of the state are in the Republican classification. Table 5.3 indicates that, in general, the Republican counties are poorer than the Democratic and Marginal counties. Of 21 counties in Kentucky which had median family incomes of under $2,000 in 1959, 15 are Republican (which is just under one-half of the 31 Republican counties). Only 4 of the 60 Democratic counties are so impoverished, and only two of the Marginal counties. The Republican counties also lagged behind in the increasing prosperity of the 1949-1959 decade. Measured by median family income, the state as a whole almost doubled (an increase of 99.36 percent). The median Republican county increased by 82 percent, the median Democratic county by 100 percent, and the median Marginal county by 93.3 percent.

9 Henderson, McCracken, and Warren counties are the major exceptions. Daviess and Kenton counties are, practically speaking, Marginal, as they only miss the above definition of Marginal by 0.1 and 0.2 percentage points, respectively.

10 According to census data, in 1939 Kentucky had 1,582 manufacturing establishments employing 76,504 persons, with an annual payroll of $89,004,000. By 1958 these figures had increased to 2,850 manufacturing establishments employing 157,754 persons with an annual payroll of $693,174,000. By 1965 manufacturing employment had increased to 192,830. Louisville *Courier-Journal*, Feb. 3, 1967. The relative decline of agriculture is indicated by the fact that in 1939 the income of farmowners was 14.5 percent of all the money earned in Kentucky, whereas in 1961 this figure was only slightly over 7 percent. *Ibid.*, Nov. 12, 1963.

TABLE 5.3

Economic Status of Republican, Democratic, and Marginal Counties

Median Family Income, 1959	Republican Counties	Democratic Counties	Marginal Counties
upper quartile	$2,957-2,449	$5,794-3,865	$5,932-3,847
lower quartile	1,324-1,833	1,432-2,860	1,504-2,637
MFI in median county	2,059	3,319	3,088
Percentage increase, 1959 MFI over 1949 MFI			
upper quartile	152-110	202-118	162-102
lower quartile	42-60	27-85	34-78
median county	82	100	93

We have now reached a convenient point at which to consider some of the changes which have occurred since 1920, and to attempt to ascertain trends which may continue in the future. The methodology used in delineating the changes occurring in the 1920-1966 period is as follows: the median of the average Republican percentage of the vote was calculated for three periods of time within the 46-year span, and comparisons were then made between the resulting medians of averages. The first period, 1920-1932, is chosen because it reflects the vote for over one-fourth of the total time span and because it was, by and large, one of prosperity. Even though the Great Depression started in 1929 and the voters reacted to it in the 1932 election, the latter election is included in the first period. This is because the New Deal did not actually begin until Roosevelt's accession to office in 1933, and the electorate could not be aware of its effects until it had been in operation. Therefore, the first election considered as occurring in the New Deal era is in 1935. The terminal date for this second period is 1944, because by then the New Deal had run its course and Roosevelt last ran for office that year. The third and last division of the 46-year period begins with the election of 1946. This year was chosen because it was the year of the first national election after the end of World War II. Table 5.4 shows how each county in the state performed in each of the three periods, how it is classified by the seven-way method of classification, and also how each county performed and was classified for the entire 46-year period.

Scrutiny of the computations for the three-way division of the

TABLE 5.4

*Partisan Classification of Counties and Median of Average
Republican Percentages of Two-Party Vote for Various Periods*

County	1920-1966	1946-1966	1935-1944	1920-1932
Jackson	SR 87.4	SR 85.4	SR 87.7	SR 89.2
Leslie	SR 82.8	SR 76.1	SR 82.4	SR 88.6
Owsley	SR 82.5	SR 80.2	SR 82.3	SR 83.9
Clinton	SR 79.1	SR 78.7	SR 75.7	SR 78.9
McCreary	SR 77.3	SR 75.5	SR 75.0	SR 80.7
Clay	SR 73.6	SR 71.0	SR 74.4	SR 75.0
Martin	SR 72.9	SR 67.6	SR 73.0	SR 78.5
Monroe	SR 72.2	SR 73.8	SR 69.6	SR 70.4
Cumberland	SR 71.8	SR 69.8	SR 71.2	SR 72.3
Rockcastle	SR 70.8	SR 71.8	SR 71.1	SR 68.7
Butler	SR 70.8	SR 70.9	SR 70.2	SR 70.5
Whitley	SR 69.7	SR 66.5	SR 66.4	SR 74.8
Russell	SR 68.8	SR 68.5	SR 67.4	SR 66.8
Laurel	SR 68.7	SR 69.0	SR 66.4	SR 66.7
Casey	SR 68.2	SR 71.1	SR 67.1	SR 63.1
Pulaski	SR 67.3	SR 69.0	SR 61.8	SR 61.4
Edmonson	SR 66.6	SR 68.5	SR 67.3	SR 61.5
Lewis	SR 66.4	SR 66.1	SR 65.2	SR 65.4
Johnson	SR 65.5	SR 63.4	SR 62.7	SR 67.7
Knox	SR 64.4	SR 62.1	SR 62.7	SR 71.3
Allen	SR 61.3	SR 60.8	SR 60.4	SR 55.8
Adair	R 58.5	SR 60.4	R 57.3	RI 53.2
Carter	R 58.1	RI 54.5	R 57.8	SR 60.9
Green	R 58.1	R 59.8	R 55.2	RI 53.3
Ohio	R 57.8	R 59.4	R 55.4	RI 53.9
Grayson	R 57.6	SR 61.4	R 55.3	RI 53.6
Crittenden	R 57.6	SR 60.8	R 59.4	R 56.6
Wayne	R 57.1	R 57.8	R 55.1	R 56.7
Lee	R 56.4	R 58.3	R 55.7	M 51.8
Bell	R 55.8	RI 50.5	M 46.8	SR 65.8
Estill	R 55.7	R 56.8	RI 53.7	M 52.1
Metcalfe	RI 54.5	RI 51.0	R 55.9	RI 53.3
Garrard	RI 54.5	RI 54.3	M 51.0	RI 53.0
Taylor	RI 53.8	R 55.5	M 50.5	M 50.6
Campbell	RI 51.9	RI 53.4	M 46.8	RI 53.4
Harlan	M 51.8	DI 44.5	SD 39.3	SR 73.2
Perry	M 51.8	M 46.7	D 43.7	R 58.7
Magoffin	RI 51.4	M 49.5	M 50.0	R 57.3
Hancock	RI 50.2	RI 50.0	M 50.5	M 49.2
Breckinridge	M 51.2	M 49.8	DI 50.1	RI 52.1

TABLE 5.4 *(Continued)*

County	1920-1966	1946-1966	1935-1944	1920-1932
Letcher	M 50.7	DI 46.4	DI 42.3	SR 61.1
Lawrence	M 50.6	RI 49.2	M 50.0	M 50.6
Fayette	M 50.4	RI 53.0	D 44.3	M 51.7
Muhlenberg	M 50.1	DI 47.3	RI 49.7	RI 51.1
Boyd	M 49.9	RI 48.7	DI 47.8	M 53.3
Lincoln	DI 49.5	RI 50.2	DI 47.0	DI 46.0
Washington	M 49.4	M 48.2	M 49.0	M 49.3
Jefferson	M 49.3	RI 49.9	D 41.3	RI 53.9
Caldwell	M 49.3	M 49.8	DI 45.4	M 49.0
Madison	M 49.2	M 48.0	DI 48.2	M 49.7
Rowan	M 49.1	DI 46.0	D 46.7	M 50.8
Greenup	DI 48.9	DI 46.9	DI 47.1	M 49.7
Fleming	DI 48.7	M 48.1	DI 48.4	DI 47.1
Hart	DI 48.6	M 47.8	DI 48.2	DI 48.2
Pendleton	DI 47.8	DI 48.1	DI 46.6	D 42.1
Mason	DI 46.8	DI 47.0	DI 45.8	D 43.8
Bracken	DI 46.7	DI 46.7	D 41.9	D 44.0
Powell	DI 46.4	DI 46.4	DI 45.4	D 43.7
Pike	DI 46.1	D 42.4	D 43.2	M 51.4
Jessamine	DI 45.4	DI 47.8	D 41.3	D 42.7
Daviess	D 45.0	M 50.0	SD 37.1	D 41.0
Kenton	D 44.9	DI 47.5	SD 36.8	M 46.1
Christian	D 44.2	SD 39.1	DI 45.6	RI 50.7
Mercer	D 43.8	D 45.6	SD 37.2	D 41.6
Warren	D 43.0	DI 46.4	SD 36.7	D 40.6
McLean	D 42.7	DI 43.9	D 40.2	SD 39.7
Barren	D 42.6	D 41.9	D 40.8	D 40.6
Larue	D 42.4	DI 46.4	SD 36.9	SD 39.6
Woodford	D 41.9	DI 42.9	SD 37.2	D 43.3
Bath	D 41.6	SD 39.9	SD 39.8	D 41.8
Boyle	D 41.5	D 42.2	SD 37.0	D 40.2
Hardin	D 41.5	D 44.8	SD 35.3	SD 37.8
Montgomery	D 41.1	SD 39.7	SD 38.4	D 40.9
Robertson	D 40.5	D 40.5	SD 40.0	SD 36.4
Bourbon	SD 39.8	SD 36.1	SD 37.1	D 44.2
Grant	SD 39.7	SD 38.9	SD 36.3	SD 37.2
Boone	SD 39.2	DI 46.7	SD 29.9	SD 29.9
Livingston	SD 39.2	SD 38.2	SD 37.9	SD 39.8
Anderson	SD 39.1	SD 39.7	SD 36.1	SD 38.9
Clark	SD 38.8	D 40.6	SD 34.5	SD 37.6
Oldham	SD 38.4	DI 45.5	SD 30.7	SD 30.3

TABLE 5.4 *(Continued)*

County	1920-1966	1946-1966	1935-1944	1920-1932
Hopkins	SD 37.8	SD 37.6	SD 31.7	D 40.9
Henderson	SD 37.4	SD 38.7	SD 26.3	M 44.6
Nelson	SD 36.8	SD 39.6	SD 33.8	SD 35.5
Webster	SD 36.4	SD 33.4	SD 32.8	D 42.7
Nicholas	SD 36.3	SD 35.0	SD 36.1	SD 35.8
Spencer	SD 36.3	SD 37.0	SD 27.9	SD 34.3
Meade	SD 36.2	SD 36.2	SD 31.8	SD 37.1
Scott	SD 35.9	SD 36.5	SD 31.0	SD 36.7
Wolfe	SD 35.7	SD 34.2	SD 34.6	SD 37.3
Trigg	SD 35.6	SD 30.5	SD 34.3	D 41.5
Lyon	SD 35.5	SD 34.7	SD 33.2	SD 37.2
Floyd	SD 35.4	SD 30.5	SD 29.7	D 41.5
Marion	SD 35.0	SD 34.8	SD 34.3	SD 35.5
Shelby	SD 34.9	SD 34.7	SD 29.7	SD 37.2
Menifee	SD 34.8	SD 34.2	SD 34.4	SD 35.6
Bullitt	SD 34.6	SD 38.5	SD 25.7	SD 31.1
Todd	SD 33.8	SD 31.7	SD 30.6	SD 37.6
McCracken	SD 33.2	SD 30.8	SD 24.8	SD 38.1
Harrison	SD 32.4	SD 31.9	SD 28.5	SD 31.1
Logan	SD 31.8	SD 32.8	SD 27.6	SD 37.8
Henry	SD 31.0	SD 29.7	SD 28.9	SD 31.7
Breathitt	SD 30.9	SD 28.7	SD 29.4	SD 37.9
Morgan	SD 30.8	SD 28.0	SD 27.3	SD 34.5
Simpson	SD 30.3	SD 30.7	SD 26.8	SD 30.2
Franklin	SD 30.1	SD 30.0	SD 23.5	SD 32.3
Marshall	SD 29.2	SD 29.7	SD 26.4	SD 27.2
Gallatin	SD 29.0	SD 27.2	SD 24.7	SD 28.0
Union	SD 27.3	SD 30.4	SD 19.5	SD 26.9
Carroll	SD 26.9	SD 26.3	SD 22.0	SD 26.0
Elliott	SD 25.8	SD 26.1	SD 23.6	SD 26.2
Fulton	SD 24.0	SD 28.8	SD 17.8	SD 20.3
Knott	SD 23.4	SD 19.9	SD 18.0	SD 23.5
Graves	SD 23.0	SD 24.5	SD 18.2	SD 23.8
Hickman	SD 22.5	SD 24.3	SD 16.9	SD 19.9
Calloway	SD 21.5	SD 24.8	SD 15.5	SD 18.8
Carlisle	SD 20.3	SD 22.5	SD 17.8	SD 14.8
Owen	SD 20.3	SD 21.4	SD 15.7	SD 19.3
Ballard	SD 19.6	SD 20.5	SD 18.4	SD 18.3
Trimble	SD 17.0	SD 18.8	SD 13.4	SD 14.0
KENTUCKY	DI 47.07	M 47.1	SD 37.2	M 43.3

1920-1966 period reveals that partisan changes have occurred in a number of Kentucky's counties, breaking the mold set by the Civil War era in many counties. The New Deal regime of Franklin D. Roosevelt caused a long-term realignment of some groups in Kentucky, as in other states. Political behavior in some counties in the post-World War II period indicates a considerable change from the earliest periods, probably of a lasting nature. The map in Figure 5.4 shows these changes and trends.

The most prominent gains by the Democrats are in a group of counties in the extreme southeastern part of the state—the great coal-mining center—and the changes here are attributable to the welfare and labor policies of the New Deal and the unionization of the mines during the early 1930s.[11] Five of these counties (Bell, Harlan, Letcher, Magoffin, and Perry) were Republican during the 1920-1932 period, with median of average Republican percentages ranging from 57 to 73. Declines during the New Deal period have been recouped to some extent, so that the counties are now Marginal. Two of the counties (Breathitt and Floyd) are traditionally Democratic strongholds made stronger by the New Deal experience, while three counties (Knox, Leslie, and Martin) have adhered to their traditional Republicanism, but with lower percentages since the New Deal. The other county (Pike) was Marginal prior to the depression and has subsequently been Democratically Inclined.

Three contiguous southwestern counties have shown consistent Democratic gains during the period since 1920. These are counties where the Negro population is relatively high (16, 17, and 22.4 percent in 1960; statewide 7.2 percent). Christian County was Republican Inclined during the 1920-1932 period, following a traditional pattern set after the Civil War and Reconstruction era. Todd and Trigg counties were Democratic during the 1920-1932 period, as had generally been the case since the Civil War. In the United States as a whole the traditional Negro attachment to the Republicans was shifted to the Democrats by the New Deal welfare programs. This is what apparently happened in these three counties.[12] It is also probably a factor in Logan and McCracken counties, where

[11] Fenton, *Politics in the Border States*, 66-68; Jasper B. Shannon and Ruth McQuown, *Presidential Politics in Kentucky, 1824-1948* (Lexington: University of Kentucky Bureau of Government Research, 1950), 111, 114.

[12] Fenton, *Politics in the Border States*, 69-71.

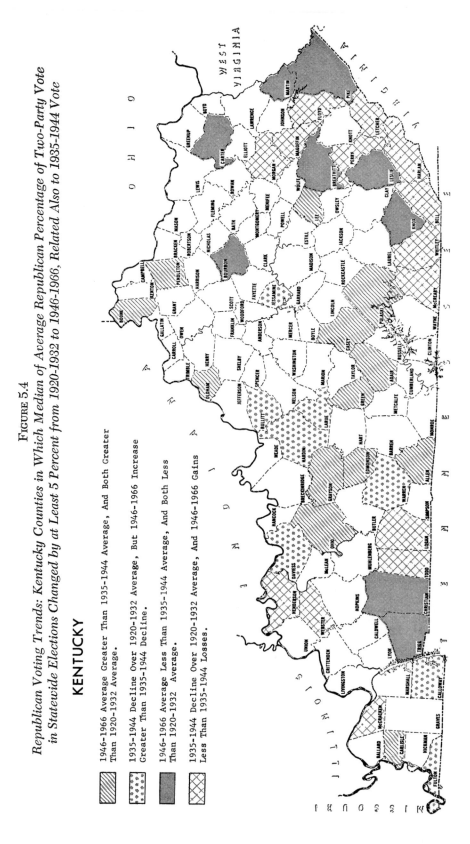

FIGURE 5.4

Republican Voting Trends: Kentucky Counties in Which Median of Average Republican Percentage of Two-Party Vote in Statewide Elections Changed by at Least 5 Percent from 1920-1932 to 1946-1966, Related Also to 1935-1944 Vote

KENTUCKY

1946-1966 Average Greater Than 1935-1944 Average, And Both Greater Than 1920-1932 Average.

1935-1944 Decline Over 1920-1932 Average, But 1946-1966 Increase Greater Than 1935-1944 Decline.

1946-1966 Average Less Than 1935-1944 Average, And Both Less Than 1920-1932 Average.

1935-1944 Decline Over 1920-1932 Average, And 1946-1966 Gains Less Than 1935-1944 Losses.

Republican losses in New Deal days have not been regained in the postwar period; the Negro population in these two counties is also above the state average.

Republican gains shown on the map in Figure 5.4[13]—most of which have occurred in the postwar period—have occurred in a variety of counties, making impossible any obvious and simple analysis. Many are traditionally Republican counties which have become more strongly Republican. They are agricultural, rural, and poor (1959 median family income ranged from $2,842 to $1,802), and the 1949-1959 increase in the median family income has not been especially great (the increase ranged from 152 to 70 percent, the increase in half of the counties being above the Kentucky increase of 99.36 percent, the increase in the other half being less). There is a more varied picture in the Democratic counties which show Republican gains. Boone and Oldham counties, which are within the category of counties with consistent Republican gains, are among the richest counties of the state in terms of median family income ($5,794 and $4,808, respectively, in 1959) and enjoyed an increase in prosperity in the 1949-1959 decade at a rate higher than the state as a whole (148 and 128 percent respectively). Both counties are near metropolitan areas and contain many suburbanites. The prosperity here is doubtless a factor in the increased Republican performance. The remaining counties show diversity in wealth (1959 median family income ranged from $4,640 to $1,930), increase in prosperity (1959 median family income increased over that in 1949 from 161 to only 27 percent), and are predominantly rural-agricultural, although six of them have substantial manufacturing operations within their borders. Daviess County is the one urban and industrial county in the group.

The Marginal counties with Republican gains show similar divergencies: median family income in 1959 varied from $4,786 to $2,498, and prosperity increased from 66 to 162 percent. Four counties are agricultural; three others are counties where about as many employees work in manufacturing concerns as work in agricultural enterprises.

Many counties where Republican gains have been less than the

[13] Only those counties where the 1946-1966 Republican performance exceeds that of 1920-1932 by 5 percentage points or more are considered. A change of less than that is deemed insignificant.

TABLE 5.5

Counties Showing Change of at Least Five Points in Median of Average Percentage of Vote between 1920-1944 and 1946-1966 Periods

Republican Gains		Democratic Gains	
	Percentage		*Percentage*
County	*Points Gain*	*County*	*Points Gain*
Boone	16.8	Harlan	14.2
Oldham	15.1	Christian	9.2
Daviess	10.8	Martin	9.2
Fulton	7.6	Leslie	9.0
Pulaski	7.6	Trigg	8.6
Bullitt	7.3	Bell	7.2
Larue	6.9	Floyd	5.8
Hardin	6.8	Letcher	5.8
Warren	6.3	Breathitt	5.7
Casey	6.0	Whitley	5.6
Carlisle	5.9	Pike	5.5
Calloway	5.8	Bourbon	5.1
Grayson	5.6	Webster	5.1
Hickman	5.4	Carter	5.0
Kenton	5.4		
Union	5.3		
Jessamine	5.2		
Taylor	5.2		

gains in the above counties, or where the Democrats have gained, have characteristics in common with, or similar to, the counties just previously considered. There is, therefore, no discernible common denominator suggesting the reasons for the changes in voting behavior.[14]

Another way of viewing changes which have occurred during the 1920-1966 period is to ascertain what differences are shown when comparisons are made between the median of the average Republican percentage of the vote in the 1946-1966 period and the same for the 1920-1944 period. This is, in other words, breaking the 46-year period into approximate halves and comparing the partisan performance in each half. It is found that in 66 counties the Republican performance for the 1946-1966 period exceeds that of the earlier period. In 52 counties, the reverse is true. Two counties show no change. Thirty-two of the counties (listed in Table 5.5)

[14] Of the remaining 76 counties, 40 show Republican postwar gains over the 1920-1932 period, 35 show losses, and 1 shows no change.

show changes of five percentage points or more;[15] 86 counties show changes of less than five percentage points.

URBAN COUNTIES: GROWING IMPORTANCE

We have indicated previously that the urban areas now comprise over one-third of Kentucky's electorate. This makes it unnecessary to comment extensively on their importance to Kentucky's politics. How do they behave politically in relation to the rest of the state? How do the two parties perform in these important areas? How have they performed in them in the period since 1920? Do the urban areas show politically relevant characteristics which are similar to those of other urban areas throughout the United States?

The definition of urban county used here will be a county that has a city with a population of at least 25,000. The election statistics used will be those for the county in which the city is located, not just the statistics for the city alone, because the county is the basic unit for reporting election statistics. Since some cities have grown to 25,000 or more since 1920, the urban statistics considered in what follows will not apply to the same group of counties for all elections. In other words, the constant is counties with cities of at least 25,000 population.[16]

The growth of urban political power is demonstrated in Table 5.6. Part of the growth is due to the inclusion of counties containing cities which have reached a population level of 25,000 (Warren in 1960, Daviess in 1940, and Boyd in 1930). This is shown by the figures resulting when these three counties are excluded from the two most recent elections: the urban percentage of the total vote in Kentucky is then 34.6 for the 1964 presidential election, and 31.2 for the 1967 gubernatorial election. These figures reveal an increase of nearly ten percentage points in the urban proportion of the total Kentucky vote in presidential elections since 1920. The correspond-

---

[15] All but 4 of these 32 counties are included in Figure 5.4 and the discussion thereof. The 4 counties, all of which show a Republican increase, are Hickman, Kenton, Taylor, and Union.

[16] Campbell, Fayette, Jefferson, Kenton, and McCracken are included in all elections. Boyd County was excluded before 1930, Daviess County before 1940, and Warren County before 1960. Under the United States Census Bureau's definition of urban (which is defined as any town of at least 2,500 population), the percentages of Kentucky's population residing in urban areas were as follows: 29.8 in 1940, 36.8 in 1950, and 44.5 in 1960.

TABLE 5.6

Urban County Vote as Percentage of Total Vote, 1920-1967

Gubernatorial Elections		Presidential Elections	
Year	Percentage	Year	Percentage
1967	36.8	1964	39.9
1963	37.0	1960	38.5
1959	32.1	1956	34.5
1955	30.9	1952	34.2
1951	32.6	1948	32.5
1947	31.3	1944	30.8
1943	30.1	1940	30.8
1939	27.4	1936	27.7
1935	24.4	1932	26.4
1931	26.6	1928	28.9
1927	30.8	1924	23.7
1923	26.6	1920	23.5

ing increase in gubernatorial elections is slightly under five percentage points. This difference in increase between the two types of elections is probably attributable, to some extent, to the fact that the urban areas contain more out-of-state "immigrants" who become interested in state elections more slowly than in national elections.

Table 5.7 contains data regarding voting in the urban and non-urban counties in Kentucky. The data show that, for the entire period since 1920, the Democratic candidates have held a very slight advantage in the urban areas. The Republicans have carried the urban counties in 18 of 32 national elections, while the Democrats have carried the urban areas in 8 of 12 gubernatorial elections during the period. In all, the Democrats have carried the urban areas in 22 of 44 elections held since 1920. A more competitive situation could hardly exist.

The most significant finding in Table 5.7 is that the Republicans have been more successful in urban than in nonurban counties in every period except the New Deal. This has been true for presidential, gubernatorial, and senatorial elections. Moreover, Republican voting strength has been greater in urban than in rural counties in every election since 1946, except the 1960 presidential and the 1951 and 1967 gubernatorial elections. The Republican percentage has been more than four points higher in the urban counties in 13 of the 21 elections during the postwar period, including those at both the state and national levels. President Eisenhower and

TABLE 5.7

Average Republican Percentages of Two-Party Vote in Urban and Nonurban Counties in Presidential, Gubernatorial, and Senatorial Elections for Four Periods since 1920

Year	Urban	Nonurban	Kentucky
PRESIDENTIAL ELECTIONS			
1964	36.8	35.1	35.7
1960	52.3	54.5	53.6
1956	58.1	52.7	54.6
1952	53.2	48.2	49.9
1948	44.9	40.7	42.2
1948-1964 Average	49.1	46.2	47.2
1936-1944 Average	40.5	43.7	42.8
1920-1932 Average	52.5	49.5	50.2
1920-1964 Average	48.1	46.7	47.1
GUBERNATORIAL ELECTIONS			
1967	51.0	52.0	51.6
1963	50.3	48.6	49.3
1959	44.5	37.0	39.4
1955	44.6	40.3	41.7
1951	45.3	45.5	45.4
1947	44.5	41.7	42.6
1947-1967 Average	46.7	44.2	45.0
1935-1943 Average	45.0	47.1	46.6
1923-1931 Average	50.1	46.8	48.0
1923-1967 Average	47.1	45.6	46.1
SENATORIAL ELECTIONS			
1966	65.6	63.5	64.3
1962	55.8	50.8	52.8
1960	59.5	58.9	59.1
1956 (Cooper)	55.8	51.8	53.2
1956 (Morton)	53.9	48.4	50.3
1954	48.8	43.9	45.5
1952	54.7	49.8	51.5
1950	49.2	43.7	45.4
1948	51.6	46.9	48.5
1946	56.2	52.1	53.4
Average 1946-1966	55.1	51.0	52.4
Average 1936-1944	40.4	42.6	42.0
Average 1920-1932	51.3	46.5	47.7
Average 1920-1966	50.5	47.7	48.6

Senator Morton ran particularly well in the urban areas, while Richard Nixon, Barry Goldwater, Governor Nunn, and, in recent years, Senator Cooper ran more impressively in rural counties than did the average Republican candidate.

Although the difference in voting results between urban and nonurban areas has not been large, it has been consistent. As Table 5.6 indicates, the urban areas are gaining an increasing share of the voting population. This means that, with the decline in the population of traditional Republican counties, a larger share of the Republican votes is to be found in the urban counties. In the 1946 senatorial, 1947 gubernatorial, and 1948 presidential elections, the average percentage of the statewide Republican vote which came from the eight counties that we have defined as urban (including Warren) was 34.6. In the 1962 senatorial, 1963 gubernatorial, and 1964 presidential elections, the average percentage of the statewide Republican vote from these same counties had risen to 40.2. Urbanization means that an increasing proportion of the electorate will reside in politically competitive areas and less in one-party areas. Because more of the one-party areas have been under Democratic control, a decline in the "safe" vote will hurt the Democratic party more. The shift in population to the cities and suburbs, therefore, seems certain to make Kentucky politics increasingly competitive in partisan terms.

URBAN COUNTIESS SOCIOECONOMIC VARIATIONS IN VOTING

Since the urban areas are becoming increasingly important in the political configuration of Kentucky and since tradition in the cities has a less potent effect on political behavior than in the rural sections of the state, it is worthwhile to look for any significant patterns of political behavior within the urban areas. Are there perceptible differences in the response of different socioeconomic groups to the appeals of the candidates of the two parties? Do any such differences in voting behavior of social groups accord with behavior of identical groups throughout the United States as a whole?

The data which follow were obtained by using census tract information applied to the precincts in Jefferson and Fayette counties (the only two counties for which such information is available). By comparing maps of voting precincts with the census maps and other census information, we can determine in a given precinct the

TABLE 5.8

Socioeconomic and Voting Patterns in Jefferson County

Median Family Income	No. of Precincts	Percentage Negro[a]	Average Republican Percentage of Vote in Precincts										
			1966 U.S. Sen.	1965 Co. Judge	1964 Pres.	1963 Gov.	1962 U.S. Sen.	1962 U.S. HR	1961 Ky. HR	1960 Pres.	1960 U.S. Sen.	1960 U.S. HR	1959 Gov.
$16,231	6[b]	7	87	83	67	68	84	75	79	79	85	80	74
12,447	1		88	82	44	66	81	70	78	77	86	74	76
10,190–10,603	5		74	71	48	54	67	55	65	57	71	56	62
9,719–9,923	7		76	75	43	52	65	53	63	53	70	53	61
9,403	5		74	67	37	48	63	52	62	55	68	55	57
9,256	5		76	77	48	56	69	61	68	61	72	61	62
8,700–8,919	8[c]		78	80	52	57	72	62	68	55	66	55	54
7,151–7,542	9		70	64	40	53	59	52	56	55	65	54	51
6,203–6,447	5		56	53	32	47	51	46	48	45	56	45	48
Median Family Income in Jefferson County $5,796													
5,513	3		55	56	36	49	44	45	50	42	51	41	46
5,478	4	42	57	53	7	25	35	34	59	39	49	40	45
5,327	2	28.6	62	61	21	41	45	43	60	39	46	40	42
5,223–5,314	6		55	54	33	52	50	48	50	45	51	46	44
4,970	5	30	55	51	17	39	43	42	55	39	44	40	43
4,509–4,571	7[d]		52	51	33	50	46	44	40	31	36	31	39
3,417	2[e]	26	70	61	44	61	56	55	56	43	45	42	47
3,232	1	23	70	65	34	56	61	58	52	46	50	47	40
2,848	1		39	37	26	33	35	32	24	34	34	33	26
2,578–2,669	4[f]	35–42	58	54	20	50	51	51	51	35	37	36	36
Coefficient of rank correlation			.766	.768	.688	.427	.716	.582	.787	.787	.936	.844	.943

TABLE 5.8 (Continued)

Median Family Income	No. of Precincts	Percentage Negro[a]	Average Republican Percentage of Vote in Precincts										
			1966 U.S. Sen.	1965 Co. Judge	1964 Pres.	1963 Gov.	1962 U.S. Sen.	1962 U.S. HR	Ky. HR	1961 1960 Pres.	1960 U.S. Sen.	1960 U.S. HR	1959 Gov.
					PRECINCTS WITH NEGRO MAJORITY								
5,430	1	87.3	68	48	3	15	26	27	70	34	46	40	45
3,893	4	72.4	55	51	14	42	48	46	58	43	48	44	46
3,406-3,816	3	82-86	63	54	6	46	54	52	62	46	49	47	52
3,064-3,254	4[g]	89-93	57	53	7	46	47	47	63	37	39	38	47
2,750	1	87	42	30	11	44	46	45	49	40	41	41	47
2,475-2,517	5[h]	91-96	57	56	12	40	48	48	64	44	46	45	52
1,932	4[j]	95	44	43	4	41	44	44	52	36	35	35	39
Coefficient of rank correlation			.617	.072	-.100	-.009	.045	-.100	.429	-.070	.634	.250	-.053

[a] No number indicates Negro percentage of less than 5.
[b] 5 in $16,321 income level prior to 1961.
[c] 7 in $8,700-8,919 income level prior to 1961.
[d] 4 in $4,509-4,571 income level prior to 1961.
[e] 1 in $3,417 income level after 1964.
[f] 3 in $2,578-2,669 income level since 1964.
[g] 3 in $3,064-3,254 income level since 1964.
[h] 4 in $2,475-2,515 income level in 1964 and 1965; 3 in 1966.
[j] 2 in $1,932 income level in 1964; 1 in 1965 and 1966.

level of family income, race, education, etc. The precincts can then be classified—here, on the basis of median family income and race—the voting behavior in them can be correlated, and conclusions can be drawn. In Jefferson County, because of changes in precinct boundaries, it was feasible to use elections only since 1959. In Fayette County, comparison of different precinct maps permitted use of elections since 1955. The results are given in Tables 5.8 and 5.9.

There is always a risk in trying to draw conclusions about the socioeconomic pattern of voting from aggregate data. The average income figures for the precincts often conceal wide variations; the precincts are seldom highly homogeneous. We cannot assume that rank-order correlations of individuals would be as high as those that have been derived from precinct data, nor can we be sure that individual voting was correlated at a higher level with income in those elections for which we obtained higher precinct correlations with income.[17] The most it is possible to say with any certainty from an analysis of Tables 5.8 and 5.9 is that the Republicans have generally drawn a higher percentage of votes in the higher income precincts of Jefferson and Fayette counties. The pattern is strong and consistent enough to lead us to speculate that the Republican party in Kentucky, like its counterpart in most states, appeals most successfully in the large cities to voters in the above-average income groups.

Although the rank-order correlations vary from one election to another, they are high (except in Negro precincts) for most of the elections under review. It is significant that high correlations were found for at least some of the elections at each of the three levels—national, state, and local. We might expect economic issues to assume greater importance in national elections, but the data in Tables 5.8 and 5.9 do not show consistently higher correlations for national elections. The wide variety of elections with high economic correlations suggests the possibility that party identification is a major factor in voting in Kentucky cities (as it usually is in this country) and that economic factors are significant in determining the party identification of Kentuckians in the largest counties.

[17] The "ecological fallacy" that results from applying aggregate data correlations to individuals has been described by W. S. Robinson, "Ecological Correlations and the Behavior of Individuals," *American Sociological Review*, XV (1950), 351-57, and Hayward Alker, Jr., *Mathematics and Politics* (New York: Macmillan Company, 1965), 102-104.

TABLE 5.9
Socioeconomic and Voting Patterns in Fayette County

Median Family Income	No. of Precincts	Percentage Negro[a]	Average Republican Percentage of Vote in Precincts													
			1966 U.S. Sen.	1966 U.S. HR	1964 Pres.	1963 Gov.	1962 U.S. Sen.	1961 Co. Judge	1960 Pres.	1960 U.S. Sen.	1960 U.S. HR	1959 Gov.	1957 Ky. HR	1956 Pres.	1956 U.S. Sen.[b]	1955 Gov.
$10,313	4[c]		69	38	56	57	72	49	67	75	53	52	43	70	67	50
9,367	4[d]		66	38	53	54	68	45	66	72	54	47	41	68	64	44
8,119	3		77	43	56	60	72	—	—	—	—	nonexistent	—	—	—	—
7,879	3[e]		65	37	51	61	67	48	64	72	54	48	38	64	59	42
7,226	5[f]		71	40	50	59	68	52	65	75	52	48	37	60	54	41
7,104	6[g]		69	42	48	60	65	47	63	71	53	46	—	nonexistent	nonexistent	—
6,934	2[h]		68	42	52	64	67	51	69	75	58	50	52	69	64	49
6,649-6,669	6[j]		69	37	48	54	64	45	67	76	55	46	41	66	61	50
6,177	3		62	37	44	52	61	40	61	68	51	43	37	60	56	42
5,809-5,841	8[k]		60	37	43	61	58	40	59	64	52	37	36	56	52	31
5,613	3		56	33	41	53	58	39	60	64	52	38	40	59	54	38
Median Family Income in Fayette County $5,377																
4,780	3	9.8	64	43	37	54	62	41	59	66	52	42	46	62	60	42
4,651	3	23.1	64	38	45	57	60	41	58	65	49	37	34	61	52	37
3,859-4,221	2	12	62	39	42	60	62	37	60	64	52	38	40	56	54	38
3,265	5	15	52	38	29	46	49	37	46	50	43	33	33	54	51	30
2,868-2,873	4[l]	36	63	48	24	43	46	35	47	51	45	36	40	53	41	33
Coefficient of rank correlation			.743	−.060	.338	.440	.908	.854	.844	.842	.754	.906	.381	.811	.800	.765

a No number indicates Negro percentage of less than 5.
b Senator Morton's race.
c 2 in $10,313 income level before 1957.
d 3 in $9,367 income level in 1956 and 1955.
e 2 in $7,879 income level in 1956 and 1955.
f 3 in $7,226 income level in 1957; 2 earlier.
g 5 in $7,104 income level in 1961 and earlier.
h 1 in $6,934 income level in 1959 and earlier.
j 5 in $6,649-6,669 income level in 1959-1957; 6 earlier.
k 7 in $5,809-5,841 income level in 1959-1957; 6 earlier.
l 5 in $2,868-2,873 income level in 1959-1961; 2 in $3,091 income level in 1956-1955.

The tables do show some interesting differences among elections, although we should be cautious about interpreting these because such correlations are imprecise. In Jefferson and particularly in Fayette County the 1963 gubernatorial and 1964 presidential elections were among those in which the correlations with income levels were lowest. Both are elections in which the racial issue figured prominently and the Republican candidate took a position that was more critical of civil rights legislation than that of the Democratic candidate. We cannot say with assurance that this issue caused a change in normal voting patterns in these two counties. But it is clear that the Republican candidates in these two elections had greater success in lower income urban precincts—compared to their success in higher income precincts—than was normally the case. There is reason to believe, on the basis of polling data in this country, that persons in the lower socioeconomic and educational strata have a less "liberal" attitude toward civil rights issues than those in higher strata. The data at least provide the basis for speculation that in 1963 and 1964 the civil rights issue was an important factor distorting the normal economic voting patterns in Louisville and Lexington. It is interesting to note that the only negative correlation in the non-Negro precincts was in the 1966 United States House of Representatives race in Fayette County, where the Democratic candidate, John Watts, had the reputation of being a moderately conservative congressman with a broad base of support in the district and his Republican opponent was almost unknown in the county.

The information that can be gained from scrutiny of the data here presented indicates political behavior in these urban areas quite similar to political behavior in urban areas throughout the United States. It has long been known that the Republicans generally draw greater support in the upper income areas and that the Democrats draw greater support in the lower income areas. In the very highest income precincts, the attraction of the Republican candidates is most emphatically revealed. Here the Republican ratio of the vote runs close to four to one in some national elections. These precincts generally show a greater solidarity for the Republican nominees than the very lowest income precincts show for the Democratic candidates. V. O. Key's observation in regard to the effects of urbanization on the creation of party cleavages along class lines is apropos: "Evidently what has happened is that a sense of class politics and class solidarity remains stable at a high level among the upper-income groups while middle- and lower-income groups vary from time to time in the degree to which class and politics are associated."[18]

It is worth noting that the correlation between economic levels and voting behavior does not hold in all elections in the predominantly Negro precincts of Jefferson County. In five of the eleven elections the correlation is negative. Perhaps there is more sophistication and awareness in the higher economic levels of Negroes and thus a greater perception that a Negro "should" vote for the more "liberal" Democratic candidates. Another complicating factor is that the Republican organization in Jefferson County has been making an intensive effort in recent years to win the Negro vote, and that effort has not been limited to the higher income Negro precincts. Moreover, urban Negroes in Kentucky have seldom voted Democratic in such high proportions as Negroes in most cities of the country, although this was the case in the 1964 presidential race.

Some precinct analysis of Covington (Kenton County) was done. The census data there covered only housing (and only within the city of Covington), and the precincts were classified according to average value of housing units or average rent. The analysis revealed a general, though limited, correlation between economic levels and voting behavior (the lower the economic level, the greater likelihood of voting Democratic, and vice versa for the Republicans). This was highest in the 1962 senatorial election between Thruston Morton and Wilson Wyatt (a coefficient of rank correlation of .785), lower in the 1960 Kennedy-Nixon presidential election (coefficient of rank correlation .656), lower in the 1960 senatorial election between Keen Johnson and John Sherman Cooper (coefficient of rank correlation .594), and lower still in the 1963 gubernatorial election between Edward Breathitt and Louie Nunn (coefficient of rank correlation .417).

A more refined analysis of voting behavior in other parts of Kentucky is not feasible without the use of interviewing techniques. We have made some effort at precinct analysis of some recent elections in other counties: urban (Warren and McCracken); coun-

18 Politics, Parties, and Pressure Groups, 274.

ties showing a postwar change in voting behavior (Boone, Oldham, and Jessamine); and Marginal counties (Harlan and Madison). The results, however, are not so significantly suggestive as to warrant detailed exposition, nor do they permit any clearcut inferences. This is basically due to the lack of any reliable and precise data by which to classify precincts. It is probable that economic factors play a significant role in voting behavior in many of these (and other) counties, but such cannot be shown by the available methods.

We conclude that no common denominator or single causative factor is apparent in those areas which have manifested changes in voting behavior in the postwar period. Rich counties, poor counties, counties in all sections of the state, urban counties and rural counties, industrial counties and agricultural counties—all show no consistent pattern of voting behavior. The enormously involved process by which the hundreds of thousands, even millions, of voters who collectively constitute the electorate of Kentucky reach a decision is not amenable to a compelling analysis. Personalities, factionalism, traditional partisan loyalties, economic status, race, religion, vote-purchasing—all these and other factors enter into the electorate's final decisions at the polls. To single out any one factor as the most significant determinant of electoral behavior is perhaps a risky undertaking, but it would appear that traditional partisan allegiance is paramount. For nearly a century this traditional allegiance has favored the Democratic candidates in statewide races. Traditional allegiances were jarred and overridden "permanently" in some sections of the state by the events of the Depression and New Deal period, and the net beneficiaries were the Democrats. Postwar changes in voting behavior in many parts of the state have been of net benefit to the Republicans, but just how "permanent" are these accretions to the Republican ranks is a question which cannot now be resolved.

STATE AND NATIONAL ELECTIONS: ARE THE DIFFERENCES SIGNIFICANT?

We earlier classified Kentucky as a competitive state, under a well-known system of classification using all statewide elections. This method of classification, however, does not take account of the fact that there may be significant differences in voting behavior in state elections as compared to national elections. This difference exists in Kentucky, where the Republican candidates have fared much better in national elections, particularly in the post-World War II period. Republican candidates have won seven of ten United States Senate elections and two of the five presidential elections, barely losing another. In contrast, the Democrats have won every gubernatorial election except the most recent. The Democrats have also dominated the state legislature in the postwar period, although Republican gains of some substance were made in 1963 and 1967. The average Republican percentage of the vote was 50.7 in national elections and only 45.0 in gubernatorial races from 1947 to 1967.

No one short answer will suffice to explain this disparity in the postwar fortunes of the two parties in Kentucky. The question is an intricate one, and we can only give several "educated guesses" about the various factors that combine to produce the disparity.

One pertinent factor is that gubernatorial elections are held in what may be called "off-off" years; that is, years in which neither presidential nor congressional elections are held. There is some evidence that the holding of presidential and gubernatorial elections simultaneously tends to result in one party's winning both.[19] Generally, the higher the percentage of the vote of the presidential candidate, the more likely his party's gubernatorial nominee will be elected.[20] Needless to say, there are deviations from this "norm," and Key presents evidence to show that such deviations have increased since the latter part of last century. Nevertheless, it is quite likely that if gubernatorial elections in Kentucky were held in years in which national elections are conducted, there would be a closer congruence of outcomes than has been the case in the postwar period.

Key also suggests that "changes in the politics of a state government may lag considerably behind alterations in the presidential voting habits of the people of the state," and elsewhere records his impression "that presidential voting preferences are more volatile than are those in state and local elections."[21] Indicating that a presidential nominee will attract support in a particular state in

[19] Key, *American State Politics*, chap. 2, esp. pp. 28-49.

[20] Key does not present any data concerning the relationship of United States Senate elections to state elections. With a votegetter such as Senator John Sherman Cooper heading the ticket, however, it seems probable that the "coattail effects" for Republican gubernatorial candidates would be impressive.

[21] *American State Politics*, 48; *Politics, Parties, and Pressure Groups*, 337.

much the same relative degree that he attracts support in the nation as a whole, he adds that "the great movements of voters from one party to the other in national elections do not in the same degree dislodge people from their customary predilections in state politics."[22] Experience in Kentucky bears out Key's impressions and assertions, as traditional voting by the Kentucky electorate benefits the Democratic candidates.

All counties but two showed a higher average Republican percentage of the vote in national elections than in gubernatorial elections in the postwar period. (It was the same in Elliott County, and not quite 1 percent less in Magoffin County.) The difference was less than 5 percentage points in 45 counties, and between 5 and 9.9 percentage points in 61 counties. The 12 counties where the difference exceeds 10 percentage points are listed in Table 5.10.[23]

Examining the counties where there is the widest disparity fails to reveal any explanatory factor. Of the twelve, eight are classified as Democratic for the period since 1920, two are Republican, and two are Marginal. Two counties, Daviess and Warren, are urban under the definition used here (containing a city of 25,000 or more), and two other counties are urban under the Census Bureau classification (over one-half of the population living in areas of 2,500 or over). Five of the counties had median family incomes in 1959 above the state average, and the remaining seven were below the state average in this indicator of wealth.[24]

This examination on the county level thus fails to demonstrate strikingly the nature of "national Republicans"; that is, persons

[22] Politics, Parties, and Pressure Groups, 337. Surveys of attitudes of individual voters have shown "that the popular vote for lesser offices is a more party-determined vote than the vote for president and varies around the normal equilibrium vote figure within a much narrower range than does the presidential vote." Philip E. Converse and others, "Stability and Change in 1960: A Reinstating Election," American Political Science Review, LV (1961), 280.

[23] The Republican average in national races was obtained by computing the median (for example, 53.4 in Jefferson County) between the average Republican percentage of the vote in Senate races (56.9 in Jefferson County), and the same in presidential races (49.9 in Jefferson County). For the entire 1920-1966 period, the Republican national average exceeded its gubernatorial average in 105 counties (less than 5 percentage points in 91 counties, and between 5 and 9.9 percentage points in 14 counties). The Republican gubernatorial average exceeded the Republican national average in 13 counties, the differences in all counties being less than 5 percentage points. In 2 counties, there was no difference.

[24] Although the Republican percentage in the 1967 gubernatorial election was above the previous gubernatorial average in all twelve of these counties, it was below the national average in all but three of these counties.

TABLE 5.10

Counties in Which Average Republican Percentage of Vote Is at Least Ten Points Higher in National Than in Gubernatorial Races, 1946-1966

County	Avg. GOP Percentage National	Avg. GOP Percentage Gubernatorial	Difference
Clay	73.6	56.6	17.0
Daviess	51.8	38.3	13.5
Logan	33.1	20.1	13.0
Henderson	40.4	27.5	12.9
Warren	48.1	35.4	12.7
Nelson	42.8	30.9	11.9
Franklin	32.2	21.2	11.0
Larue	49.0	38.5	10.5
Bracken	48.4	38.2	10.2
Clark	43.5	33.3	10.2
Oldham	47.8	37.7	10.1
Martin	70.7	60.7	10.0

who vote Democratic in gubernatorial elections and who vote Republican in national elections. The data presented above on the analysis of precincts in urban counties also fails to identify any such group. No doubt voters of all kinds behave differently in national and state races (Republicans as well as Democrats, as indicated by the results in the 1959 gubernatorial election and the 1964 presidential election). Also, there appears little doubt that an important reason for the superior Republican showing in national races can be attributed to the immense personal popularity of Senator John Sherman Cooper. Large numbers of registered Democrats will vote for him but will not vote for any other Republican. This is indicated by his consistently higher percentage of the votes received, and more dramatically in the 1966 election, when he carried 110 of the state's 120 counties, including 17 counties which had never before given a Republican candidate a majority in the period since 1920.

Another contributing element in the compound which together helps to explain the contrast in outcomes of state and national elections in Kentucky is finances. Possession of money is not a sufficient condition for obtaining victory, but it is certainly a necessary condition. The fact that gubernatorial elections are held in off years in Kentucky has meant, in this connection, that the Republican gubernatorial nominees have been handicapped by the possession of funds which are small in comparison to the funds available to the Democratic nominees. This is a situation which apparently prevails in all states which follow the off-year schedule for state elections: the minority party is deprived of the benefits of national money flowing into the state on behalf of the presidential and congressional candidates.[25]

Another factor relevant to the poor Republican performance in state races stems from the quality of the party organization vis-a-vis that of the Democrats. Key points out that in many states holding gubernatorial elections in presidential election years, the gubernatorial candidate of the dominant party may be able to win, even though the opposite party's presidential candidate carries the state. One of the factors contributing to this split voting, in Key's opinion, is "that the party entrenched in power has, by virtue of the organization built up over a long period, a capacity to resist the effects of national tides."[26] This condition is reinforced, of course, when gubernatorial elections are held in years in which there are no national (presidential or the off-year senatorial) elections.

In the 1967 gubernatorial election the Republican campaign was well organized and well financed; the party reported campaign expenses that were not far behind those reported by the Democratic party. The advertising campaign, particularly on television, was more skillful than that used in the Democratic campaign. Louie B. Nunn, the Republican candidate, was elected governor by a margin of over 28,000 votes, and Republican candidates for four of the other statewide offices were elected by much narrower margins. The Republicans failed to win the lieutenant governorship, however. During his campaign, Nunn made efforts to overcome the liability of the divisive May primary and to win broad Republican support. He also sought to take advantage of the apparent unpopularity of the national Democratic administration, and told voters that "a vote for Nunn is a vote against LBJ." As Table 5.7 demonstrates, Nunn won a smaller percentage of the urban vote than any of the winning Republican presidential or senatorial candidates in the period since World War II, but in the nonurban counties his percentage was higher than the average postwar

25 Key, *American State Politics*, 42-43. A high Republican party official said that in 1963 the state party received no money from the national Republican party. The Democratic gubernatorial nominee won by some 13,000 votes that year.

26 *Politics, Parties, and Pressure Groups*, 338.

Republican vote in national elections. Nunn's urban weakness was largely attributable to his narrow margin in Jefferson County, where there was apparently lingering resentment over the primary election. His greatest rural gains occurred in western Kentucky, where he made deep inroads into the normally large Democratic majorities.

CONCLUSIONS

We have considered the variegated aspects of the voting behavior of the Kentucky electorate for the past several decades. The infinitely involved process by which the hundreds of thousands of voters who are the state's electorate make up their minds is not amenable to any simple or obvious analysis. Rather, there is a multiplicity of factors which enter into the process. We have shown that traditional party loyalties dating from the Civil War are an important element in this process. We also have seen some of the changes which have subsequently occurred that have affected the process of voting in Kentucky.

The one change which seems destined to have the greatest effect upon patterns of voting is industrialization and increasing urbanization. Urbanization tends to have an unsettling effect upon tradition, and this includes traditional voting behavior. Over one-third of the electorate now lives in urban counties, and population trends suggest that almost certainly this proportion will increase in the future. We have seen that the urban areas are predominantly Marginal; either they have been so since the period under analysis (1920) or, for the counties which have become urbanized during this period, they have shown signs of becoming increasingly more competitive. (McCracken County is the one exception.) The rural counties, nearly all of which are either traditionally Republican or Democratic, are losing population (especially the Republican counties) or are showing only an insignificant increase (the Democratic counties as a whole).

This increase in the voting power of the urban counties points to an increasingly competitive statewide politics. While it is impossible to prove the cause-and-effect relationship, it is fairly clear that the improvement in Republican fortunes in the period since World War II is related to the increasing urbanization and industrialization of Kentucky.

While an increasingly competitive statewide politics can only be good news for Republicans (since they are the minority), it is not necessarily a cause for despair to the Democrats. The 1964 presidential election showed that a deviation from traditional voting patterns can benefit Democratic candidates. It simply means that more voters are willing to give more consideration to factors other than the party label before casting their votes.

6 | Legislative Politics

The Kentucky General Assembly, like most state legislatures, has suffered from constitutional malnutrition. The framers of the 1891 constitution, conscious of legislative mistakes and corruption, were determined to place limitations both on the specific powers of the legislature and on its freedom of action. They included in the constitution detailed provisions on taxation, local government, and the regulation of business, among other things, all of which restrict the legislature's freedom of action. The constitution also limits the legislature to one regular, 60-day session every two years. Special sessions may be called only by the governor, who may specify the subjects that can be considered in such a session. Senators are elected for staggered four-year terms, and representatives serve a two-year term.

The Kentucky constitution has created an environment in which it is difficult, if not impossible, for the legislature to thrive as a coequal and independent branch of government. Unless the governor decides to call special sessions, the legislature functions for only 60 days every two years. The only interim body is the Legislative Research Commission, which supervises the preparation of staff studies but does not make legislative recommendations. Because the legislative sessions are so brief and infrequent, the committees seldom try to hold extensive hearings or to take the time for careful deliberation, major legislation is often passed with little debate, and other bills often fail simply because the clock runs out before they can be passed. Because time is so short, the legislature devotes most of its attention to the governor's program and relatively little time is spent studying the measures initiated by its own members. Another consequence of the brief, infrequent sessions is that new legislators are unable to learn the intricacies of the legislative process and the technicalities of procedure. Furthermore, because of the high rate of turnover, a great many legislators in any session are inexperienced and unskilled, and therefore have to depend heavily on the leadership and advice of others—the governor, floor leaders, other members, or lobbyists. Although there are several factors that contribute to undermining the independent authority of the legislative branch, none is more important than the constitutional restrictions.

LEGISLATORS

As in other states, most Kentucky legislators are businessmen, lawyers or other professional men, and farmers. The business or professional man who is self-employed and perhaps has partners who can carry the load in his absence is obviously more available to spend several months in Frankfort than the wage earner in a factory or store who is sure to lose money and perhaps even his job if he is elected to the legislature. As long as the regular legislative session is from January through March, the farmer can serve without seriously interfering with planting and harvesting. The lawyer, the insurance agent, and some other businessmen ofter anticipate that their legislative service will make them well enough known to attract clients, and some of them hope to benefit from contracts with the state or with other companies doing business with the state.

In Kentucky (as Table 6.1 shows) lawyers constitute twice as large a proportion of senators as of representatives. This is a common pattern, but in Kentucky the proportion is lower than in most state legislatures, for the number of lawyers has been declining in the Kentucky legislature, particularly in the House, where the percentage dropped from 21 in 1952-1954 to only 13 in the three years, 1958, 1962, 1966. The large number of businessmen include a wide variety of retail and wholesale merchants (more numerous than in other states where data are available) and a large number of insurance and real estate agents (comparable to other states). The number of school teachers and administrators in the Kentucky

TABLE 6.1

Occupations of Legislators[a]

Occupation	Number Senate	House	Percent Senate	House	Median Percent in 8 Other States[b]
Business owners and managers	74	181	32	36	33
Merchants (retail, wholesale)	40	93			
Bankers	7	4			
Insurance and real estate	12	53			
Morticians	5	7			
Contractors	5	10			
Manufacturers	4	5			
Coal mine operators	1	3			
Truckers		4			
Credit managers		2			
Lawyers	73	80	32	16	30
Other professional, technical	24	88	11	18	9
Doctors, dentists, etc.	8	8			
Teachers, principals	8	39			
Ministers, church workers		10			
Social workers		2			
Newspaper and radio	6	8			
Public relations, advertising	1	9			
Accountants	1	4			
Engineers		8			
Farmers	37	86	17	17	13
Craftsmen, foremen, operators	4	22	2	4	4
Railroad workers		13			
Other skilled workers	3	7			
Labor union agents	1	2			
Salesmen and clerks	7	20	3	4	5
Industrial laborers	0	6	0	1	1
Other, retired, unknown	9	17	4	4	5
Total	228	500			

SOURCE: *Kentucky Government Directories;* Malcolm E. Jewell and Samuel C. Patterson, *The Legislative Process in the United States* (New York: Random House, 1966), 108.

[a] Senate, 1944-1966; House, 1952, 1954, 1958, 1962, 1966.

[b] California, New Jersey, Ohio, Tennessee, Wisconsin (all 1957), Indiana (1961), Washington (1951), Pennsylvania (1958).

legislature, particularly in the House, is surprisingly large (larger than in other states) in view of the conflict between teaching schedules and legislative service. The proportion of farmer-legislators varies more from state to state than do other categories, and the percentage is slightly above average in Kentucky, probably because it is more heavily agricultural than the average state.[1]

In recent sessions (1954, 1960, and 1966) half of the senators have been over 50 years old; representatives have been divided into three almost equal groups: those under 40 years, those in their forties, and those 50 or older. About three-fourths of the senators in these three sessions have attended college, as have almost two-thirds of the representatives. The proportion of college-trained legislators has been growing gradually in recent years and is likely to continue to grow, both as a result of a new generation of legislators and the increasing representation from urban counties.

Legislative turnover is higher in Kentucky than in most states, though it has been declining.[2] In a period of eight elections, 1947-1961, half of those elected to the House and 41 percent of those chosen for the Senate had had no previous experience in the legislature. In the elections of 1963 and 1965 the proportions of inexperienced legislators dropped close to one-third. (See Table 6.2.) The

TABLE 6.2

Turnover in Legislature, 1947-1961 and 1963-1965 (in Percentages)

	1947-1961		1963-1965	
Status of Legislators Chosen in Each Election	*Senate* *(N-152)*	*House* *(N-800)*	*Senate* *(N-38)*	*House* *(N-200)*
Reelected to Senate or House	32	39	40	56
Elected after period of absence or after service in the other house	27	12	26	10
Elected without previous legislative service	41	50	34	35

proportion of senators who had served in the previous session from the same district was only one-third in the first eight elections and rose to 40 percent in the last two. Most of the remaining one-fourth of the senators had experience in the House during the previous session or earlier, and a few had served in the Senate during an earlier term. The proportion of representatives who were reelected was higher, 39 and 56 percent in the two periods. Almost half of

[1] Malcolm E. Jewell and Samuel C. Patterson, *The Legislative Process in the United States* (New York: Random House, 1966), 106-10; John C. Wahlke and others, *The Legislative System* (New York: John Wiley and Sons, 1962), 490.

[2] Jewell and Patterson, *Legislative Process*, 120.

those who had served at an earlier session but had their tenure interrupted came from the districts where the rotation policy was followed. Not only is the proportion of freshman legislators high in Kentucky, but also the number of those who have served for long periods of time is relatively small. In three sessions (1962-1964) there were an average of only 9 senators (out of 38) and 12 representatives (out of 100) who had at least eight years of previous legislative service.

Why do members leave the legislature? Approximately one-half of the incumbents sought reelection to their seats, but one-third of the senators and just over one-fourth of the representatives who sought reelection were defeated, most of them in primary elections. (See Table 6.3.) (The complications of reapportionment require exclusion of the 1963 election.) One factor reducing the risk of

TABLE 6.3

*Fate of Incumbent Legislators in Elections, 1947-1961
and 1965 (in Percentages)*

Status of Incumbent Legislators in Each Election	Senate (N-171)	House (N-900)
Reelected to Senate or House	32	41
Defeated in primary election for same seat	15	11
Defeated in general election for same seat	1	4
Retired as a result of district rotation agreement	12	16
Ran for another state or legislative office	1	4
Retired voluntarily	39	24

defeat has been the low level of electoral competition. In the 1947-1965 period (excluding 1963), 26 percent of the incumbent Democrats in the Senate and 35 percent of those in the House had no opposition in the primary. Among those with opposition, 31 percent were defeated. The risks of defeat in the general election are considerably smaller. In the 1947-1965 period both parties contested 42 percent of the House elections, the Democrats were unopposed in 47 percent, and the Republicans had no opposition in 11 percent. In the Senate there were bipartisan contests in 46 percent of the elections, and Democrats and Republicans ran unopposed in 42 and 12 percent, respectively, of the elections. In 1967, however, there was bipartisan competition for 73 percent of the House seats and 75 percent of the Senate seats. Not only were a majority of seats uncontested in the general election, but in most districts one party was so dominant that the other party never elected a candidate. In the 1947-1959 period there were only 4 Senate and 14 House districts in which both parties elected legislators, although 2 more districts in the Senate and 7 more in the House were added to this list in 1961, mostly as a result of the Republican breakthrough in Jefferson County. The most competitive districts, in a partisan sense, have been those in the metropolitan counties, particularly Jefferson, and those districts that are on the borderline between counties traditionally Democratic and Republican. The 1962 reapportionment has increased the proportion of seats contested by both parties because the usually competitive metropolitan counties have gained representation and the number of overwhelmingly Democratic and Republican districts has declined.

The proportions of districts with party turnover and with two-party competition in Kentucky are roughly comparable to those found in other states of the Border and Upper South, but these levels of competition are much lower than those in most northern states.[3] Incumbent Democratic legislators in Kentucky had about the same chances of encountering opposition, and of losing, in the primary as did those in Tennessee, Florida, and South Carolina. They were more likely to be opposed or defeated in the primary than were legislators in Texas and North Carolina, but less likely than legislators in Louisiana and Alabama, where the primaries are highly competitive.[4]

To explain adequately the reasons why about half of the incumbent legislators in Kentucky do not seek reelection would require interviews with all of them, and probably some former legislators would find it difficult to provide a single, clear, accurate explanation of their decision not to run. Among those who did not run, over one-third in the House and almost one-fourth in the Senate represented districts in which there was a rotation agreement among the various county committees of the dominant party requiring that the nomination go to a person in another county after one or two terms. (Included in these totals are all those who retired in districts having two-year rotation plans and those in districts with four-year

[3] Ibid., 80-82.

[4] Malcolm E. Jewell, Legislative Representation in the Contemporary South (Durham, N. C.: Duke University Press, 1967), chap. 2. It should be noted that reapportionment has increased the proportion of seats in metropolitan counties, where two-party and primary competition is usually higher than in rural counties.

plans who retired when it was time to switch counties.) Some of these (in the House) ran for the Senate, and others subsequently ran for their seat when it again became their county's turn. There are occasional examples of two members, from different counties, taking turns for long periods of time. It should be emphasized, however, that the great majority of legislators who retire in conformity with a rotation agreement do not return to the legislature in any subsequent session. The incumbent occasionally challenges the rotation principle, usually without success, although party leaders throughout a district may agree to support a legislator who holds an important leadership position.

Not every legislator who retires from the legislature in conformity to a rotation agreement would have run for another term if there had been no agreement. One legislator who had cited such an agreement in publicly stating that he would not be a candidate confided in an interview that the pressures of work in his law office would have made it very difficult for him to serve a third consecutive term. Probably many legislators would be unable to say with any certainty whether or not they would have run for reelection in the absence of a rotation agreement. Such an agreement creates a framework for legislative service and imposes a pattern on legislative careers. It may even have the effect of attracting to the legislature men who are willing to serve for only short terms. Although we cannot say how many legislators would have run again in the absence of rotation agreements, we can show, as noted below, that the proportion of legislators who are reelected is much lower in rotation districts than in other districts of the state. The net effect of the rotation policy, we must conclude, is to increase turnover and reduce the proportion of experienced men in the legislature. Rotation agreements have been feasible in the past in the two-county House districts (the maximum size) and in Senate districts containing a few counties. These agreements are likely to become less frequent as a result of the new apportionment adopted in 1962, which increased the number of counties in both Senate and House districts, and as a result of the certainty that district boundaries will be redrawn—and rotation patterns upset—every ten years.

Legislative office, particularly in the lower house, may be a steppingstone to some other office. In the nine elections being surveyed there were 6 legislators who ran for statewide office (such as attorney general or secretary of state), and there were 31 representatives who ran for the Senate. (These totals are included in Table 6.3.) Six other representatives who ran for the Senate were conforming to rotation agreements (and are included in Table 6.3 in the category of those who retired because of such agreements). It was not feasible to determine how many other legislators ran for judicial or county office, although a check of two election years showed that only one legislator won a county office. It is probable that complete data on legislators retiring to run for other positions would increase the percentages listed in Table 6.3 very slightly. Except for representatives who run for the Senate, relatively few legislators apparently leave in order to seek other elective offices.

Most of the legislators who do not run for the legislature or for any other office and who are not bound by rotation agreements can be classified as having retired voluntarily, though this is not exactly appropriate as a description for the two or three incumbents, on the average, who die in office during each legislative term. Among those retiring voluntarily during the period of 1947-1965 (except 1963), 30 percent of the senators had completed two or more terms (at least eight years) and 21 percent of the representatives had completed three or more terms (at least six years). On the other hand, 70 percent of the senators and 55 percent of the representatives who retired voluntarily did so without seeking a second term. It is easy to speculate on the reasons why legislators decide not to run again. Some find it necessary to devote more time to their business, and others decide that they have served long enough to accomplish their main objective of gaining the publicity that will attract clients. Some, who view legislative service as a civic responsibility (like serving on a fund-raising drive), decide that they have done their duty. Others find that legislative service is boring or become frustrated because they have little sense of accomplishment —perhaps because their party or faction is in the minority. The record of turnover suggests that relatively few Kentucky legislators seek a career of legislative service.

Without interview data it is impossible to weigh the importance of these various reasons or to discover others that might have significant influence. It is possible to show that the rate of reelection has varied among different groups of legislators. (The data cover House elections, 1947-1961.) The lowest rate was among legislators from counties with rotation agreements; only 19 percent were reelected, all of these after one term in districts where the agreement permitted a second term. In the other nonmetropolitan counties 41 percent of the legislators were reelected, and another 18 percent sought reelection unsuccessfully. In this group of counties the rate of reelection was 44 percent for Democrats and 32 percent for Republicans. Although a larger proportion of Republicans was defeated in general elections, the contrasts resulted mostly from the smaller proportion of Republicans who sought reelection. The highest proportion of reelected legislators, 57 percent, was in four metropolitan counties: Jefferson, Fayette, Kenton, and Campbell. Although the risks of electoral defeat were greater in these counties, there were fewer defeats in the primary, in part because of the strong party organizations in Jefferson County. The major reason for the contrast is the high proportion of metropolitan legislators—70 percent—who sought reelection.

We conclude that the high rate of turnover in the Kentucky legislature results principally from the high proportion of members who drop out voluntarily after one or two terms, either because they never intended to serve a longer tenure or because their legislative experience proved to be disappointing. A second factor is the rotation system, which has been more prevalent than in most states. Defeat at the polls is a third factor, but one which assumes less importance in Kentucky than it apparently does in most states. Although it is impossible to predict whether the turnover rate will rise or fall, it is probable that the reasons for turnover will change in importance, largely as a result of periodic reapportionment based strictly on population. The rotation system will be used in fewer districts. A larger proportion of legislators will be elected in metropolitan areas, where the rate of turnover has been least. But the metropolitan legislator, particularly from Jefferson County, is losing some of his electoral security, both because of the decline of party organizations that have minimized primary competition and the growth of Republican strength that will guarantee closer two-party competition.

GUBERNATORIAL LEADERSHIP AND DEMOCRATIC DOMINANCE

Although six Republican governors have served terms in Kentucky (elected in 1895, 1907, 1919, 1927, 1943, and 1967), the Republican party has never won a majority in the Senate and has won control of the House only twice, in 1895 and 1919. During the administration of Republican Governor Willis the Republicans had 15 seats in 1944 and 17 seats in 1946 in the 38-member Senate. They elected 44 out of 100 House members in 1944, but only 31 in 1946. With this large a delegation, the Republican legislative party was relatively effective and was more cohesive than usual, but when the Democratic party returned to power, Republican legislative strength was reduced to about one-fourth of the seats. From 1948 through 1962 the median Republican membership was 9 in the Senate and 25 in the House, and never exceeded 10 senators and 27 representatives. Most of these members came from the traditional Republican counties in the southeast. Not until the 1960s, when the Republican party won in several metropolitan counties and reapportionment enhanced the importance of these victories, did the Republican legislative party make significant gains.

The fact that the Republican party was a badly outnumbered minority for so many years in the legislature had important effects on both parties in Kentucky. Republican legislators not only lacked the votes necessary to pass bills, but they were not even strong enough to create issues by forcing debate and votes on the floor. To a large extent, they stopped trying to be an effective opposition party, and many of them cooperated with the governor in order to get patronage and roads and other projects for their districts. The Democratic majority, on the other hand, ran the legislature as if it were a one-party body. Committees were organized with little concern for maintaining an equitable balance between the parties. The strong gubernatorial leadership that has characterized modern legislative politics in Kentucky has been facilitated by the absence of a strong minority party and by the governor's ability to win the votes of Republican legislators with favors.

Sources of Gubernatorial Power. The governor of Kentucky, in his exercise of legislative leadership, is one of the most powerful and successful governors in the United States. There is no single, simple explanation for his legislative influence; it has many roots. The constitution and statutes contain few of the restrictions found in some states, other than the ban on successive terms. The weakness of the Republican party has created a vacuum of opposition to Democratic governors in the legislature. Patronage, though declining in importance, has traditionally been available to the governor. Perhaps most important, several strong governors have vigorously exercised the formal and informal powers of their office, setting precedents for their successors to follow. The people of Kentucky, and the legislators, have grown accustomed to strong leadership from the governor's office.

The constitution gives the governor the power to recommend to the legislature "such measures as he may deem expedient," and the governor makes these recommendations in an address at the start of the session and sometimes in additional appearances before the legislature. The governor, and no one else, may call a special session, and he may specify the subjects to be considered at such a session. Most governors in recent years have called several special sessions during their terms to deal with problems that have arisen since the regular session or that the legislature failed to handle previously. Governor Combs called five special sessions during his term. The threat of calling a special session is often used by the governor and his lieutenants as a technique of persuasion when an important bill appears to be in jeopardy in the closing days of a regular session. As in most states, the governor has a veto power that is almost absolute in practice. In four legislative sessions, 1960 to 1966, only one of the governor's 69 vetoes was overridden. Only an absolute majority in both houses is required to override a veto, but the governor's political allies in the legislature are usually strong enough to block such action. Moreover, most legislation passes during the last ten days of the legislature, when the governor can delay a veto until after adjournment; if the governor's supporters cannot block a bill that he opposes, they are often able to delay it until the closing days of a session, when a veto will become final. The governor's item veto for appropriation bills is potentially important, but it is rarely used because the governor's budget is seldom changed by the legislature.

Any governor's legislative influence is affected by his authority within the executive branch. In some states many of the executive departments are run either by elected officials or by boards whose members serve staggered terms, and consequently the governor is unable to hire and fire many of his key officials. Although Kentucky has a number of elected officials, most major agencies are directly under the governor's authority because he can appoint and replace their heads. It is particularly important that the governor has such control over the highway department and the budgetary agency. Unlike most governors, the Kentucky governor does not have to get confirmation of the Senate for his appointments. The governor's executive authority is an asset in his effort to present a firm budget and a cohesive legislative program to the General Assembly. It also means that legislators will be indebted to him, and not merely to the heads of agencies, for the patronage and the local projects that are dispensed to them.

The constitutional sources of power are important, but they are not so exceptional as to explain fully why the governor is unusually influential in the Kentucky legislature. More important is the use that has been made of informal power. The governor makes promises during his campaign for the nomination and election, and most of these are legislative promises. He also makes commitments and becomes indebted to various groups that support him, and these groups confront him with legislative proposals when the campaign is over. Additional parts of the legislative package are initiated by the executive agencies. Because the governor's influence in the legislature is widely recognized, all of those who have any claim on the governor seek his endorsement for legislative proposals. Most legislators believe that the newly elected governor has a general mandate from the voters and that his proposals deserve attention, although they may argue that he has no mandate to enact a particular bill that they dislike.

The governor's mandate is an uncertain one, his supply of political capital is not unlimited, and there is never enough patronage to go around. Consequently, he has to decide which bills will be "must" legislation, which he is willing to fight for. There are usually only a few pieces of top priority legislation in any session, and the governor will normally exercise significant pressure only in support of these. Often, when agencies of government or interest groups seek his support for other bills, the governor will encourage them to start a lobbying campaign and will observe the results. If the response is favorable, the governor will adopt the bill as part of his program and work for its enactment; if there is too much resistance, he will take a neutral position. Occasionally, of course, the governor must retreat and compromise even on "must" legislation, although sometimes when he is defeated on a relatively minor bill he will make an unusual effort to reverse the result and restore his prestige. The governor's resources in the legislative struggle are large and varied but not inexhaustible, and some of them are consumed in each battle. The wise governor does not become overcommitted and spends his resources cautiously.

The men who transformed the American governor from a nonentity to a powerful executive and a legislative leader were governors, like Woodrow Wilson, Theodore and Franklin Roosevelt, and Robert LaFollette, who recognized that public opinion was a powerful force that could be mobilized to support their programs. Recent Kentucky governors have utilized the press, radio, and television, and have toured the state, explaining their legislative programs to the public. Although a governor cannot match the president's ability to attract public attention, he has many invitations to speak across the state and many opportunities for personal salesmanship. In theory the governor hopes to arouse enough support for his legislative programs so that the voters will put pressure on legislators to pass administration bills. In practice the governor's program is so diverse and many of the issues so complex that it is unrealistic to expect many voters to become interested in a wide variety of bills. The governor may emphasize a few issues, such as the education and highway programs that Governors Combs and Breathitt endlessly explained to the voters. If the governor is successful, most voters will support these broad programs and will conclude that the governor is doing a "good job." The legislator is likely to support the governor's program, not so much because of mail from the voters on specific issues, but because he realizes that the governor's popularity is high and the public thinks the governor should be given a chance to carry out his program. The governor's prestige with the people becomes an important determinant of his success in the legislature, particularly during the second legislative session of his term, when his resources of patronage are low.

Despite the importance of the governor's popular prestige, it is too tenuous a foundation to provide the only basis for a legislative program. In some two-party states the governor's party provides disciplined, cohesive support for his program, but that has not usually been the case in Kentucky. Because the Republican opposition has usually been ineffective and the Democratic party has been divided by factionalism, Democratic governors have neither needed nor been able to depend on cohesive Democratic support for the controversial parts of their program. Because the Democratic governor is a factional as well as a partisan leader, factional loyalties have influenced the votes of many Democratic legislators on issues involving the governor's prestige. In theory, the governor should be able to depend on legislators who have been identified with his faction and to encounter opposition from members of the opposing faction, but there are other factors that complicate the situation.

During the first legislative session of the Democratic governor's term he usually can rely on his factional allies, but he also has voting support from many legislators who have been identified with the opposing faction. Because he can dispense patronage and favors and affect legislation for the next four years, the governor is in a powerful position to attract converts from the opposing faction. But as his term progresses, the battlelines are drawn for the next gubernatorial primary, and some legislators defect from the administration faction because of dissatisfaction with the rewards they have received or because of a belief that the governor is unpopular in their districts. It is in midterm that the Democratic governor is most likely to make endorsements in the legislative primaries, and these have the effect of intensifying the factional conflict. In the second session those legislators who won with the governor's endorsement are indebted to him and are committed to support his program. The governor seldom demands an advance commitment to support many specific bills (in part because priority decisions about legislation have not yet been made), but a general commitment of support is expected from those who are endorsed. In 1961 many candidates were committed to oppose any exemptions to the sales tax, being advocated by Chandler; in 1965 senatorial candidates were expected to vote for rules changes that would strip the lieutenant governor of his control over committees. Aligned against the governor in the second session are those legislators who won by defeating candidates endorsed by the governor. By making endorsements in the midterm primary the governor gambles on winning a more solid base of support and takes the risk of creating an opposition block more antagonistic than any existing during the first session.

In the 1958 session of the legislature, the factional division within the Democratic party was unusually deep and, on some issues, Governor Chandler's faction was outnumbered. Chandler had tried to defeat some legislators in the 1957 primaries, but his efforts had been ineffective, and his policies had aroused strong antagonism among the Jefferson County Democratic delegation. During the 1958 session a number of the "rebels" in the Democratic party met in regular caucuses. The rebels had only 17 votes in the Democratic caucus that nominated a House speaker, but in the Senate they had a 16-12 majority in the caucus that enabled them to select the president pro tem. The rebels challenged Chandler's budget, attacked his plan to transfer the Health Department from Louisville to Frankfort, and opposed legislation on highway work, among other things. Although their strength varied from issue to issue, on some rollcalls the rebels had the support of a majority of Democrats. Chandler was able to gain enactment of most of his controversial bills only because he was able to secure the votes of most Republican legislators.

In the 1960 session of the legislature Governor Combs was in firm control and carried out an ambitious legislative program; there was little evidence of factionalism in the debates and rollcalls. During the 1962 session the factional conflict was centered in the Senate, where a small band of Chandler supporters kept up a running attack on the Combs administration. A coalition of Chandler Democrats and Republicans challenged the administration on a relatively small number of issues. The Senate rollcalls on seven administration bills can be used to illustrate the factional division. The votes on these seven rollcalls were scalable, with a coefficient of reproducibility of 0.97, when two particularly unpredictable Republicans were omitted.[5] At one extreme were a group of 17

[5] Scale analysis is a technique used for measuring the voting of legislators on a series of rollcalls. An underlying assumption of this technique is that all of those who vote perceive the same issue to be at stake in all of the rollcalls. In this case the issue would be support for or opposition to the administration, because the administration's prestige was deeply involved in each issue. The rollcalls would be arranged in order, depending on the size of the proadministration vote. If, for example, the administration had the support of 75 percent of the senators on bill A, 50 percent on bill B, and 25 percent on bill C, in an ideal scale every senator who voted for the administration on bill C would also support it on bill B, and all those voting for it on both bills B and C would also do so on bill A. In practice, scales are rarely perfect, but the coefficient of reproducibility measures the number of responses accurately predicted by the scale out of the total number of responses, and an index of at least 0.90 is considered scalable. All those legislators who voted the same way on all rollcalls (disregarding errors in the scale) receive the same score and are grouped as one type or category.

reliable administration supporters, all but one Democrats, only two of whom voted once against the administration. At the other extreme were several groups of legislators, including most of the Republicans. Two Democrats always opposed the administration, and five other Democrats, clustered in three categories, voted against the administration at least half of the time. Most of the Democrats who had received Comb's backing in primaries were consistent administration supporters, and two of the three who had defeated administration candidates were either consistent or frequent opponents.

In the House the factional conflict less often came to the surface in debate and attracted less public attention, probably because the half dozen or so Chandler Democrats were so outnumbered in the House. A group of 13 rollcalls may be used to illustrate the effect of factional loyalties. All of them involved either important administration bills or proposals that were strongly opposed by the administration. The rollcalls are not scalable, because there was no consistent pattern of opposition, but the contrasts between the most frequent supporters and opponents of the administration are worth noting. All of the consistent opponents and most of those frequently voting against the administration were Republicans. Among the Democrats there were 30 who always supported the administration and 31 others who did so with only one or two exceptions; in these groups were 32 of the 34 Democrats who reported in questionnaires that they had the administration's endorsement in the primary. (See chapter 4.) Three Democrats voted this regularly for the administration even though they had run against an administration candidate in the primary. The nine Democrats most frequently aligned against the administration (on from four to eight bills) included four who had overcome administration opposition in the primary. Following the rollcall that caused the largest number of opposition votes the administration leaders persuaded a number of legislators to change their mind and won a reversal on a second rollcall. If the opposition votes of those who switched are not counted, the number of Democrats who always voted with the administration on the 13 rollcalls is increased from 30 to 41, an even more impressive demonstration of the governor's success.

In the 1966 session of the legislature, Governor Breathitt was able to maintain control and win passage of most bills in his legislative package, although on some issues factional alignments were evident. Factionalism can be illustrated by a scale analysis of voting within the House Democratic party on a group of issues on which the administration's prestige was at stake. These include strip mining, civil rights, constitutional revision, and automobile inspection, for example. These 12 rollcalls are scalable, with a coefficient of reproducibility of 0.94 if six Democrats with irregular voting patterns are left out. There were 30 Democrats who supported the administration with but one or two exceptions, 19 who did so on most occasions, and 8 Democrats who voted against the administration on a majority of the rollcalls. In chapter 4 we identified 33 representatives who had the governor's support in the primary (and were reelected); 20 of these were in the group of the most consistent legislative supporters of the governor's program, and only 2 were among those usually opposing it. Among the 11 who won the primary over the opposition of the governor, only 2 supported him regularly, 4 did most of the time, and 5 opposed his programs a majority of the time.

In the course of a legislative session many of the governor's bills pass with little opposition or with opposition that is not organized along factional lines. It is evident from an analysis of rollcalls that when there is a major confrontation along partisan or factional lines the Democratic governor is usually able to hold his forces in line and at the same time win some votes from the opposition faction and often from the Republican party. It is also evident that some legislators who have been identified with the opposing faction, even including some of those whom the administration opposed in primaries, join the administration forces when the session begins. In factional and partisan battles, the odds seem to favor the governor.

A Republican governor faces a partisan and factional situation different from that which confronts a Democrat. The Republican party is not burdened with the legacy of factional divisions, and a Republican governor can expect a high degree of cohesion from his legislative party. During the administration of Republican Governor Willis (1943-1947), the minority Republican party in both houses provided a high level of support for the administration's bills. The major handicap facing a Republican governor is the inability of his party to win a majority in the legislature. During the first session of Governor Nunn's administration (1968) the Republicans had 14

Senate seats out of 38 and 43 House seats out of 100. As Republican organizational efforts become more successful, future Republican governors may hope to win legislative majorities, but it is common for a minority party to have less success in legislative races than in contests at the statewide level. Any governor whose party has a legislative minority must be able to win some votes from the opposition party, either by making compromises with the opposition leadership or by persuading some majority party legislators to split with their leadership and support the governor. The traditional factionalism in the Democratic party may be an asset to a Republican governor, though the previous Republican governor, Willis, frequently was defeated in legislative battles with the Democratic party. In the 1968 session, Governor Nunn did not have an extensive legislative program, but he won enough Democratic votes to gain passage of his budget and his increased tax program without any changes.

Undoubtedly a major reason for the governor's advantage is that he, and no one else, is in a position to offer the legislator a variety of favors. We use the term *patronage* to refer to the whole range of favors that are available: clients for the legislator's business or jobs for his relatives, jobs and other favors for his most important constituents, and state projects designed to benefit the entire county or district. Patronage serves in various ways to keep members of the administration faction in line. Some members are tied to the administration only by bonds of patronage; these are the least dependable, the most likely to defect because of dissatisfaction with the favors received. Those legislators who have long records of identification with the administration faction are likely to receive patronage as a fringe benefit. It may occasionally be necessary to provide state projects for their counties in order to demonstrate to the voters the advantages of their loyalty to the administration. When additional votes are needed, the governor may offer patronage to members of the opposition faction; the stronger the governor's political prestige and the more decimated the ranks of the opposition, the greater are the chances that the governor's offer will be accepted.

For many years Republican legislators were susceptible to the governor's offers of patronage, and it was common in Frankfort to refer to some of them as the governor's men. Whenever a political party is badly outnumbered for a prolonged period in a state or a county, the minority politicians are likely to give up hope of winning and some of them will succumb to the temptation of seeking crumbs from the majority table. Until recently most of the Republican legislators came from the depressed areas of southeastern Kentucky, where the need for roads and other state projects was particularly acute. They realized that their constituents were more interested in gaining tangible benefits for the county than in having a legislator who played a vigorous opposition role. If they could gain some of these benefits from a Democratic governor, they saw no reason to wait an indefinite number of years for a Republican governor.

During the 1966 session, a Republican legislator from Casey County took the floor to describe why he had to support the administration. He came to Frankfort with a petition from 800 of his constituents asking to have a 55-year old bridge rebuilt, and when he went to talk to the governor's assistant about the bridge, he was asked to support the administration's budget bill. He told his colleagues: "If you fight the administration, you won't get too much for your people. I'm a Republican—what do I have to work with? And if I come into the House and vote against the Democrats I'll get mud in my face for my people—that's all I'll get. What can I do? If I go against them I'll have no chance of serving my people."[6]

During the second session of the Chandler administration, when the governor lost the support of a majority of Democrats on a series of crucial votes, he was able to win most of the battles because he had support from most of the Republicans. As the session progressed, he was able to consolidate this support. Shortly before the rollcall on a bill authorizing the highway department to undertake certain kinds of construction work without using private contractors, Chandler was invited to attend a Republican House caucus. At the meeting he thanked Republicans for their support in the 1956 and 1958 sessions and warned them that without their backing on this bill he would be unable to provide the roads, parks, and industrial development that he hoped to make available for their counties. Twenty-one of the 22 Republicans at the caucus voted for the bill; two others left before the governor arrived and voted against it. Although almost two-thirds of the Democrats were against it, the bill passed by a single vote. Republican assistance was also vital in

[6] Louisville *Courier-Journal*, Jan. 13, 1966.

a series of rollcalls on the budget. One Republican legislator said he supported the governor's budget in return for a written promise of a road. He said, "That's what you call reciprocity. My people need that road. . . . If I can get it for them, they don't care how I vote on matters such as the budget."[7] Another Republican from eastern Kentucky subsequently reported: "One of the five National Guard armories in the state is in my county—a Republican county— even though several large Democratic counties were trying hard for it. Why was I able to get it? Chandler's budget passed by one vote and I voted for it."[8] Although the Combs and Breathitt administrations were less dependent on Republican votes, they continued the effort to attract the rural Republican legislators with offers of patronage. As we shall see, the resistance of the Republican legislative party to such offers grew as the proportion of those elected from metropolitan counties grew.

Since the passage of the merit system law in 1960, the amount of job patronage available for the governor to dispense has been sharply limited. As we have seen, this patronage is handled through the contact man in each county, who is seldom a legislator. The legislator who wants to get a state job for a political ally, a friend, or a relative has to compete with other political leaders in the county. If he brings a constituent in search of a job to the governor's office, one of the administrative assistants can write a note to the personnel department asking that the man be given a routine test, but he seldom can do anything more. When the administration is seriously concerned about keeping the support of a legislator, however, it can often find some way of assisting the legislator or his relatives. A private firm, such as a contractor, doing business with the state may be persuaded to hire a legislator's son or brother-in-law. The state negotiates a number of personal-service contracts without bids, with engineering firms, for example; it buys insurance and hires lawyers for certain kinds of work; and firms doing business with the state need legal services, insurance, and performance bonds. Almost one-third of the legislators are engaged in the practice of law or the insurance business. In 1960 the Kentucky legislature passed a conflict of interest law, however, that places limitations on the governor's ability to provide personal patronage for legislators. The

[7] *Ibid.*, Feb. 12, 1958.
[8] *Ibid.*, Feb. 20, 1966.

law prohibits legislators from being hired by state agencies (without resigning from the legislature), having any contractual relations with the state except as a result of competitive bidding with public notice, receiving compensation for representing any person before a state agency, and having an interest in any contracts that are pertinent to matters on which they have a vote, among other things.

The legislator may find himself indebted to the administration without seeking or wanting favors. One legislator said, "When I first came up here I used to boast of how independent I was: I didn't have any relatives on the payroll and I had only a small law practice. They snuck behind me and put my sister-in-law on the payroll without my knowing it and she thought I was responsible. And then I have had my business clients come to me and express the hope that nothing that I do in Frankfort will put them in an embarrassing position with the state."[9] Job patronage has declined in importance, but there are a variety of ways by which an imaginative governor and his staff can make it profitable for legislators to cooperate with the administration. It is impossible to calculate how extensively these techniques are used, and it would be inaccurate to attribute most of the governor's power to his ability to "buy" legislators, but this is one of the sources of gubernatorial power that cannot be overlooked.

It is easy to understand why legislators of both parties, particularly from the poorer sections of the state, are willing to vote for the administration in return for state projects in their counties. Their success in getting such projects will impress constituents far more than their voting record. The scope and variety of state services has grown in recent years, but at the same time there have been increasing limitations on the governor's freedom to select the counties that will benefit. As we noted in chapter 2, the allocation of highways, parks, colleges, hospitals, and other state projects is increasingly influenced—if not determined—by expert advisers and by federal officials, neither of whom show much interest in the governor's political problems. But the governor's discretionary authority continues to have some importance even though it is no longer absolute, and legislators still turn to him for help even though they recognize the limitations on his power. The governor has fewer jobs to distribute and less freedom in authorizing state

[9] *Ibid.*

projects than he once had, but he is still the only one to whom legislators can turn for various kinds of patronage. If the currency of patronage has been devalued, it is still being minted only in the governor's office. If there are fewer legislators who are controlled by the governor through the device of patronage, it remains true that most legislators want something from the governor's office during the course of a session. The various forms of patronage have declined in relative importance because the governor is relying more on influencing public opinion and on creating factional allies through endorsements in the primary; but, skillfully handled, patronage is still an important tool of gubernatorial leadership.

During the 60-day session legislative business occupies a large portion of the governor's time. Even though he has administrative assistants who also concentrate on legislative business, it is necessary for him to make the strategic decisions about selecting priority legislation and determining what concessions and compromises are necessary. He meets frequently with the leaders and he also confers with rank-and-file legislators who are seeking his support for a bill or whose votes he is seeking on his priority legislation. When the legislature is acting on important business, members can usually see someone from the governor's office sitting in the gallery, and occasionally the governor is there too. When the need is urgent, the governor is even found in the corridors outside the legislative chambers, talking to members. On the final day of the 1966 legislative session Governor Breathitt spent the morning talking to senators in and around the Senate chamber and spent the afternoon talking to representatives just outside the House chamber; the result was final passage of a public utilities tax measure that had appeared to be doomed.

Some of the members are vitally interested in the passage of bills that they have introduced. It may be a local bill of concern only to one county, or it may be a bill with statewide importance that does not conflict with the governor's program. By threatening to block this bill or by offering to get it passed, the governor and his legislative leaders may insure the member's support for some of the governor's bills. In some sessions the governor's strategy has been to delay members' bills as long as possible in order to strengthen his bargaining position while his program was being passed. Some members are immune to these tactics, because they do not have any bills in which they are deeply interested, while almost all members (at least all Democrats) have some interest in patronage. These tactics also sometimes backfire; the governor may lose the votes of members who resent the delay of their bills.

The Organization of Majority Power in the Legislature. Because of the governor's interest not only in passing his program but in controlling the legislative timetable, he needs the close collaboration of legislative leaders. It has become an established practice for a Democratic governor to select those he wants chosen as speaker of the House and as Democratic floor leaders, who run the legislative machinery with a firm hand. The governor's inability to get his choices approved has been a clear sign that his legislative influence is in jeopardy. This occurred in 1958 when Governor Chandler's choice for president pro tem of the Senate was defeated. Democratic governors have also exercised a voice in the choice of key staff members, such as the chief clerk of each house. The governor has consulted leading legislators and has usually been sensitive to legislative preferences, but the legislators in turn usually have gone along with the governor once he has made a firm decision. In 1964, for example, the governor selected the speaker, who was a close friend, and the majority leader; he suggested that two other aspirants for the floor leader's job serve as assistant leaders; and he accepted the choice for caucus chairman suggested by rank-and-file Democrats. At the start of the 1966 session the governor negotiated for some time before replacing the incumbent House floor leader. Although the change was unpopular among some legislators, most seemed to share the views of one Democrat who said, "I wish he'd just go ahead and tell us who he wants. That's what we're all waiting for." In the 1968 session Republican legislators quickly acceded to Governor Nunn's suggestions for filling party leadership posts.

In the Senate the lieutenant governor may share in the choice of legislative leaders. Governor Combs and Lieutenant Governor Wyatt cooperated in decisions about organizing the Senate. When Harry Lee Waterfield was elected lieutenant governor on a ticket with Governor Breathitt, Waterfield was able to exercise considerable discretion in the selection of leaders as well as committees. He chose as floor leader Casper "Cap" Gardner, who had been identified with the Chandler faction and had been a leader of opposition forces during the Combs administration. After the break between Breathitt and Waterfield, the governor's choices were approved by the Democratic caucus for the 1966 session.

The Democratic governor's influence in the legislature has been implemented further by the selection of a high proportion of administration supporters to the most important standing committees. In the House the selection has been made by a committee on committees, consisting of the speaker and the Democratic floor leader and caucus chairman. In the Senate the power has alternated between the lieutenant governor and a committee on committees. The Democrats established a committee on committees in 1944 when the lieutenant governor was a Republican and continued the practice in the Clements, Wetherby, and Combs administrations. During Chandler's administration, Lieutenant Governor Waterfield had the authority to make committee assignments, but his successor, Wilson Wyatt, did not want such authority. Waterfield regained the power in the 1964 session, but after his break with Governor Breathitt, the control over committees became an issue in the 1965 primaries. In the 1966 session the administration forces succeeded in reestablishing the committee on committees, consisting of four Democratic leaders in addition to the lieutenant governor. Except for Waterfield's independent authority in the 1964 session, the committees in recent years have been selected by leaders who were handpicked by the governor. In some cases the governor has made specific suggestions for committee assignments, and in 1966 Governor Breathitt was reported to have played an unusually active part in submitting names of committee members to the leadership.

The legislative rules authorize the committee on committees to assign bills to standing committees. In the Senate, Lieutenant Governor Waterfield had this authority in the 1956, 1958, and 1964 sessions. In practice, the most important bills, both those favored and those opposed by the administration, have been assigned to a few committees. Consequently the leadership has been able to stack these key committees with men who are completely reliable. It has not needed to worry about the exact balance of power on the remainder of the committees, and frequently it has been able to satisfy the wishes of most of the members concerning assignment to these committees.

Even though the concentration of most important bills in a few committees seems like an effective means of maintaining control by the leadership, another device has been used during the last 15 days of a regular session and throughout special sessions. All existing committees have been superseded during this period by a rules committee in each house, which has assumed jurisdiction over all bills that are introduced or that have been introduced previously but have not yet received final passage in that house. Although the membership has been chosen to insure that a majority of those on the rules committee were administration loyalists, the large size of the committees—sometimes as much as one-half of the legislators—has made it more difficult to control. In 1964, for example, the House rules committee refused to vote out a civil rights bill despite a personal appeal by Governor Breathitt.

A detailed analysis of the 1964 session provides an example of the concentration of legislative work among a few committees, which can be found in any session of the legislature. During that session 43 percent of all Senate and House bills were originally referred in the House to the rules committee, 32 percent were

TABLE 6.4

Committee Referral of All Bills and of Bills That
Became Law in House of Representatives, 1964

Committee	Percentage of All Bills (N-639)	Percentage of Bills That Became Law (N-195)
Rules[a]	43	53
Kentucky Statutes No. 1	4	9
Kentucky Statutes No. 2	3	2
Kentucky Statutes No. 3	3	3
Elections	4	3
Education	3	2
Revenue and Taxation	3	2
Public Health	3	1
Roads and Highways	3	5
Courts and Legal Procedure	3	2
County Government	3	2
All Other Committees (34)	25	18

[a] These totals include only those bills originally referred to the rules committee, and not those referred first to another committee and sent to rules in the last 15 days of the session.

referred to 10 other committees, and 25 percent went to the remaining 34 committees, 5 of which received not a single one. Among the most active committees were three Kentucky statutes committees, which handled much of the priority administration legislation. If we look only at those bills that became law, the workload was even more concentrated. (See Table 6.4.) During the 1964 session of the Senate, the rules committee received 41 percent of the bills, the ways and means committee received 11 percent, another seven committees got 36 percent, and the other ten committees had 12 percent (each receiving at least one bill). These committees had jurisdiction over approximately the same proportions of those bills that became law. If we take into account rules committee action on bills previously considered by another committee as well as those handled under original jurisdiction, the committee in the Senate acted on 59 percent of the bills that became law, and in the House the figure was 57 percent.

During the 1964 session the Republicans were represented on most House committees, including the six most active ones, approximately in proportion to their House membership, which was 37 out of 100. The Republicans had only one member out of ten on the courts and legal procedure committee, however, and not a single member on the three Kentucky statutes committees, even though the House rules adopted by the Democratic majority required that committee memberships be distributed "in proportion to the representation of each political party in the House." A total of 20 Democrats were named to the three Kentucky statutes committees (5 of them to two of these), and with two exceptions they were men who had a high record of proadministration voting in the rollcalls that we used earlier to test administration loyalty. One of the two exceptions was Fred Morgan, a former speaker and veteran member of the Chandler faction. Of these 20 men, 11 had run in the 1962 primary with Combs' support (according to their responses on questionnaires), 4 others were clearly identified with the Combs faction, and only 3 had been opposed by the Combs administration in 1962. In the 1962 session the membership on the three Kentucky statutes committees was more widely distributed, but there was only one Republican out of 28 members, and a large majority of the members voted solidly with the Combs administration. In 1966 the 13 members of the three committees (6 of them on two of the committees) included only one Republican; most of the members were either leaders or loyal members of the administration faction.

The House rules committee has usually consisted of all or most of the representatives with previous legislative service. In 1960 all but seven of the veteran members were on the rules committee; those left out included four of the nine Republicans with previous service. In the 1962 and 1964 sessions the House rules committee included all of the members with previous service and no freshmen. The Republicans had only 9 of 35 members in 1962 and 16 of 40 members in 1964, in both cases less than their proportion of the total House. Because Republican membership in the House was growing in these years, the policy of including all members with previous service had the effect of keeping Republican membership on the rules committee relatively small, and the leadership made no effort to exclude antiadministration Democrats from the committee.

In 1966 the Democratic leadership was confronted with a problem; the number of representatives with previous service, which had averaged about one-half, totaled 75, and included 23 Republicans. A rules committee of this size would be unwieldy. The Democratic leadership chose 39 of the 52 Democrats and only 12 of the 23 Republicans to the rules committee. The Republicans chosen included some of the most vociferous critics of the administration; those omitted included several of those who had more often cooperated with the administration. At least four of the Democrats omitted from the committee had run in the 1965 primary with Breathitt's support; four others had been opposed by Breathitt. The administration's tactics backfired. Eleven of the 13 veteran Democrats who were excluded from the committee formed a "rebel" group within the House and were joined by 6 others, some of whom had long been associated with the Chandler forces. Many of those who joined the rebels resented the administration pressure that they had been subjected to during the session, particularly with regard to bills concerning mining. The rebel group, which was able to outvote the administration when it was aligned with the Republicans, succeeded in delaying or defeating some administration bills in the closing days of the session. All of the Democratic legislators whom we found opposing a majority of the governor's bills, in the scale analysis, and a number of his inconsistent supporters were in the rebel group. The rebellion illustrated the weakness of the large rules committee as a technique of administration control. Not only is a large committee difficult to control, but when approximately half of the representatives are put on the committee, those who are left off believe themselves to be "second-class citizens," deprived of a voice and a vote in the body where the most important decisions are being made. Once it became necessary to omit veteran Democratic members, most of whom had often supported the administration, a rebellion followed naturally.

In the Senate the administration leaders have usually appointed a large rules committee, not limited to veteran members, as well as a few small committees of administration loyalists to handle major legislation. This was the pattern in 1960, when the rules committee included 24 of the 30 Democrats and 2 of 8 Republicans; most of the excluded Democrats had been Chandler supporters in the 1958 session. The 1962 rules committee included 23 Democrats and 4 Republicans. Earlier in this chapter we described the categories of senators resulting from a scale analysis of rollcalls on seven administration bills in 1962. There were 22 senators in the three categories that most regularly supported the administration, and 21 of them (including one Republican) were placed on the rules committee. Only 4 of the 13 senators classified in other groups gained a place on the committee. In both 1960 and 1962 there were two small Kentucky statutes committees made up of administration leaders and loyalists.

This pattern of Senate committee assignments was broken abruptly in 1964 when Lieutenant Governor Waterfield made the selections. The Republicans, with one-third of the Senate membership, had approximately one-third of the seats on both major and minor committees (except rules). There were no Kentucky statutes committees, and no other committees under tight administration control. The 13-member rules committee had only three Republicans. Among the ten Democrats, six were identified with the Chandler-Waterfield faction. Chairmanship of the other major committees was divided, with a majority headed by administration supporters. The split between Breathitt and Waterfield did not begin to develop seriously until late in the 1964 session, shortly before the rules committee was named. When a special session was called in 1965 to pass legislation on property-tax assessment, the Senate was sharply divided between

Breathitt and Waterfield forces. When the bill appeared to be stuck in the rules committee, the Senate voted (22 to 12) to enlarge the rules committee to include all senators. In 1966 the administration leadership named a rules committee of 14 Democrats, almost all loyal to the governor, and 5 Republicans.

Even though Republicans have usually been given little or no representation on major committees in the Senate, they have often received chairmanships of several minor committees in the Senate, though not in the House. In 1960 the number of Senate committees was increased from 19 to 38 in order to make every senator a chairman. The practice continued in 1962. Republicans chaired such committees as aviation, classification of towns and cities, and child welfare and social work. In 1964 Waterfield named 3 Republican chairmen, out of 19 committees; and 3 were chosen out of 21 chairmen in 1966.

By maintaining control over those committees that handle most important legislation, a Democratic administration has had a good chance of blocking bills that it opposed and in getting floor action on its measures. Although it has occasionally been defeated, the administration usually has commanded enough votes on the floor to win passage of its priority legislation. There is always the risk, however, that administration bills will be drastically changed by amendment on the floor. Legislators who are unwilling to vote against a bill may go along with amendments to it despite the governor's opposition. In order to minimize the risk of unwanted amendments being passed, the legislative leaders have regularly included in the House rules a provision that a previous question may be adopted by a majority of those voting. When the previous question has been moved, 20 minutes of debate is permitted—equally divided between proponents and opponents, no further amendments may be offered, and a vote is taken on the bill and any pending amendments. A similar provision exists in the Senate rules; except that a majority of the elected senators is required to pass the motion. The usual practice of the majority leader is to call up a bill, to move any amendments desired by the administration, and then to move the previous question. Once the motion has been adopted, the presiding officer sometimes allows more than the 20 minutes of prescribed debate, but the ban on further amendments is rigidly enforced.

At the start of each session in the House, when the rules are adopted, a motion is usually made to change the provision requiring a majority of the elected members to adopt a previous question motion. Because the administration has insisted on adoption of this change, it has often been one of the earliest tests of administration strength. During the 1956 and 1958 sessions, a vote of 51 House members was required to cut off amendments, and the rebels took advantage of this to harass the Chandler administration. In the 1960 session the Combs administration leaders won adoption of the rule to cut off amendments by a simple majority (often referred to as the "gag rule"). Those opposing it that year were all the Republicans, several Chandler Democrats, and a few anti-Chandler "rebels." In 1962 the opponents included all but two of the Republicans and seven hard-core Chandlerites: in 1964 all but two Republicans and no Democrats voted against the "gag rule." Again in 1966 the rule was adopted, this time by a straight party vote, but ten days before the session ended, a coalition of Republicans and rebels succeeded in changing the rules to require the vote of 51 members to move the previous question.

At the start of its 1968 session both houses of the legislature adopted a new set of rules, which had widespread, bipartisan support. The rules were designed to strengthen the legislature and, specifically, to make its committees more effective. The number of substantive committees, which had averaged 28 in the Senate and 44 in the House during the previous four sessions, was reduced to 14 in each body. The jurisdiction of each committee was spelled out in the rules, in an attempt to reduce the arbitrary authority of the committee on committees in assigning bills. The rules committee in each house was restructured into a small bipartisan leadership committee with authority throughout the session to schedule the order in which bills, once reported by the substantive committees, would reach the floor. No longer would the rules committee supersede other committees during the closing days of the session. Moreover, the substantive committees were authorized to meet between sessions, as subcommittees of the Legislative Research Commission. The Republican party was given a proportionate share of seats on all the substantive committees, and in the Senate it received three chairmanships. Moreover, the Republican committee members were assigned by Republican rather than Democratic leaders.

TABLE 6.5

Republican Legislative Candidates and Legislators from Metropolitan and Nonmetropolitan Districts, 1948-1968[a]

	Average 1948-1958		1960		1962		1964		1966		1968	
	Met.	Non-met.	Met.	Non-met.	Met.	Non-met.	Met.	Non-met.	Met.	Non-met.	Met.	Non-met.
SENATE												
Total Seats in Senate	8	30	8	30	8	30	9	29	11	27	11	27
Senators to Be Elected	4	15	5	14	3	16	6	13	5	14	7	13
Republican Candidates	3½	10½	5	9	3	6	5	7	4	5	7	10
Winning Republican Candidates	½	4	0	4	2	3	2	6	3	1	4	6
Total Republican Seats	½	8½	1	7	2	7	4	9	5	7	7	7
HOUSE												
Total Seats in House	19	81	19	81	19	81	28	72	28	72	28	72
Republican Candidates	16	38	15	29	14	38	25	32	28	33	27	53
Total Republican Seats	3	21	1	19	9	17	16	21	16	20	17	26

[a] Dates refer to the years in which the legislature meets; the election is the previous year. Half of the senators are elected every two years.

These new rules, if continued in future sessions, should give the legislature a greater measure of independence from a governor of either party and should protect interests of both legislative parties.

We have seen that the Republican party, with only about one-fourth of the legislative seats, was for many years unable to function effectively as an opposition force or to develop its own legislative program. Because of their dependence on the governor for patronage and state projects in their districts, many of the Republican legislators supported the Democratic administration consistently on its priority measures. In order to break its administration shackles, the party needed to elect not only more legislators but more who were able to exercise independence.

Table 6.5 traces the recent changes that have occurred in the size and composition of the Republican legislative delegation. From the 1948 through the 1958 sessions, the party averaged almost exactly one-fourth of the membership in each house. The four major metropolitan counties (Jefferson, Fayette, Kenton, and Campbell) had 8 senators and 19 representatives. Although the Republicans ran candidates consistently for every seat in Jefferson County and contested almost two-thirds of the seats in the other metropolitan counties, these four counties had an average of only three Republican representatives and had a single Republican senator in only three of the six sessions. In the 1960 session the metropolitan counties had one senator and only a single representative. Among the nonmetropolitan House districts electing Republicans, which averaged 21 from 1948 through 1958, were 17 districts that always elected Republicans. In the Senate there were 7 districts that were consistently Republican, out of an average of 8½ nonmetropolitan districts represented by Republicans. The Republican legislative party was dominated by members from the rural counties, principally in the southeast, that were traditionally Republican.

In 1961 the Republican party won the local elections in both Jefferson County and Louisville, and in the process elected 9 of 11 representatives and won both of the Senate seats for which an election was scheduled. In 1963 the legislature was reapportioned, and the result was to further change the balance of urban-rural power within the Republican party. Under the reapportionment, 13 House seats were transferred from rural counties to seven urban counties. Nine of the lost seats were normally Democratic, three were Republican, and one was Marginal. Ten of the seats went to four Marginal counties: six to Jefferson, two to Fayette, and one each to Campbell and Boyd. The other three went to western counties that are normally Democratic in House races. In the Senate, Jefferson County gained two seats, Fayette gained one, with the probable loss of one rural Republican seat (as well as one Democratic and one Marginal seat). Reapportionment guaranteed a loss of rural Republican representation, and it created the potential for metropolitan Republican gains if the party could maintain its strength in Jefferson County and make inroads into the other metropolitan counties. In 1963 the Republican gubernatorial candidate fell short of victory by only 13,000 votes, but his gains were less impressive in Jefferson County than in other parts of the state. The Republicans won a single Senate seat and 10 of 17 House seats in Jefferson County, a smaller proportion than in 1961, but gained 6 House seats in the other metropolitan counties. In the rest of the state the Republicans gained eight House seats, mostly in rural counties, while losing four from reapportionment. In 1965, when the Republicans again won the local elections in Jefferson County and Louisville, they elected their candidates for all 3 Senate seats at stake as well as for 14 of 17 House seats, but suffered losses in the other metropolitan counties.

The 1967 results were similar to those in 1963. The Republicans lost three House seats in Jefferson County but gained two Senate and four House seats in other metropolitan counties; in the rest of the state the Republicans made a net gain of six House seats. The Republicans won legislative seats in most of the counties carried by Nunn, including substantial majorities in most metropolitan counties that went Republican. The Republican party contested 17 of 20 Senate seats and 80 of 100 House seats. There were only four seats (all in the House) with no Republican candidate but with majorities for Nunn—most of them in northeastern Kentucky. The failure to win a legislative majority in 1967 resulted principally from the fact that the party had only a large minority of votes in most of the western Kentucky districts and consequently won very few seats there despite its increased voting strength.

The Republican losses in traditional areas that resulted from reapportionment have been balanced by gains in some Marginal rural districts that resulted from the party's unusually strong showing in the 1963 and 1967 gubernatorial races. In the metropolitan counties that benefited from reapportionment, the Republicans have greater organizational strength and a continuing potential for legislative victories, but the number of legislative seats is likely to fluctuate, perhaps by wide margins, from session to session. In Jefferson County, where the outcome of legislative races seems to be tied closely to state and local elections, it is likely that the fluctuations in Republican legislative strength will be particularly great, but the party is not likely again to be reduced to the single representative it had from 1954 through 1960.

In the 1962 session the metropolitan Republicans became, for the first time in many years, a vocal minority in the legislative party. In the 1964 and 1966 sessions the metropolitan Republicans held almost half of the party's seats, and were frequently able to pick up enough support from other Republicans to constitute a majority. We can illustrate the changing balance of power in the Republican legislative party by reviewing changes in the leadership structure. In recent years there have often been wide-open contests in Republican caucuses and incumbent leaders have frequently been replaced at the start of a session. In the Senate most of the top posts have been held by rural Republicans, but in the 1962 and 1966 sessions senators from Jefferson County were selected as caucus chairmen. In the 1958 and 1960 sessions of the House the top three leadership posts were held by Republicans from eastern rural districts, but in 1962 a Republican from a western rural district was chosen, and subsequently defeated in 1964. In both the 1962 and 1964 sessions Jefferson County Republicans were selected as caucus chairmen. When the House Republicans caucused before the 1966 session, the 16 members from metropolitan areas were prepared to take command. They had enlisted support from one other urban representative (from Boyd County) and from two rural members— enough to give them a narrow majority. The caucus selected James Caldwell of Jefferson County as floor leader, Don Ball of Fayette County as caucus chairman, and a rural representative, Harry Hoe, as the whip; the caucus also selected two more metropolitan members to new posts as assistant floor leaders. In 1968, the Senate

Republican caucus chairman came from Jefferson County and in the House, the floor leader, caucus chairman, whip, and one of two assistant floor leaders came from metropolitan or urban areas.

Most of the Republicans who were elected from metropolitan counties in the 1962, 1964, and 1966 sessions did not have previous legislative service. They had not experienced the frustrations of belonging to a hopeless minority, nor had they grown accustomed to trading their votes for benefits from the governor's office. Moreover, they came from metropolitan constituencies with needs that were very different from those in eastern Kentucky. Voters in the major cities were more likely to feel the effects of important state-wide programs than to be impressed by the individual projects that a governor might offer in return for legislative support. As a practical matter the large size of legislative delegations from metropolitan counties made it difficult for the governor to negotiate with the members or for any single legislator to claim credit (in a convincing fashion) for any state benefits the county received. The metropolitan legislators were more interested in state politics than most of their rural colleagues, and several of them had political ambitions above the legislative level. They were conscious of the party's need to build a record in the legislature that would attract public attention and win public approval. Much of the initiative for developing alternatives to the administration's programs came from the metropolitan Republicans, and in some sessions it was these members who most often opposed the administration on roll-call votes. Divisions in the Republican legislative party did not follow metropolitan-rural lines precisely, but this was the best single predictor of voting behavior.

Those Republicans who were most interested in developing an effective opposition believed that the party, particularly in the House, needed institutional devices to serve these purposes: to carry out studies on administration bills and on issues that might lead to Republican bills, to provide a forum for discussions that might lead to greater party cohesion, and to attract the voters' attention to the party's record and stand on issues. In 1964 the House Republicans established a legislative review committee to study pending bills and recommend those on which a partisan stand should be taken. A more active group was the legislative policy committee, which prepared or endorsed a number of bills that constituted a

Republican program in the legislature. Many of these bills were introduced with the joint sponsorship of most Republican members. Both committees were dominated by urban members.

During the 1962 session Republican legislators from both houses met in a joint caucus (which bore the title of joint policy committee), and during the 1964 and 1966 sessions the House Republicans held regular caucuses. In 1966 these meetings were open to the press. It is difficult to judge the effectiveness of the caucus because its deliberations did not usually become public, even when they were open to the press. The caucus was used by the leadership and the various study committees to explain proposed legislation. It provided an opportunity for discussion that showed whether or not there was anything approaching concensus among the members on an issue. When there was a high degree of consensus, the members sometimes voted to take a formal stand on a bill, although they deliberately avoided any effort to bind the membership to support a caucus recommendation. In 1964, however, the House Republican caucus ousted the party whip because he had voted against a bill to establish a permanent fiscal watchdog committee in the legislature.

After defeat of the bill to establish a legislative watchdog committee on fiscal affairs in the 1964 session, Republicans in both houses established a joint committee to serve the same purpose. It continued to meet after the session, and it provided the party with a vehicle for criticizing the financial practices of the Democratic administration. In the 1966 session the legislature established such a committee, and the Republicans selected two members who had had experience on the party's watchdog committee.

In an effort to attract some public attention to its legislative proposals and its record, the Republican legislative party has made increasing use of statements to the press. It has issued a platform of proposed legislation at the beginning of sessions and a commentary on the record of the legislature—and its contribution to that record—at the end of the session. Early in the 1965 general election campaign a group of 40 Republican legislative candidates issued a campaign platform that included a number of specific commitments regarding legislation.

A nine-point legislative program offered in 1962 included several proposals for changing taxes, a broad statement on civil rights, a proposal to remove highway department employees from politics, and a suggestion that all state buildings fly the American flag. The party had little success in enacting its program, although it did win passage of a bill to extend the filing deadline for the veterans bonus. The Republicans were usually divided, sometimes almost evenly, on those administration bills that were controversial. There was no block of consistent administration supporters among the Republicans, and only a few members who regularly opposed the administration. The metropolitan Republicans more often supported the priority administration bills than did the rural members; but on several issues in which the partisan interest was most obviously strong, such as the gag rule and the investigation of several charges of scandal in state government, only a few rural Republicans supported the administration.

In 1964 the Republican legislators in the House issued a platform that emphasized increased support for education, cuts in the income tax and other incentives for new industry, greater economy in government and more careful budgetary review, and a change in the timing of state and local elections to coincide with federal election years. In the House (where the size of the Republican delegations makes analysis more useful), the Republicans voted with complete or near unity on several motions that clearly served the party's interest, including opposition to the gag rule and abolition of the three Kentucky statutes committees that had no Republican members. The Republicans also had substantial unity on several bills implementing the party's platform on elections, taxation, and budgetary procedures, but the defection of several members weakened the party's effectiveness on several rollcalls involving the budget. With several members dissenting in each case, a majority of Republicans succeeded in delaying speedy action on the budget, voted unsuccessfully against cutting off amendments to the budget, and then approved its final passage. On a motion to establish a permanent legislative watchdog committee to review fiscal affairs, the Republicans split 27 to 5; the bill was defeated, but it had enough Democratic votes to have passed if the Republicans had supported it unanimously. The Republicans were most seriously divided on the major administration measures. The most controversial issue of the session, which split both parties, was a civil rights bill on public accommodations, which died in the rules committee. Republicans voted 18 to 11 against bringing the bill out of committee, with support for the bill coming almost entirely from metropolitan Republicans.

The divisions among House Republicans in the 1964 session can be illustrated by use of a scale that includes ten rollcalls. These include votes on the gag rule, the Kentucky statutes committees, several votes on the budget, the watchdog committee, a road bond issue, and a commission on economy and efficiency to be appointed by the governor. There were 21 Republicans in three groups who either voted consistently against the administration, or supported it on only one or both of two bills: the bond issue and final passage of the budget. Fifteen of these 21 represented metropolitan counties. The other 13 Republicans, only one from a metropolitan county, supported the administration and opposed the majority of the Republicans on one or more of the other issues. Included in this latter group were several Republicans, mostly from eastern Kentucky, who rarely voted with their party colleagues on those issues that involved a direct clash between the administration and Republican legislators.[10]

During the 1966 session the Republican party did not have many opportunities to force floor action on the legislative proposals included in its platform enunciated during the 1965 elections, but several of these objectives were achieved: a legislative audit committee was established, a law was passed to regulate campaign spending, and greater support was given to the minimum foundation program for teachers' salaries. The Republican legislative delegation was more successful than in the past in maintaining unity on issues that were of major interest to the party. For example, the House Republicans voted with complete or near unanimity on setting up a legislative audit committee, amending the rules to make it harder to shut off debate and amendments, gaining more Republican members on the Legislative Research Commission, and seeking to permit amendments to the budget bill.

The Republicans in the House were divided during the 1966 session on most of the major bills presented by the administration, however. Only two Republican representatives opposed the civil rights bill and only six opposed the strip mining bill, but the

---

[10] The coefficient of reproducibility for this scale was 0.96, with three members who voted only a few times being omitted.

party was deeply divided on the issue of constitutional revision. A scale analysis shows that there was some consistency in the pattern of Republican voting on a group of eight rollcalls, including these and other important issues. The division within the party, as in previous sessions, was along rural-urban lines, but on these rollcalls it was the legislators from metropolitan counties who most often supported the administration. Fourteen of the 18 Republican representatives who most often supported the administration came from metropolitan counties, but there were no metropolitan Republicans among the twelve most frequently opposed to the administration.[11]

In the 1968 session of the legislature the Republicans had the largest proportion of seats since 1944. In the 1967 election Republican gains in Fayette and Campbell counties were almost offset by losses in Jefferson County; consequently, the biggest gains were in smaller urban and several rural districts. The party remained divided along urban-rural lines, but the responsibility of providing support for a Republican governor gave the legislative party more incentive for minimizing its differences and attaining unity than had been the case during the years of Democratic administrations. The only votes during the session that directly involved the governor's prestige were those taken on his budget and his tax program, and on these crucial rollcalls the governor never lost more than one or two Republican votes, while winning enough Democratic votes to be successful.

[11] The coefficient of reproducibility was 0.93, with three inconsistent Republicans omitted.

7 | Kentucky in Transition

Anyone who attempts to forecast political developments in a state like Kentucky that is in transition runs the risk of making either of two mistakes. One mistake is to exaggerate the factors that perpetuate the status quo and cause resistance to change. The other is to assume that, because the signs of longrun changes are already visible, these changes will become effective tomorrow. Kentucky is in the process of becoming a predominantly urban state with a flourishing two-party system, but it has been moving toward urbanization more slowly than most states, and the immediate obstacles in the path of a two-party system remain formidable.

The analyst of Kentucky politics must also avoid the error of ignoring or blurring the diversity that characterizes the state. Mountain politics in eastern Kentucky still differs in style from the politics of the Bluegrass or western Kentucky. Family traditions are stronger, political loyalties are different, and social and cultural patterns are unique in the mountain areas. There are important differences in the other rural sections of the state between those communities that are continuing to decline in population and those that have been able to attract some industry and to maintain population levels. The three major metropolitan areas—Jefferson, Fayette, and Kenton-Campbell—differ widely among themselves, but they share several characteristics that distinguish them from most smaller counties: a high level of income and a growing and increasingly cosmopolitan population.

The trend to the cities will continue in Kentucky, and by 1970 more than half of the population will be urban, as defined by the

Census Bureau, but Kentucky is likely to continue to remain one of the less urbanized states in the country. The metropolitan areas, particularly Jefferson and Fayette, will continue to grow. The proportion of persons living in the four largest counties, which rose from 26 to 33 percent between 1950 and 1966, will probably reach 35 or 36 percent by 1975. Several other urban counties are growing rapidly: Daviess, Christian, Warren, and Franklin, and several small counties adjoining the metropolitan ones. The decline in the population of rural counties, particularly in eastern Kentucky, can be expected to continue. But for several decades the population of Kentucky is likely to remain rather equally balanced between urban and rural.

There are some states today in which the interests of the rural and small-town voters can be almost completely ignored by political candidates, but that is not likely to be true in Kentucky for many years to come. The two political parties will have to continue to devise programs and recruit candidates with an appeal to voters in the cities and suburbs, the small towns and the farms. The growth of metropolitan areas is certain to affect the political life of Kentucky because the needs of the metropolis differ from those of the smaller cities and towns. The viewpoints and attitudes of Kentucky voters may not change as rapidly as the population changes, however. Many of the new residents of the large cities come from rural Kentucky counties. In 1960 there were about 113,000 persons over five years old who had moved into the four largest counties within five years, and almost half of these came from other Kentucky counties. The impact of migrants from the rural eastern and south-central counties of Kentucky is particularly strong in Fayette County; in 1960 there were almost 5,000 residents of Fayette County who had lived in one of these counties in 1955, and they constituted 14 percent of all the persons who had come into Fayette County during the five-year period. In the same period less than 6 percent of the newcomers to Jefferson County came from eastern or south-central Kentucky.[1] Probably many of these new urbanites and suburbanites retain their old political attitudes and loyalties for a number of years, and often they retain close ties to families who remain at home. Urbanization may have the effect of weak-

---

[1] Bureau of the Census, *Census of Population, 1960: General Social and Economic Characteristics*, Table 82, p. 19-206. Data on migrants from eastern and south-central counties come from the Department of Sociology, University of Kentucky.

ening traditional voting habits, but the effect is often gradual and is most likely to be noticeable among younger voters.

PROSPECTS FOR EMERGENCE OF THE REPUBLICAN PARTY

The time is propitious for the emergence of the Republican party as a political force that is capable of competing for votes in state elections on equal terms with the Democratic party. A number of factors suggest that a highly competitive two-party system is about to become a reality in Kentucky. Some half million voters, from 49.8 to 54.3 percent of the total, voted for Republican presidential candidates in the elections of 1952, 1956, and 1960. The voters of Kentucky have elected Republicans to the United States Senate in five elections starting in 1956, with a popular vote ranging from 434,000 to 644,000 and by percentages of from 50.3 to 64.4. Perhaps most significantly, in 1963, 436,000 voters, 49.2 percent of the total, voted for a Republican candidate for governor, and in 1967, 454,000, or 51.6 percent, elected a Republican governor. We do not have survey data available to tell us whether most of the Republican votes in these recent elections have come from the same voters or whether a somewhat larger number have been voting Republican with somewhat less consistency. In either case, it is evident that a majority of those Kentuckians who usually go to the polls have cast at least one Republican vote for a major office in the last few years, and it appears to be true that a very large minority of the frequent voters have voted Republican quite consistently in recent elections.

Voting is largely a matter of habit,[2] and previous voting patterns in the state suggest that most Kentuckians have been lifelong Democrats or Republicans, casting a habitual vote for one party. A majority of these traditional voters have been Democrats. During the last decade some of these lifelong Democrats have cast one or more votes for Republican candidates. Once the habit of voting for one party has been broken, it becomes easier to cross party lines again and again, and the voter begins to approach the polling booth in a more independent frame of mind. The habitual Democratic voter

[2] Angus Campbell and others, *The American Voter* (New York: John Wiley and Sons, 1960); Philip E. Converse, "A Major Political Realignment in the South?" in Allan P. Sindler, ed., *Change in the Contemporary South* (Durham, N.C.: Duke University Press, 1963), 195-222.

who has voted for Dwight Eisenhower, Richard Nixon, or John Sherman Cooper is a potential Republican voter in state and local elections. Once the voter has begun to question his unswerving loyalty to one party, the other party has a chance of winning his support if it offers the right candidates and runs effective campaigns in state and local elections.

The Republican party has also gained votes in recent elections from new members of the Kentucky electorate. Those who have come to Kentucky, and particularly to the metropolitan centers, from other states have included a number of voters who consider themselves either Republicans or Independents. Table 7.1 shows

TABLE 7.1

Proportions of Republicans, Independents, and Democrats Having Certain Characteristics among a Sample of Fayette County Voters (in Percentages)

Characteristics of Voters	Republicans	Independents	Democrats
Those who grew up in northeast or midwest states	24	24	10
Those who grew up in Kentucky	64	67	74
Those who grew up in Republican counties in Kentucky	9	5	8
Those with at least some college education	75	55	59
Those who are professional or businessmen	36	25	29
Those 50 years old or above	32	34	41
Those 30 to 49 years old	56	46	46
Those 18 to 29 years old	12	20	13
Those who are registered as Republicans	79	14	1
Total number	(146)	(112)	(244)

the higher proportion of non-Democrats among persons in Fayette County who were raised outside Kentucky. At the time of the 1960 census, 7 percent of the state's population had been living in another state five years earlier.[3] In addition, the new voters who join the electorate every year at the age of 18 are likely to be less bound by tradition than older generations. Almost one-fourth of the Kentuckians of voting age were under 30 years of age in 1960, and the proportion in that age category is growing. It is true that younger persons are usually influenced by the political loyalties of

[3] *Census of Population, 1960*, Table 82, p. 19-206.

their parents, but as they leave home and frequently take jobs in other parts of the state, they are less likely to be bound by local political customs and traditional family loyalties. Table 7.1 shows that one-fifth of the Independents who were polled in Fayette County were under 30, compared to about one-eighth of the Democrats and Republicans.

It is impossible, in the absence of statewide survey data, to determine what proportion of the Republican votes comes from new voters in the state and what proportion comes from Kentucky natives who used to be consistent Democratic voters. It is also impossible to tell how many former Democratic voters are not only changing their voting habits but are beginning to think of themselves as Republicans. It is probable that the decline in traditional voting patterns and outmigration from eastern Kentucky counties have reduced the number of traditional Republican voters. Although the absence of survey data conceals information on changes in individual voting habits, it is obvious from the election returns that some Republican candidates for both state and national office are winning majorities or at least large minorities in large numbers of counties that used to be Democratic by substantial margins. This change is most evident in the rural counties of the Bluegrass and in western Kentucky. The most significant gain made by Louie Nunn in his 1967 gubernatorial race was in the counties of the far west, most of which have regularly gone Democratic by 70 to 75 percent; the Democrats won only 56 percent of the vote in the first congressional district, incorporating the western counties. It is evident that in the traditionally Democratic rural counties of Kentucky enough voters have abandoned traditional voting patterns to make these counties important targets for Republican candidates in the years ahead.

Of equal or greater importance as a source of additional Republican votes are the metropolitan counties in Kentucky, which are steadily growing in population. These counties contain a large and growing number of voters in the high-income, white-collar, managerial, professional, and technical groups. It is these groups of persons who are particularly likely to vote Republican and who have provided the Republican party with its urban and suburban base of support in other parts of the country. Tables 7.1 and 7.2 provide some limited data about the nature of metropolitan Republi-

TABLE 7.2

Party Identification of Persons Voting Republican in 1963, 1964, and 1967 among a Sample of Fayette County Voters (in Percentages)

Voting Behavior	Total Number	Republicans	Independents	Democrats
Republican vote all 3 times	77	80	12	8
Republican vote 1 or 2 times, no Democratic vote	85	49	27	24
Republican vote 2 times, Democratic vote 1 time	44	32	30	39
Republican vote 1 time, Democratic vote 1 or 2 times	69	22	29	49

cans. They are based on a 1967 survey of 505 respondents, who were selected at random from among registered voters in a number of the most heavily Republican urban and suburban precincts in Fayette County. It is evident from the tables that persons who identify themselves as Republicans are the most consistent Republican voters, and that a substantial proportion of Democrats and Independents have occasionally voted Republican. Compared to Democrats and Independents, those who identify themselves as Republicans are more likely to have a college education, to be engaged in business or a profession, and to be in the middle age bracket. Almost one-fourth of the Republicans and Independents came from states outside Kentucky (and outside the Border or the South).

The metropolitan counties are vital to Republican growth for other reasons. Here the party is likely to find wealthy individuals, dedicated to the Republican cause, who are willing to provide the funds necessary for large-scale campaigns. Here there are many persons, particularly lawyers and businessmen, who have the training and background that make them suitable candidates for public office on the Republican ticket. The large concentration of voters in metropolitan counties provides the party with an incentive for developing a strong organization for use in national elections, one that can be utilized in state and local elections as well.

In Jefferson County the Republican organization has been built carefully over a number of years, and today it is a powerful group, under able leadership, solidly entrenched in the city and county government. There is every reason to assume that, whatever changes in electoral fortunes occur, the Jefferson County Republican organization will remain strong and will play an increasingly important part in the state party organization. Although Republican organizational growth has been slower and leadership less effective in Fayette, Kenton, and Campbell counties, the potential Republican vote in those areas is so large that party organization growth would appear to be inevitable in the years immediately ahead.

There are several remaining obstacles to the growth of the Republican party in state politics, and the most important is the continued importance of the Democratic primary. It has long been evident that the decisive point in the electoral process has been the Democratic primary. In races for state offices many Democratic primaries have been closely contested, and the winners have usually won the general election easily. The importance of the Democratic primary has been obvious not only to political scientists and politicians but also to the general public. The Democratic primary attracts public attention and interest, while contests in the Republican primary—if they occur—are usually one-sided and are ignored. At the start of the general election campaign the winner of the Democratic primary is not only better known than his Republican opponent but is likely to have already attracted considerable support from potential Republican voters. It is true that the Republican candidate in some elections can attract substantial numbers of voters from those who supported the loser in the Democratic primary, but the Republican party pays a price for this windfall because its campaign tactics must be adjusted to conform with the results of the Democratic primary. In this sense the Republican party is a prisoner of the Democratic party system.

Because the importance of the Democratic primary is widely recognized, many persons who normally vote Republican register as Democrats in order to have a voice in the primary election. The closed primary system in Kentucky makes it impossible for them to switch registration frequently and thus excludes many normally Republican voters from participation in the Republican primaries. In 1965 only 32.4 percent of the voters were registered as Republicans, compared to 65.7 percent Democratic and 1.9 percent Independent. But the Republicans have usually polled between 40 and 60 percent of the vote in statewide races. In the 1956 and 1960 presidential elections the number of votes cast for the Republican candidates exceeded the number of registered Republicans, even though less than three-quarters of the registered voters went to the polls.

When persons who often vote Republican are registered as Democrats, they are hidden from the sight of Republican campaign workers who are trying to get out the vote, collect campaign contributions, or solicit other kinds of help in a campaign. One important consequence of this practice of Democratic registration is that Republican primary elections can be decided by a relatively small number of voters who may not be representative of the total number of usual Republican voters in an election. This has not been a significant factor in the past because Republican organization leaders have usually agreed on one Republican candidate, who has won the primary with little or no serious opposition. But the growth in Republican strength has made the party's nomination more attractive to potential candidates and has made closely contested primaries more likely. The 1967 gubernatorial primary, for example, was the first close Republican contest for that office since 1951.

Republican voters are most likely to register as Republicans in those counties, particularly in eastern Kentucky, where there are frequently contested Republican primaries at the local level. A much lower proportion of Republican voters register as Republicans in the metropolitan areas. The result is to give the metropolitan Republican voters a relatively weak voice in the party's primaries and to reduce the chances that the party will select a candidate who can make the strongest appeal to urban voters if the primary election is contested. This can be illustrated by comparing Republican registration and voting figures in two groups of counties: the 4 metropolitan ones (Campbell, Kenton, Jefferson, and Fayette) and 17 counties in the southeastern mountain area (that constituted the Republican eighth congressional district during the 1950s). In 1965 the metropolitan counties had 139,000 registered Republicans; the mountain counties had 136,000. In three recent elections (1965 presidential, 1962 senatorial, and 1963 gubernatorial), the metropolitan counties regularly polled more than twice as many Republican votes as the mountain counties did; in 1963, for example, there were 139,000 Republican votes cast in the metropolitan counties and only 61,000 in the mountain counties. In part this contrast is a result of the inflated registration rolls in the mountains, but the difference can also be illustrated in the few contested Republican primaries of recent years. In a close Republican gubernatorial primary in 1947, the 17 mountain counties cast 36,000 votes, compared to 27,000 in the 4 metropolitan counties. In the 1967 gubernatorial primary, the Republican party organization in Jefferson County made an intensive effort in behalf of County Judge Marlow Cook, and as a result about half of the registered Republicans in Jefferson County voted, but in the other three metropolitan counties only about one-fourth of the registered voters went to the polls. In the mountain counties, and in the remaining parts of the state, about 30 percent of the registered Republicans voted. The total vote in the 4 metropolitan counties exceeded that in the 17 mountain counties (62,300 to 42,300), but this contrast was much smaller than the difference between the two groups of counties normally found in the Republican vote cast in general elections. The growth of two-party competition and the increased importance of statewide Republican primaries will probably cause a steady increase in the proportion of voters registered as Republicans outside traditional Republican counties.

FUTURE OF DEMOCRATIC FACTIONALISM

It is part of the state's political folklore that Kentucky Democrats would much rather beat each other than defeat the Republicans, and it is easy to assume that Democratic primaries will continue to be characterized by bitter contests and factional alignments despite the growing strength of Republican opposition. But the development of a strong two-party system in which control of state government frequently changes hands will probably lead to the erosion of factionalism as a pervasive feature of the Democratic party.

The most obvious reason why the growing Republican party threatens Democratic factionalism is that in a closely competitive two-party system the winning party is frequently the one that is most successful in maintaining unity. It is almost certain that some members of a losing faction will support the other party in the general election, and as the Republican party grows stronger, this factional tendency could lead to the perpetuation of Republicans in the governor's office—a development that would eventually cause alarm in Democratic ranks. One of the characteristics of a two-party system, and a factor that helps to regenerate the opposition party, is that all of the persons and groups who eventually grow disillusioned with the party in power throw their support to the opposition. This is true even if these dissidents have little in common with the leaders of the opposition. They must support the opposition party, at least temporarily, because there is no place else to go if they want to be politically effective. In Kentucky politics it has been the opposition Democratic faction, rather than the Republican party, that has performed this function of mobilizing those who have split with the administration faction. Once the Republican party succeeds in establishing its claim to be *the* opposition party, then it is likely to attract most of those who are dissatisfied with the administration faction. It will gradually gain a monopoly of the effective opposition. In the 1967 gubernatorial election it took a major step in that direction.

Democratic factionalism has been very largely a contest between the "ins" and the "outs." The administration faction has maintained cohesion because it controlled the machinery of government, under the strong leadership of the governor, and the opposition faction has frequently been able to unite behind a single gubernatorial candidate because this was the only hope of regaining power. When the Republican party controls the governorship, however, the Democratic factional leaders will lose the sanctions and incentives that have enabled them to maintain a measure of cohesion within their respective factions. Another factor that may undermine factionalism is related less to the growth of Republican strength than to the growing political effectiveness of the governor and his increasing success in winning the nomination for his chosen successor. The Combs administration succeeded in choosing a successor in 1963, and the Breathitt administration had similar success in the 1967 primary—the first time in modern political history in which there have been three successive gubernatorial primary victories by one faction.

Probably the most important reason for predicting the gradual demise of Democratic factionalism is that it is no longer functional; it has outlived its usefulness. The factions have not consistently represented distinctly different socioeconomic interests, nor have they taken sharply distinct and consistent positions on major issues. In specific elections one faction may be described as more liberal and one as more conservative, but these labels cannot be applied accurately over the long run to the two factions. The factions have served one clear purpose for the voters by enabling them to distinguish between the "ins" and the "outs," to cast a vote in support of—or in protest against—the faction that is in power. The growth of an effective two-party system will transfer this function to the two parties and will make the Democratic factions dysfunctional for the operation of the political system.

It is always risky, in the absence of survey data, to try to read the voters' minds, but many Democratic politicians believe that the voters have grown weary of factions. Many voters probably never recognized that factions served a valuable purpose and provided them with useful clues to an understanding of state politics. Instead they seem to have viewed factionalism simply as a personal struggle for power among individual politicians. Voters in the older generation—or many of them—seem to have shared a sense of loyalty to such men as Chandler, Clements, and Waterfield. But a new generation of voters has entered the voting booths, and we may doubt how many of them have inherited the factional loyalties of their parents. The thousands of voters who have moved into Kentucky, particularly into the cities, bring with them no heritage of factional loyalty and little respect for this quaint Kentucky tradition.

The outcome of the 1967 Democratic primary can be interpreted as a sign that voters are losing interest in factionalism and, more significantly, that they are less inclined to vote for an opposition faction in order to bring about a change of government in Frankfort. Although, as the Democratic defeat in November was to demonstrate, many voters believed it was "time for a change," the administration's candidate for governor won a majority in the primary. His principal opponents, A. B. Chandler and Harry Lee Waterfield, apparently won support from many voters who had traditionally supported their factions. But both Chandler and Waterfield had been prominent in Democratic politics for decades; neither was a new face. It seems likely that many of the voters who wanted a new administration, a "new look" in state government, were not convinced that the opposition leaders in the Democratic primary could offer it. The turnout in the 1967 Democratic primary was the lowest since 1951 and was only two-thirds of the primary vote in 1963, but the turnout in the general election was one of the highest in history for a gubernatorial race. This contrast tends to support the thesis that many voters in 1967 perceived the Republican party as offering a clearer alternative than dissident Democratic candidates to the Democratic administration.

POLICY IMPLICATIONS

It is easier to predict changes in the structure of the Kentucky political system than it is to visualize the effects that these changes will have on public policy. We might speculate that a two-party system will offer the voters clearer policy choices than they have enjoyed under the Democratic factional system. In some election campaigns the two factions have presented some clearly distinguishable policy alternatives to the voters, but there is no evidence to indicate how many of the voters have accurately perceived these alternatives. From the voter's viewpoint, political parties have greater continuity and greater visibility than do factions. If the leaders of the two parties consistently take contrasting positions on issues, the voter seems likely to become more aware of these differences than would be true in the case of factions. If the stands taken by the state parties on the major socioeconomic issues resemble the positions of the national parties, the voter's task is simplified.

We have suggested that the policy differences between parties are more likely to be accurately perceived than the policy differences between factions. But there is no certainty that the Kentucky political parties will develop policy positions that are clearly distinct. The political parties in a state are likely to be issue-oriented when they represent distinctly different interests. In most of the northern industrial states, for example, the Democratic party in recent years has represented the middle- and low-income groups in the cities, members of labor unions, and ethnic minorities; the Republican party has represented higher income voters in the cities and many of the residents of the smaller towns and rural areas. This partisan division of interests is the one that took shape during the New Deal era, and it persists today in most northern states, though it is unlikely to be a permanent phenomenon. The important point is that the two political parties are more likely to have cohesive, and contrasting, stands on issues if each represents a relatively homogeneous coalition of interests.

At present each of the Kentucky political parties represents a collection of interests that is so diverse as to make agreement on issues difficult. This results in large part from the fact that party loyalty of so many Kentuckians is a matter of tradition, and these loyalties seem to have been less affected by the political revolution of the New Deal than is true in most states. The Kentucky Democratic party includes middle- and low-income voters in the cities, union members, and some Negroes; but it also includes a large proportion of more conservative members: higher income residents in the cities and the large proportion of rural voters in the central and western parts of the state. The strongest traditional Democratic counties, in the western part of the state, are mostly rural ones. Although many of these traditional Democrats have voted Republican in some of the recent national elections, most seem to cling to their Democratic identification and usually vote Democratic in state elections. Although the lower income urban voters are usually Democratic, they are not organized as effectively as in many northern cities; in Louisville the weakened Democratic organization no longer can "get out" as much of the lower income vote that was so effective in the past.

The Kentucky Republican party represents interests that are even more diverse. The traditional Republican counties in the southeastern mountain area rank among the lowest in the state in levels of income, education, and urbanization; they are the areas of declining populations and economic stagnation. Some of the Republicans who have been leaving these counties have moved to the metropolitan areas of Kentucky. The major *new* source of Republican votes is in the rapidly growing cities and suburbs, among the voters with high levels of income and education, the members of the business, technical, and professional classes. In a sense both types of Kentucky Republicans are conservative, but they are sharply different in background and interests, and we can expect that in the years ahead they will differ sharply in the expectations they hold concerning the responsibilities of state government.

Neither political party in Kentucky is sufficiently homogeneous in the interests represented to provide the basis for a high level of cohesion regarding issues.[4] In the past, the Democratic governor has usually been able to exercise strong enough partisan control to insure a high degree of cohesion within his legislative party on those issues that he considered important. In a sense, this has been unity imposed from the top rather than unity that grows naturally out of agreement among the interests represented by the party. If the legislature develops greater independence with the growth of the two-party system, it is possible that such disciplined legislative party voting will become less frequent. An increase in competition between two legislative parties has been conducive in some states to greater party cohesion, but in Kentucky it appears likely that the legislative alignments that develop in the legislature on major issues are likely to be bipartisan in nature.

Political scientists in recent years have devoted more attention to efforts to measure the effects of growing party competition and reapportionment on legislative output and public policy. The results of these explorations have been ambiguous.[5] It has proven difficult to demonstrate, by means of statistics, that either increased party competition or reapportionment leads to precise and identifiable changes in public policy. Most of the statistical analyses have been based on interstate comparisons rather than on before-and-after studies of an individual state. It is probable that changes in both competition and apportionment have such complex consequences that they will produce different results in each state. Population trends and reapportionment are likely to force greater legislative attention to the problems of the cities, even though it is impossible to predict just what kinds of legislative decisions will be reached regarding urban problems. These trends are also likely to bring

---

[4] A poll conducted in the most heavily Republican precincts of Fayette County in October 1967 showed that, on several questions concerning the role of government and attitudes toward civil rights, supporters of Ward were only slightly more liberal than supporters of Nunn. Persons who identified themselves as Democrats were more liberal than Republicans in their attitude toward governmental activity, but differed little on civil rights questions.

[5] Thomas R. Dye, "Malapportionment and Public Policy in the States," *Journal of Politics*, XXVII (1965), 586-601; Richard I. Hofferbert, "The Relation between Public Policy and Some Structural and Environmental Variables in the American States," *American Political Science Review*, LX (1966), 73-82; Richard E. Dawson and James A. Robinson, "Inter-Party Competition, Economic Variables, and Welfare Policies in the American States," *Journal of Politics*, XXV (1963), 265-89; Thomas R. Dye, *Politics, Economics and the Public* (Chicago: Rand McNally, 1967).

about changes in the balance of power within both political parties as the traditional bases of support are eroded and both parties become more urban in character.

Reapportionment may make state government more responsive to urban needs, without assuring the adoption of any specific urban policies; similarly, two-party competition may make government more responsible to the people, without causing any predictable changes in policy outcomes. A two-party system at the state level may be more responsible in the sense that it simplifies the voter's task and makes it easier for him to assess responsibility for the actions—or inaction—of government. It must be admitted that this is only a theoretical advantage; we know very little about voters' perceptions of state government, and we do not know how these perceptions differ with variations in the nature of the party system. But it seems reasonable to speculate that among the consequences of an increasingly competitive party system in Kentucky will be a higher level of governmental responsibility and an enhancement of the voters' ability to exercise ultimate control over the policy choices made by state government.

KENTUCKY: A MODEL FOR THE CHANGING SOUTH?

The development of a two-party system is not, of course, a trend that is unique to Kentucky. The Republican party is growing, more or less quickly, in every border and southern state. Because the two-party system has deeper roots and has become stronger in Kentucky than in most southern states, we might expect recent political history in Kentucky to serve as a model and provide us with clues to the probable course of two-party development throughout the South. In reality, however, Kentucky differs from most southern states in a number of ways, some of which make it an unlikely model for others to follow.

The most obvious difference is that Kentucky has had many of the characteristics of a two-party system ever since the 1872 election. From 1896 through 1928 the two parties were almost evenly balanced, except for Democratic control of the legislature. It was the New Deal that brought about Democratic dominance in the politics of Kentucky. The two-party system in Kentucky today is being reborn, rather than born. Because of its political heritage,

Kentucky has a substantial minority of voters with traditional Republican loyalties, a characteristic of only a few other southern states such as Tennessee, North Carolina, and Virginia.

The Republican party is better established in Kentucky, but its recent rate of growth has been less dramatic than that of the Republican parties in such states as Texas, Florida, and South Carolina. The political situation is less explosive and the revolt against the national Democratic party is less widespread and much less bitter in Kentucky than in the states of the Deep South. The major reason for this difference is that the Negro population in Kentucky is smaller and racial issues have stirred up much less turmoil in Kentucky than in the Deep South. Administration leaders in Kentucky have supported, rather than resisted, desegregation; and the pace of desegregation has become a significant political issue only in the gubernatorial election of 1963. In the Deep South, the Republican party must take account of public opposition to civil rights measures and must make difficult decisions about how to exploit these attitudes. In Kentucky, the Republican party can choose to avoid racial issues or, as in Louisville, it can afford to deliberately seek Negro support without risking the opposition of most white voters. The different racial climate in Kentucky reduces the Republican party's opportunity for dramatic shortrun gains, but it also spares that party from the most difficult dilemma that confronts its counterpart throughout the states of the Deep South.

Although the Kentucky Democratic party has been divided into factions for many years, the party is not so deeply split along ideological or interest-group lines as the party in several other states, such as Texas, Florida, or Georgia. The recent Democratic administrations have been much less conservative than those in many southern states, and as a consequence a liberal opposition wing has not developed within the party, comparable to that in Texas, for example. The Democrats are not deeply divided in Kentucky over racial issues, as they are in Alabama, Georgia, and Arkansas; in no recent Kentucky Democratic primary have the gubernatorial candidates emphasized conflicting views on desegregation or civil rights issues. Although the Kentucky Republicans have generally been able to win support in the November election from some supporters of the losing Democratic factional candidate, this has usually been a temporary alliance. Those Democrats who have shifted permanently to the Republican party have not come exclusively from one Democratic faction. There is no parallel in Kentucky to the tactical and often quiet alliance that sometimes exists between Republicans and liberal Democrats who cooperate to oppose the conservative Democratic establishment in power, as in Texas for example.

Kentucky, in short, may be a more likely model for some of the states in the Border and Upper South rather than for the states of the Deep South. It is also an imperfect model for states like Texas and Florida whose populations are heavily concentrated in large metropolitan areas. Although some of the political trends in Louisville are similar to those in some Florida and Texas cities, the major cities in Kentucky are not large enough to permit the urban Republican parties to play quite as dominating roles in the state party as is possible in those states.

If Kentucky experience is of any value for our understanding of two-party growth in the South, it is not because other states can be expected to duplicate that experience exactly, but because we can gain a fuller understanding of the changing South only by recognizing its variety and studying the many ways in which political change occurs in the several southern states. Because this change has started earlier here than in most southern states, Kentucky provides us with some clues or guidelines for studying southern two-party politics.

The experience in Kentucky to date emphasizes the critical importance of the large cities to the growth of southern Republican parties. The Jefferson County Republican party's success in winning both local and legislative seats dramatizes this fact and shows that a strong urban party organization can accomplish more than just winning votes for national and state candidates. Although the existence of a block of traditional Republican voters is of great importance in winning statewide electoral majorities, experience in Kentucky demonstrates that this traditional vote may be a source of disunity. It may cause divisive primaries and create splits within the party's legislative delegation. Political scientists are well aware that a majority party primary which is usually vigorously contested constitutes a major obstacle to the minority party, and Kentucky experience serves merely to reinforce this conclusion. Despite growing Republican party strength, a large number of regular Republican voters remain registered as Democrats. Because the law requires a closed primary and makes it difficult to shift party registration quickly, many persons who usually vote Republican are excluded when the Republican party has one of its rare hotly contested primaries. The choice of the Republican nominee, as in 1967, is in the hands of only one segment of the Republican party, a segment in which the rural and traditional Republicans are over-represented.

Experience in Kentucky suggests that southern Republican parties for many years will continue to have difficulty in recruiting candidates for local and legislative office, particularly outside of the cities. Where such candidacies seem hopeless, local Republican leaders will often prefer to run only a few candidates (to avoid arousing the sleeping Democratic giant) or will try to negotiate a deal with the Democratic power structure to win a few political crumbs in return for not making an intensive campaign effort.

With the election of a Republican governor in 1967, we will be able to measure the impact of the two-party system on the structure of government. We can anticipate that legislative procedures and practices will change and the legislature may acquire greater independence and vitality as a consequence. The two-party system should make political decision-making more visible and more meaningful to the voter. It is too early to tell whether this will help to roll back the clouds of apathy and indifference that obscure the operations of state government from its citizens and that contribute to cynicism and alienation regarding state government. It is clear that most state governments do not yet have a great enough impact to persuade their citizens that the states are making a significant contribution to solution of the problems facing modern government.

There is a two-party trend throughout the South that will probably continue until it has irrevocably changed the political face of every southern state. But the experience of Kentucky suggests that the rate of change will vary in every state, and that the Republican party is likely to suffer reversals in most states before the two-party system is firmly established. The observer of

Kentucky politics must be impressed both by the strength of the forces that are bringing about change and by the powerful hold of political loyalties and traditions, in a state where change is obvious to the most casual visitor but traditions lie deep in the history and character of the people.

Index